ASPECTS
IN
ASTROLOGY

ASPECTS IN ASTROLOGY

A GUIDE TO UNDERSTANDING PLANETARY RELATIONSHIPS IN THE HOROSCOPE

SUE TOMPKINS

Destiny Books
Rochester Vermont

Destiny Books
One Park Street
Rochester, Vermont 05767
www.InnerTraditions.com

Destiny Books is a division of Inner Traditions International

Library of Congress Cataloging-in-Publication Data
Tompkins, Sue.
    Aspects in astrology : a guide to understanding planetary
relationships in the horoscope / Sue Tompkins.
        p. cm.
    Includes bibliographical references and index.
    ISBN 978-0892819652
    ISBN 0-89281-965-0
        1. Aspect (Astrology) I. Title.

BF1717.2 .T66 2002
133.5'3044—dc21

                                                    2002074027

Printed and bound in the United States at Lake Book
Manufacturing, Inc.

10 9 8 7 6 5 4

To

Liz and Adam Matar with love
and to the memory of my father,
who always wanted to write a book

Sue Tompkins has been a practising consultant and teacher of astrology since the early 1980s and lectures widely at home and abroad. She runs the London School of Astrology as well as a busy astrological and homoeopathic practice in central London.

CONTENTS

Part Two: A Planetary Cookbook

6. Sun Aspects

7. Moon Aspects

8. Mercury Aspects

9. Venus Aspects

Acknowledgements

With thanks to everyone who has helped me directly or indirectly in the writing of this book. Students, teachers, clients, colleagues, partners, lovers and friends. Everyone from the Faculty of Astrological Studies during the 1980s and especially Lindsay Radermacher, Babs Kirby and Mike Harding for their insight, support and encouragement. Neil Robertson for introducing me to computers (way back in the Dark Ages) and being so great generally. Faye Cossar for many a meal and astrological chat. Dianna Coward for, amongst other things, designing my chart form, and Janet Spencer for giving so much in all those analytical hours. Steve Eddy from Element Books for his help in the Element edition of the book and Doreen Montgomery and Julia McCutchen for the new Rider edition. Thanks too to Frank Clifford for his insight and for helping me update the data section.

INTRODUCTION

I started studying astrology in the 1970s and like most students, then and now, when I discovered it, got quite obsessed. I never thought of it as having career potential; I was just fascinated and, not being in any particular hurry, my apprenticeship was long and slow. As I progressed in my studies, qualified and started seeing clients, it became obvious to me that the most important facet of the horoscope, the bit that one urgently needed to understand and be able to describe, was aspects – and yet, I couldn't find much in the way of contemporary material on the subject.

Even then there was much that was excellent on the market as to the nature of planetary combinations. Stephen Arroyo for example on the outer planets and Liz Greene on these and Saturn. Charles Carter's book *Astrological Aspects* was and still remains a classic in the field but is a little out of date and does not include Pluto. Bill Tierney's book *Dynamics of Aspect Analysis* is invaluable for the subject of aspect patterns, so much so that the writer has not attempted to comment further on these. So *Aspects in Astrology* came about because I needed to know more, and as I began teaching I realised that students needed to know more too. So I set about my own low-key empirical research and what follows is the result of that.

Much of the art of astrological interpretation lies in the capacity of the astrologer to bring different symbols together and synthesise them. At every step of the way, this is what the interpreter is doing. The astrologer considering, for example, Mercury in Sagittarius in the 4th house has to bring together their understanding of the planet, the sign, the 4th house, *and* the houses that are ruled by Mercury. The average student of astrology can usually manage to juggle around with these different factors but when presented with the fact that Mercury is not isolated but is in fact in 'aspect' – that is, forming a relationship with other planets or points in the chart – can feel totally overwhelmed. This is not surprising. Interpreting aspect configurations is a very complex business and not easy, even for the most experienced practitioner.

Nevertheless such interpretation is worthy of effort for it is the aspects that provide the energy in the chart, the energy that transforms the horoscope from the description of a lifeless puppet into something symbolising an alive and vital human being, complete with conflict and joy. Above all else in the chart, the aspects describe the *prima materia*, the raw stuff out of which every individual has to build their life. Horoscopes can be set up for anything; their use is not confined to the study of human nature and human life but whatever the birth-chart depicts — the time of an event, a question, a live being. The aspects describe the drama, they describe *what actually happens*. And in terms of people, aspect configurations describe what psychologists call 'complexes' (groups of interacting symbols), of which the psychologist C.G. Jung commented that it is not so much people who have complexes but complexes who have people. In other words, aspects play a large role in describing what might be termed our 'fate' inasmuch as they describe what we *have* to deal with.

The birth-chart by its very nature is unique and has to be viewed as a whole; thus it must be clear that any astrological 'cookbook' such as this one is always going to have its limitations, interpreting as it does one piece of information out of the context of the rest of the chart. Nevertheless, the interpreter has to start somewhere and it is hoped that this book will provide some help.

PART ONE

THE PRINCIPLES
OF ASPECT
INTERPRETATION

CHAPTER ONE

THE PLANETS

The following notes on each planet are an attempt to revise and highlight some of the basic key issues that are associated with each.

SUN

Our sense of identity, what we consider important, what we are proud of, what we seek to put our heart into. Vitality. Importance. Pride. Illumination. Recognition. Our will, purpose, future goals.

It's difficult, for me anyway, to define exactly what the Sun signifies. Sometimes it is described as the significator of the self. Perhaps it depends on what is meant by the term 'self' but personally I interpret the word in the Jungian sense, as meaning an individual's Whole Self, including the unconscious as well as the conscious parts. In which case, the 'self' must surely be at least the whole chart and perhaps something outside the confines of the horoscope which nevertheless also encompasses all that is within it. In any event, the Sun does seem to act as a strong integrating factor in the overall map – the leader or conductor of the orchestra, so to speak. It does seem to describe the 'core', the heart of the person and is rather as the nucleus is to the atom. Not that this core can ever be truly known, which is perhaps why the deepest meanings of the Sun remain elusive.

More simply though, I believe the Sun contributes to our 'ego', what we know ourselves to be, the person we think we are, the person we *identify* with. So that planets aspecting our Sun affect the way we identify ourselves. Do we have a 'good' opinion of ourselves or do we have a poor self-image? Do we have an image at all? Aspects to our Sun throw light on these questions. Planets aspecting our Sun will also tend either to compound or deny our 'Sun sign'. Jupiter tightly aspecting the Sun might exaggerate our Sun sign characteristics for example, whilst Saturn might inhibit or suppress them or urge us to define more closely just what these characteristics are.

Just as the Sun in the sky provides light and heat, anything that is touched by the Sun in our charts is at once *illuminated* and warmed. Whatever the planet is, the spotlight is put upon it and it is given both power and strength. Aspects work both ways of course so, conversely, aspects to the Sun, especially 'hard' aspects from 'difficult' planets, seem to sap the strength and power of whatever the Sun individually represents for us – a bit like wearing dark glasses on a sunny day perhaps.

Whilst the Ascendant and its ruler seem to describe our journey in life, the vehicle we are travelling in and the way we have to go, the Sun is more descriptive of the true *purpose* of our going, as well as some of the challenges we are likely to meet along the way.

The Sun has a strong future orientation in as much as it describes where we are heading, as opposed to the Moon, which has a lot to say about where we are coming from.

One of the keywords for the Sun is 'will'. Along with Mars, the Sun does describe our will, our inclination, future intention, wish and desire. The desire to be ourselves, to become a certain type of character, to do something with our lives. More simply, the Sun seems to describe our purpose, and the lifetime goal and task of recognising and consciously living that purpose. The house and sign of the Sun are certainly areas which we find important, and usually the most important areas of life. When a planet is touched by the Sun that planet is rendered especially important to us too, and that planet will often say something about how we want to be seen, and the ease or difficulty with which we might accomplish this. For example, Sun square Saturn will usually have important authority issues in their lives and people with this contact will usually want to be seen as an authority in some area, whilst at the same time they may find it difficult to accept authority from others or be able to grasp it for themselves.

It is the solar principle which says: 'I want, this is my purpose, my intention, my direction.' Where you find the Sun is where you say, 'Here I am, here I want to be a force to be reckoned with. Here I want to be myself. Here I want to be special … I want to be unique, and I want to be an individual in my own right.' If the Sun describes our inclination and direction to do something, aspects to it will show what impedes this happening, what stops us from doing our own thing and what helps us to make the best of ourselves.

The Sun is a part of oneself that centres on oneself, the Sun is 'self-centred'. Aspects to the Sun describe the ease or difficulty which we have in being self-centred and 'self-conscious'. The ease or difficulty we may have in recognising or accepting ourselves.

Where we find the Sun in a chart is where we seek to glean our identity, where we want to be recognised; and in being recognised our identity is reinforced. And if we are not able to get recognition, more negatively, we might just go in for plain old attention-seeking. This works with houses and can just as easily work with aspects too. Some simplistic examples may be appropriate here; Sun–Mars might say: 'Notice me, I'm strong'; Sun–Neptune: 'Notice me ... look what a saviour I am,' or, 'Look what a victim I am. Can't you save me? Don't you feel sorry for me?' Sun–Uranus: 'Notice me ... I'm different from you'; Sun–Saturn: 'Notice me ... people don't usually.' And so on. We tend to glory and bask in our Sun. We also glory in, and are proud of, whatever is signified by the planets that it touches.

As any astrology textbook will tell you, the Sun describes our vitality, our will and our creative self-expression. I have always found this term 'creative self-expression' to be rather an elusive one but nevertheless planets aspecting the Sun certainly do contribute to the way in which we seek and are able to express our own individual uniqueness. The Sun sign and solar aspects certainly do have bearing on our vitality, our basic 'life-force' and may therefore contribute, along with Mars, to our ability to shrug off disease.

The Sun is also described as the hero. Whatever the Sun is doing in the chart will say something about the challenges that the hero within us all is fated to meet. Jungians use the word *individuation* to describe this process. According to the *Oxford English Dictionary* the word 'individuate' means: '... to form into an individual or distinct entity, to give individual organisation or form to. To distinguish from others of the same species.'

Arguably, this is what the Sun is about; the hero's purpose is about becoming a distinct individual. To become oneself, the person one really is somewhere inside. The acorn can only ever become an oak tree, as Liz Greene would say. But each oak tree is unique and its potential uniqueness exists in a latent form inside the acorn. So the Sun seems to symbolise the process of finding one's identity. Planets aspecting the Sun will not only help define what the hero looks like but will describe the challenges that this inner core of the person will meet. All the helpful and not so helpful inner figures who may accelerate or impede the process.

The Sun is also one of several symbols in the horoscope for the father. The biological father, the man that generated life and also the person who provided (or didn't) an early model for the child's sense of identity.

MOON

Feelings, reaction, response, mother, home, food preferences, domestic habits, habits generally. Where we retreat to. Our place of safety. How we feel nurtured and how we nurture others. Accommodation.

The Moon represents our urge to nurture and be nurtured, our urge to care for, cosset and protect. And it is the infant within us all that even in adulthood is sometimes dependent, needy and requiring protection. Aspects to our Moon have a great deal to say about the ease or difficulty which we may have in nurturing others or in finding sanctuary and safety for ourselves.

The Moon will describe, especially by sign, what will calm us, comfort and sustain us; the aspects will show what supports or gets in the way of this happening.

The Moon, along with the IC and its ruler, describes where we are coming from in the widest sense; our emotional background, our roots, history and heritage. It can also describe our behaviour, in that it points to how we used to behave as a child in response to cues in the environment and how we still tend to behave, perhaps out of programming or force of habit. The Moon and its aspects will often describe how we quite unconsciously, automatically in fact, react and respond to stimuli. The Moon with Mars might, for example, react very quickly or angrily, tending always to be ready to leap into action. Moon–Saturn will appear controlled in its reactions and will respond cautiously and carefully.

Aspects to our Moon will describe the ease or difficulty with which we express our feelings, as well as the nature of those feelings. Our feelings may have much to do with our heredity and also the feeling tone that surrounded us when we were growing up, a feeling tone that we may have been unconscious of but absorbed nevertheless.

The Moon describes our home and domestic preferences in general. Our home is our *accommodation* and our Moon describes how we accommodate others in the widest sense, how we adjust and adapt ourselves to the people and life-situations that we encounter. Ideally, we should react to different people and experiences individually, for each new situation calls for something different: a different spontaneous emotional reaction and a different behavioural response.

The Moon is also the significator of home in the sense that our home provides us with a place to retreat to, a place which provides emotional anchorage, a place where we can feel safe and be ourselves; a place where we can flop around in slippers and behave in whatever way we choose, safe from the eye of the outside world. The Moon also has bearing on how 'at home' we feel with ourselves, and this in turn affects how we respond to others and how others respond to us.

We tend to retreat to whatever our Moon describes because it is familiar. After all, it does describe roots, where we are coming from. The Moon should describe how we felt safe as a child, and even if we didn't feel particularly safe (perhaps we have difficult contacts to our Moon from, say, Saturn, Uranus or Pluto), we will still tend to gravitate to whatever our Moon represents, for the planet describes habitual patterns which we get attached to. It's rather like having a cigarette with a coffee: if you do it often enough, you get to the stage where you cannot really enjoy drinking a cup of coffee unless it is accompanied by a cigarette.

As well as describing the domestic environment in which we feel most comfortable, our lunar aspects will also usually say something about how easy or difficult we are to live with, as well as how easy or difficult we find living with others. This again has much to do with our capacity for adjustment and the extent to which we feel emotionally safe. If we feel it's safe to be ourselves then we can usually behave in a more spontaneous manner and are more able to adjust to others' differing life-styles, different habits (especially domestic habits!), mood swings and so on.

The Moon is a major significator of the mother. Clearly, we all have a biological mother and our Moon will describe our experience of her. It will also say a great deal about our experience of all our early caretaking, which in turn will affect many of those factors already mentioned. In charts of children who have been fostered by several or many families, or perhaps lived in institutional care, the Moon in the child's chart (together with the MC–IC axis and their rulers) will usually describe all the different caretakers, as well as the 'real' mother, albeit in different ways. So the Moon describes our early experience of mother, whoever that person or persons may have been. The Moon is concerned with that aspect of parenthood which says: 'I will accept you, no matter what. I will protect you, care for you. I will emotionally hold you and provide a place of safety where you can explore and express your feelings, and it doesn't matter what your feelings are, I will hold them, and accept them. I will provide a cushion for your fears, your rage, your anxieties.'

We can receive this kind of nurturance from anyone and in an ideal childhood will receive it from at least several people. Nevertheless, our first bond is with our mother, if only because for purely practical reasons it has to be so, for we are carried around within her, we absorb her feelings and her moods in the same way as we are nourished by her food.

She is the first person we are bonded to and therefore the first person to whom we turn for unconditional acceptance. So the Moon does seem to describe Mum but it also describes what our early experience of nurture was in general, and as such it can be a significator for father and for a whole host of other caregivers — though where the Moon is a significator for a caregiver other than the biological mother, this is usually clearly stated in the chart, through house placements, house rulerships or other factors.

In any event, our Moon — by sign, house placement and planetary aspect — will have much to say about how we felt as a child, and more especially whether we felt safe. How we feel safe now, how we feel protected, how we protect and care for others and the ease or difficulty with which we are able to do so — all these are especially influenced by the Moon.

MERCURY

Thought, speech, writing. Communication. The rational mind. Opinions. Making connections. Siblings. School. How we learn.

As significator of all forms of communication, the natal Mercury and its aspects will describe the way in which we communicate who we are, at least on a non-feeling, verbal level. When Mercury touches a planet or point in our chart, we are more strongly urged to write, talk or simply think about that facet of ourselves, than where no aspect exists. Mercury connects different parts of the chart to each other and acts as a kind of agent. Thus the planet has an important function in terms of consciousness-raising. Mercury picking up Saturn for example, may suggest a greater opportunity for the individual to contact, think about and communicate their fears. Mercury can be seen here as enabling the individual to become more conscious of those things that Saturn represents for them. Thus even stressful aspects to Mercury can be seen as potentially helpful for growth, for by making contact to different planets in the chart, Mercury offers us the opportunity to dip in and out of various aspects of our psyche.

There are of course many routes to greater consciousness and Mercury perhaps only offers one of them but it is an easy one to get hold of. Mercury has a *naming* function. If we have a name for something we can get hold of it more easily. We can talk about it to other people and so look at it from different points of view and generally amplify what it might mean for us. Conversely, aspects to Mercury can also show what gets in the way of our learning about ourselves and, of course, learning generally. With Mercury–Saturn, fear may get in the way of self-knowledge and the education process as a whole. With Mercury–Mars, anger and too great an impulsiveness might be at odds with the acquisition of self-knowledge. And so on.

Areas of life uppermost in our minds are shown by our whole chart and not just by the sign and house of Mercury; thus the mind of an individual whose chart has a strong 7th house or Libran emphasis will often naturally gravitate to thinking and talking about their relationships, irrespective of whether Mercury is also in the 7th house of Libra. Nevertheless, the sign, house and aspect relationships of natal Mercury will contribute to what we think, talk and generally communicate about. More important, our Mercury will describe *the way* in which we communicate those things uppermost in our mind. Our Mercury shows the lines upon which our thinking is likely to run. Our own particular mental wavelength.

Like any other planet in the natal chart, Mercury can never be found in its pure form; it is always coloured by a sign, a house and other factors. But if Mercury were available in a pure form it would describe the completely rational and objective mind. A mind free not only of any distortion or bias, but of any kind of moral reasoning too. For Mercury is not concerned with the rights or wrongs of a given situation. The realm of principles, ethics, meaning and morals comes under the umbrella of Jupiter, the planet which rules the signs opposite to those ruled by Mercury. Mercury was messenger of the Gods, but was not a God himself, and it is the Gods who make judgements, who ask what it all means. Mercury is simply concerned with information – and quite unconcerned with the usefulness or otherwise of that information, and perhaps not even bothered about whether it is true or not.

Mercury also has a lot to say about our opinions. We can never know all there is to know about any given subject, so any judgement we make is always going to be based on insufficient evidence, on opinion. Our opinions reflect what we believe to be the case, based on what knowledge we have and the particular lines we tend to think along anyway. We know that there is no such thing as objective knowledge. The sign of our Mercury and, more especially, aspects to that planet will contribute to or detract from our ability to get as near to objectivity as possible. Objectivity and rationality are required in order to avoid bias and prejudice but they come from the opposite place to feelings and can be overvalued. A world without feelings and values is not only impossible to imagine but would be grotesque even if one could. The relative prominence of Mercury in our chart, and aspects to it, may say whether we tend to undervalue or overvalue rational thought.

Hard aspects to an individual's Mercury may suggest that their opinions are likely to be tested, challenged and disagreed with by others, or that they expect them to be challenged, whereas soft aspects suggest the reverse. Sometimes the lack of dissension may be because of the way that the individual expressed their ideas and opinions in the first place. The person with soft aspects is less likely to feel threatened if disagreed with and so can often express themselves more easily. They are less likely to feel vulnerable in the Mercury areas of life and so will be less bothered if others do disagree. They may even enjoy it. Easy aspects may also suggest that the opinions held will be reinforced by other people or by other aspects of the individual's personality (as described by the planets concerned) which may have an investment in their thinking along a particular groove. However, since opinions must always be based on insufficient evidence or understanding, then perhaps, whilst not a pleasant experience, it is no bad thing to have our opinions challenged, as may be the case with the hard aspects. (The challenge may come from within ourselves or from outside.) For therein lies the possibility of the mind and our ideas being stretched and broadened. As always, the soft aspects, especially the trine, can give rise to complacency, whereas the hard aspects offer the potential for growth.

The extent to which any of us change during a lifetime is debatable, but certainly our attitudes and opinions can change and it is Mercury which enables this to happen. And any changes that we do introduce into our behaviour or life-style must, quite obviously, follow a change in attitude. *Energy always follows thought.* Viewed in this way, it could be argued that Mercury holds the key to progress itself.

Mercury is primarily concerned with making connections. Intelligence cannot be defined; perhaps there is no such thing. IQ tests show the ability of a human being to do IQ tests, rather than anything as nebulous as 'intelligence'. Perhaps if IQ tests reveal anything it is the individual's ability to make quick connections – an ability that can be taught, and which is clearly Mercurial. School, whose significator is Mercury, is the primary place where making connections is taught. School is also the place where we learn to gather, process and communicate information. Here we learn how to communicate and how to read and write. Here we learn about language on all levels. The sign position and aspects to our Mercury will have a lot to say about how we learn and what might impede, obstruct, support or accelerate this learning process. Our Mercurial aspects will also have a bearing on what we learn in the widest possible sense.

Mercury is also significator of transport, and transport is merely a means of moving someone or something from one place to another, a means of connecting A to B.

Mercury is also a significator of brothers and sisters and it is astonishing how accurately the planet does describe, along with the 3rd house, an individual's sibling relationships. A child will often learn a lot from its brothers and sisters, who also often act as agents, or intermediaries between each other and the parents.

VENUS

Co-operation. Giving. Sharing. Compromise. Beauty. Love. Value. Comparison. Art. Taste. Means of exchange. Money. How we seek to make ourselves and others happy.

Venus symbolises our urge to co-operate and share with others; our desire to give and harmonise; to love and be loved. Aspects to our Venus may shed light on how important being popular and fitting in may be to us.

Planets contacting Venus will describe what supports or gets in the way of our being able to achieve this co-operation and harmony. A person with Venus squaring Uranus, for example, may find that the urge to be independent, individualistic and unique (Uranus) feels at odds with the desire to fit in and harmonise with everyone else. Or, we could say that there is an urgent need (square) and thus tension caused because the individual is impelled to integrate their need for relationship with their need for independence and freedom and the two impulses seem at variance. Ultimately though, the person may find that there is actually greater freedom within relationship than without.

We all have what can be termed 'relating' problems and problems which revolve around giving (Venus) and taking (Mars). Aspects to our Venus (together with Mars) will suggest the nature of those problems and offer ways in which they might be worked through, integrated and healed. People with a highly focal Venus, particularly if it is at the expense of a strong Mars, for example, may tend to be overly co-operative and yielding – so much so that personal principles may fly out the window and the individual find themselves fulfilling the needs of others at great personal expense. Planets contacting Venus may suggest a tendency to over-compromise or a tendency to under-compromise and usually a mixture of these in different situations. The planet picking up Venus will have a lot to say about why this occurs. The Venus principle wants peace; unchecked by other planetary principles it may seek peace at any price. Venus will also make the best of things and tend to look at things in the most favourable light. As Charles Carter says: 'Venus tends always to see points of likeness and common interest and to gloss over and remove differences.'

On the surface, Venus may appear to be all 'give' and Mars to be all 'take' and it can therefore seem that Venus is the 'Goody' and Mars the 'Baddy'. Traditionally, of course, they are known respectively as the lesser benefic and lesser malefic. But it is not usually that simple: Venus wants to give, often because it wants to be given something in return – usually, love, popularity or money; the Mars principle takes but is honest about it and in taking, Mars is also often giving. If we give someone a present and they take it and respond favourably to it, we feel pleased and happy. In taking, the recipient is also giving.

Venus says, 'I want what you want,' whereas Mars says, 'I want what I want.' Because they work as a polarity, neither planet should be examined in isolation but always needs to be looked at as one of a pair. Venus is concerned with peace partly because it is non-competitive.

Whereas the Moon is a symbol for the mother, Venus represents the young woman (and Mars the young man) and it is often useful to look at Venus in terms of the existence of this inner figure and her dialogue with other inner figures in the chart.

Venus is concerned with relationship, with our ability and need to give and receive affection, with how we are in social situations generally and, more particularly, in social situations which could have a romantic or sexual outcome. Our Venus will describe how we seek and manage, consciously or not, to attract others. Venus–Uranus, for example, may attract people through being different and unusual. To others, Venus–Uranus may appear magnetic and full of surprises and that's what they find attractive.

How we seek to attract others and the way in which we value ourselves, in turn has a bearing on our appearance, how we dress, do our hair and generally try and make ourselves as attractive as possible. All these are Venus dialogues too. Venus–Uranus may seek to look different from most other people. For Venus–Saturn the whole issue may be surrounded by fear; they may feel inhibited and 'dress down'. Each combination will of course yield many different outcomes. The important thing is not so much how the person dresses, for example, but what kind of statement is being made by their choice of dress. As always the nature of the planets in the dialogue will describe the why as well as the how and what.

Venus is concerned not only with appearance and all aspects of taste but more especially with value: how we value ourselves and others; what we value generally and why. The planet acts as a barometer of our personal sense of beauty and aesthetic appreciation. Venus is also the significator of money; money is something we pay for those things we value, it is also a means of exchange, and above all else Venus is concerned with 'means of exchange' on all levels. Some astrologers associate Jupiter with money but I have never found this to be the case though Jupiter is the significator of wealth in the widest sense. Jupiter is not concerned with material values in the way that Venus is.

Because Venus is concerned with the appreciation and creation of that which is pleasing or beautiful, Venus is also a significator of art and music. The arts are – amongst other things – concerned with pleasure, which is another Venus preoccupation. In fact, our Venus has a great deal to say about how we are able to derive pleasure, and perceive beauty in all of life's rich and varied guises. And as such, Venus is an indicator of the way and extent to which we are able, or allow ourselves, to enjoy life in the widest possible sense. Our sign, house and aspects patterns of Venus will have a bearing on what makes us happy; what we like and don't like, and why; what gives us pleasure and makes us happy; how we seek to make others happy, give them pleasure and show them we value, appreciate and love them. Aspects to our Venus will describe what impedes or supports our ability to make ourselves or others feel loved, valued and happy.

Another important point about Venus aspects is that when Venus touches a planet it will *soften* it. No matter what that planet represents, the touch of Venus will render it softer, more pliable and easily shaped. Issues of potential comfort, ease, luxury, sweetness or gentleness will reinforce or impede the expression of that other planetary principle.

MARS

Survival, resourcefulness and courage. Endurance and fight. Assertion. Daring. Competition. Action.

Mars is traditionally described as the lesser malefic. Personally I am not fond of these benefic and malefic terms. All energies are fundamentally beneficial and necessary, though all can work negatively if we don't handle them properly.

We certainly need Mars, for the planet's central concern seems to be with the *fight to survive* on all levels. For some people, the best way of surviving is keeping quiet or avoiding an issue, whilst for others, it's rolling the sleeves up and jumping headlong into the fray. Correct use of the Mars principle can make for courage and endurance. Courage does not necessarily, of course, mean aggression or fighting. Courage means facing those things we are frightened of. For some it might be brave not to fight but instead to admit that one is vulnerable and frightened. The Mars principle also enables us to 'rough it', to stand firm when the going gets tough. We need Mars to cope with pressure and to avoid buckling under the stresses and strains of everyday living. Aspects to our Mars, along with the sign and house placement, will suggest what tools we have to defend ourselves with and how able we feel to use those tools and maintain our position in given situations. Difficult Mars aspects may suggest that we find it difficult to defend ourselves, for whatever reason. Mars coupled with Saturn for example, automatically suggests that fear gets in the way of self-defence. On the other hand, Mars contacts may describe a tendency to be too eager to defend ourselves, perceiving threats from outside where none were intended. Again, the planets contacting Mars will indicate what it is all about.

Mars is concerned with assertion. To assert oneself is to declare one's interests, to affirm, to be positive, to maintain one's position, one's individuality, in the face of pressure or resistance not to do so. This does not mean riding roughshod over people. This is a common misuse of Mars energy and explains why the planet has such a poor reputation. Since being assertive means being pliable and having a healthy respect for the needs of others, good practice in assertiveness skills requires the use of the Venus principle as well as that of Mars. But if we concentrate on just the Mars end of the spectrum, it is easy to find reasons why we may find it difficult to be assertive. These can be linked to planets that might be paired in the horoscope with Mars. Perhaps we find it difficult to be assertive because we want to be popular (Venus) and think that we cannot be both. Perhaps we lack confidence or are fearful (Saturn). Perhaps we feel impotent (Saturn). Maybe taking the easy way out seems much more attractive (Venus). And so on.

The Mars principle not only helps us fight off unwanted pressure from the outside world but can also enable us to cope with internal psychological conflict. It is Mars that keeps us out of mental hospital as well as Mars that often puts us in there, when the pressure is too great. The planet must also have some bearing on the body's ability to fight off disease and ill health. Apart from anything else, Mars will describe our desire and will to survive. Fighting for life implies being attached to living and so perhaps Mars, together with Venus, can be used as a barometer of our ability to enjoy life.

Mars is also a planet we can associate with all forms of *competition*. Sport is a good vehicle for expressing the competitive spirit, for in sporting or exercise situations we can compete with ourselves as well as with others. Research suggests that people who engage in regular exercise tend to feel better about themselves and often have an improved self-image. There is also often greater self-sufficiency and less of a tendency to blame other people for one's misfortunes. Exercise keeps us healthy.

Aspects to our Mars will indicate what we feel about the whole area of competition in all its various guises. Perhaps we vibrate more to Venus than to Mars, in which case competition is not likely to be an issue, though survival may be. Or we may be very competitive and handle this by getting into legitimate competing situations − or conversely we may find the whole issue so fraught that we avoid competition altogether because not being best is too painful to contemplate.

The Martian impulse is a selfish one, inasmuch as it is concerned with going out and getting what we want. Aspects to our Mars may indicate what we learnt about being selfish when we were young. Some people are taught very strictly in childhood that it is wrong to be selfish (perhaps Mars with Saturn) and then find it difficult in later life to allow themselves to want something or be able to ask for it. Others are raised in a very competitive environment (perhaps Sun–Mars or Ascendant–Mars) and are taught, or pick up cues, that the only way to survive is to push oneself forward. In later life they may find it difficult to trust in the process of sitting back and allowing, believing that one must push all the time. The permutations are endless but they can mostly be traced to the Mars aspects in the birth-chart. The same applies to anger; our Mars aspects will describe, along with the Mars sign, the way in which we express our anger and passion about things and the ease or difficulty we may have in doing so.

Accidents will usually have been caused, at least in part, by the action of Mars. Accidents are usually the result of misplaced energy and are also perhaps, often the result of unexpressed anger – frustration that can find no outlet. Mars is also traditionally associated with fever and, indeed, has dominion over 'heat' generally, as well as all areas about which we may get 'hot'. 'Hot under the collar' as in anger; 'hot' as in sexually aroused.

Mars is an indicator of our drive to dare to do something. As soon as we dare to do something we are vulnerable, because we might lose or fail. Our Mars will show where, how and in what way we may dare to show our strength. Pure Mars energy is very vulnerable, for it impels us to go out and get something – impels us to dare. And when we have dared, our cards are on the table; what we want is clearly expressed and can be denied to us.

Mars is also a significator, along with Venus, of our sexuality, but whereas Venus relates to the harmony of sexual union and to sensual pleasure, Mars relates to that part of sexual life which involves forcing the issue: the chase, conquest, penetration. Again, this incurs vulnerability: one only has to consider the male sexual organ to understand how vulnerable the Mars principle is.

Aspects to our Mars, along with its zodiacal sign, will have bearing on what we may find sexually exciting ourselves, as well as what others may find exciting about us. Aspects to our Mars will have much to say about our sexual fears and fantasies and how best we might deal with these.

Mars will also quicken the expression of whatever planet it touches in the birth-chart. That planet will be speeded up and the individual will be impatient to express it. There will also be a strong impulse to express whatever it signifies. In this area, if in no others, the person may come on strong. The Mars principle converts very easily into action and the individual will often seek to act physically on whatever the contacting planet represents. Mars contributes, along with the Sun, to the notion of the *will*, which the *Oxford English Dictionary* defines as 'that facility or function which is directed to conscious or intentional action'.

Because the Mars principle is so honestly go-getting, when it is prominent it often contributes great spirit and gusto to the personality, though unrestrained it can also suggest much forcefulness. Prominent Mars aspects will increase the fiery quality of a chart and can help to offset some of the problems that a lack of this element may indicate.

JUPITER

Expansion, inflation, exaggeration. Wisdom, wealth, meaning. Beliefs of all kinds. Vision, faith, confidence. Greed.

In some ways Jupiter aspects are the easiest to interpret, for one of Jupiter's most reliable major characteristics is its tendency to *expand* whatever it touches. The planetary principle contacting Jupiter, whatever it is, is simply made bigger. And it's important to remember that bigger doesn't necessarily mean better. If Jupiter expands what it touches it will also exaggerate and inflate already difficult aspect patterns in a chart, often turning a merely stressful configuration into one which is potentially lethal.

In accident and disaster charts for example, Jupiter is nearly always very prominent. Classically in such charts there will be difficult contacts between the planets traditionally associated with violence and accidents – Mars, Uranus and Pluto; but inevitably Jupiter will also be involved in the pattern. There may be many reasons for Jupiter's involvement, including perhaps the fact that such disasters raise many moral, religious and philosophical questions. And we might remember that Zeus was a warlike God, hurling, as he did, thunderbolts and lightning from the top of Mount Olympus. More simplistically though, we can just remember the idea that Jupiter will expand whatever principle it touches in the horoscope.

Our Jupiter position by sign, house and aspect will describe where we seek to grow, to expand and to find meaning in life. Where we seek to be expansive and to do things in a Big Way and the areas in which we need quite a bit of space in order to do so.

Above all else, Jupiter represents our ability to grasp *meaning*. Jupiter urges us to look beyond the immediate facts and the current situation and see a deeper meaning, significance and purpose. Clearly, in holding any kind of beliefs (whether they be religious, philosophical, political or whatever) we are having to do this. Every time we try to see the meaning or purpose behind an event, we are calling upon the principles of Jupiter or the 9th house. When Jupiter contacts a planet in our chart we tend to philosophise about the things represented by that planet; we ask what that planetary principle actually means. And we want to spread our wings in that area, take as much as possible on board, travel tremendous distances with it.

Our Jupiter aspects also say a great deal about the nature of our beliefs and the manner in which we convey these. Aggressively with Mars, cautiously with Saturn. Jupiter with Mars might suggest that we fight for our beliefs, fight against others' beliefs, whilst Jupiter–Saturn might describe us as having to work hard to have beliefs in the first place. Mars–Jupiter might describe belief in winning, in being competitive, belief in the importance of taking initiative, whilst Mars linked up with Saturn might describe belief in the importance of responsibility, belief and trust in form, in matter, in what one can actually see.

Thus aspects to our Jupiter will have a great deal to say about what we believe in and how we deal with our beliefs. To find meaning and purpose in life is a need which cannot be too highly estimated. We can cope much better will all sorts of atrocities and pain in our lives if we can believe that our suffering has some sort of higher purpose. The world's major belief system is religion and our Jupiter contacts will have much to say about our relationship with God, whatever we might personally mean by that term. Jupiter is also of course the significator for all belief systems, and not only religious ones, but certainly beliefs that people pursue with a religious zeal – politics for example.

We are often told that human beings create God in their own image, and so it can be seen that our Jupiter contacts also describe the way and extent to which we may tend to 'play God' in our own lives. When we believe that ours is *the* belief system we are not only being very arrogant but 'playing God'. This is of course a distortion of the Jupiter principle, which in fact knows that 'God' embraces all: all religious expressions or observances; all political inclinations and all the different world-views that each of us do and do not hold. Contacts to our Jupiter, along with planets in or ruling our 9th house, will describe the ways in which the Jupiter principle may be distorted; the way in which our personal belief system is geared. Easy aspects may describe the fact that we can easily discern meaning in life although we may be complacent about what we do believe. With the easy aspects others are less likely to challenge our beliefs, for they represent our lines of least resistance, what we fall back on, what supports us, rather than beliefs which on some level we feel uncomfortable with and thus might tend to over-express. Difficult contacts usually suggest that we are uncertain or unclear about our beliefs and that they will be challenged. In the long run such challenge may make our belief system much more rounded. Hard aspects and sometimes conjunctions may mean that we have to work very hard to find meaning in life or that we go overboard in trying to prove that our beliefs are the right ones.

Jupiter also describes faith in the larger sense and as such is an indicator of our feelings of inner faith, confidence and buoyancy. When Jupiter forms a soft aspect to a planet in our chart we generally feel gently expansive and optimistic in relation to what the planet signifies. With the hard aspects we may be over-optimistic in that area or uncertain about how much faith we actually have, but in any event, we feel forced to 'try our luck' in that area.

Jupiter is also associated with wisdom. To be wise we have to have knowledge and information – but also, the capacity for understanding these in the light of the greater whole. Jupiter represents that function which enables us to see the grand scheme of things, the wider implications, and in seeing those wider implications we are in a better position to make wise judgements. Aspects to our Jupiter may describe what impedes, accelerates or gets in the way of our being able to glimpse the larger picture.

Jupiter is also associated with the broadening of one's mind, understanding and wisdom, and as such it has rulership over long-distance travel and higher education, both of which can broaden the mind. Aspects to our Jupiter, along with 9th house planets and rulers, will have much to say about our urge for, and experience of, travel and education.

Where we find Jupiter is also where we tend to be greedy. When Jupiter contacts a planet in our chart, we tend to want more (and perhaps can give more) or whatever that planet signifies. It is also often an area where more and more is available to us. Thus Jupiter is associated with wealth. When we are wealthy we abound in something which is valuable. Our Jupiter aspects will describe the ease or difficulty with which we attain, use or recognise wealth. They will also show, together with the sign and house placement, what the nature of that wealth might actually be.

SATURN

Fear, control and denial. Authority. Discipline. Time. Learning things the hard way. Responsibilities. Duties.

Beyond all else perhaps, Saturn represents *fear*, and many of the problems and difficulties surrounding this planet can be traced to this single root principle. When Saturn contacts a planet in our chart we tend to be frightened of expressing those things symbolised by that planet. More than that, we feel *unable* to express them, for we feel awkward in that area of ourselves – awkward, clumsy and severely hampered.

Naturally enough, we don't usually want people to see a part of ourselves that feels to us like an awkward, clumsy animal for it doesn't occur to us that others might perceive it as acceptable or even beautiful. And even if they did, what good would that be, for it is our perception of ourselves which decides most things. Little wonder that Saturn has been linked with the Jungian idea of the 'Shadow' – that part of ourselves which we not only attempt to hide from others but successfully conceal from ourselves as well. We hide Saturn by attempting to package up our fears into some socially acceptable form or by pretending that we are adept in this awkward area of ourselves. So whilst Saturn may well describe our Achilles' heel, we can often manage to hide this aspect of ourselves, even from ourselves. It is important to realise this way of dealing with Saturn when considering Saturnian contacts in the natal chart, for at first glance the individual may not seem particularly awkward in this area of their lives and may even appear very sophisticated and adept at dealing with it. The sophistication isn't always 'false' either, for eventually we can become genuinely very adept at those things that were initially our biggest problems. Turning lead into gold as the alchemists would put it. But this comes only after time and only after lots of effort. And after facing our fears and perhaps suffering numerous disappointments.

When we do learn things the hard way, and through experience, we generally know about them thoroughly; we become an 'authority' in that area. And this is what Saturn seems to insist upon, that we deal with the issues, whatever they are, thoroughly. For as always Saturn, unlike Jupiter, never lets us get away with anything.

So contacts from Saturn to another planet in our chart can describe, when we are older at any rate, a real understanding of what that planet represents. On the other hand, we can merely pretend that that understanding exists. How do we now the difference? When merely acting with our Saturn (though not of course consciously doing so) we tend to express the planet involved in a controlled and *formulated* kind of way. We tend to behave how we think we should behave in the given circumstances, how society would expect us to behave. What is missing is spontaneity of self-expression; the 'false' and inevitably socially acceptable response is usually rather boring and, whilst saying all the usual things, lacks sincerity somehow. It is rather like a child writing a typical 'Thank You' letter for a Christmas present – a kind of 'formula' response.

Discovering what our Saturn represents is inevitably a long and painful process. Like everything, pain too seems to have some purpose, for it is our pain that tells us that something is wrong inside ourselves. Pain tells us that there is a wound somewhere that demands our attention. Fear too has its purpose. It is fear that makes the rabbit freeze or the antelope run. Freezing or running are *defence* mechanisms. Defences protect us, rather as clothes protect us on a cold day. Our Saturn contacts can describe us as being underdefended or overdefended in various aspects of life. As children, we have a special need of our defences, and childhood is the prime time for building them, but as we get older some of those defences may become inappropriate, even strangulating. We can never look into a distant horizon if the first thing that our eyes hit is a brick wall. When Saturn contacts a planet in our chart it is often as if we have built a brick wall around those things that that planet represents. And for many people with difficult Saturn aspects in their charts, much of the adult life has to be spent slowly taking the wall down, brick by brick. For confronting the Shadow has to be done slowly and with great care and respect.

When we are 'overdefended', when we have surrounded ourselves with rather too much brick wall, we will have locked away a lot of the potential in our lives, for here, we are too frightened to take risks. This is also one of the reasons we can associate Saturn with pain, for when in pain we usually feel better if we can relax and let go. It is often the holding on that is painful, but with our Saturn contacts we are often frightened to let go.

Our defences have protected us up until now and we believe they always will, whereas now is usually the time to let go.

Another Saturnian principle is control and this too is often attributable to fear, for when we are frightened we often attempt to control whatever is going on. We also want things very clearly defined. When Saturn touches a planet in our chart we will tend to seek definition of whatever that planet represents. Venus–Saturn for example is frightened of not being loved, so may push their partner to define their feelings. Do you love me? How much? Will it last for ever? This of course does not usually yield the required response, for feelings cannot be quantified or defined in this way and the partner may not want to be forced into responding in this way in any case. So classically the Venus–Saturn type will go away feeling unloved and unappreciated to sit in a room by itself and face another lonely evening wailing that nobody cares.

Saturn problems can often be traced to childhood issues. In childhood we often feel denied those things that planets contacting Saturn represent. And because we feel denied them, we crave them for evermore. They can become the very reason for our existence. We may have been denied in childhood through no one's 'fault', merely through some seemingly cruel twist of fate, a fate that we can eventually be grateful for, once we have got through our first faltering steps.

Although our childhood cannot be held 'responsible' for problems in adulthood, exploring some of the themes in our early life is necessary in order for us to make peace with our past and to enrich our future. But childhood images are useful for Saturn contacts anyway, because planets contacting our Saturn often feel as a small child does when confronted with the stern voice of authority. For example, Mercury–Saturn people often feel as if they are in an examination room being tested every time they meet a learning experience, even if in fact their school years were not especially gruelling, and did not include grim examination conditions. But the image is helpful and one which we can dialogue with.

The idea of feeling denied something and craving it, is also, I think, a useful one, for when Saturn touches a planet we do tend to crave those things that that planet represents. With the Sun we may crave recognition; with the Moon nurturance, a home and a family; with Venus, love and affection; with Jupiter, faith, and so on.

Saturn contacts by house, aspect and, to a lesser extent, sign, describe those areas where we lack confidence, where we feel we *ought* and we *should* do better. Often we apologise for those areas of our chart which Saturn touches, and in apologising we are not only expressing regret but are saying that we don't think we are good enough. Sometimes we also offer some sort of justification for our 'faults' and in doing so are defending ourselves.

As many an astrology teacher has noted, this is the part of the chart where we seem to have an internalised schoolteacher always sternly telling us to work harder, do better, be better, try harder. Saturn denies, delays, restricts, restrains, generally slows down, even cripples at times, the development of whatever it touches. The purpose of all this denial and restriction is often to test the validity of what we are doing or what we think we want.

In contrast to Jupiter, which often describes where we feel confident or where we go to to feel good and to find meaning, Saturn describes the place where we tend to feel the least comfortable, most fearful, most awkward and most vulnerable.

In order to get a feel for Saturn one can reflect on the metal lead, which it rules. Lead is extremely heavy, dull in appearance, and enduring – it does not corrode easily, for which reason it was once used in water pipes and is still used in roofing. Like lead, Saturn lends an inert, immobile quality to whatever it touches in the chart. Saturn will also slow down the development of whatever it touches but it will also insist that that development is thorough and that no short-cuts are taken. Saturn may appear dull, but it bestows endurance. It insists that time is taken. Saturn is also concerned with rules and regulations (again, with doing the 'right' thing), with duty, responsibility and discipline. Rules and regulations in the wider sense are designed to protect the individual and society as a whole. Parental laws are also designed to protect the child and to educate the youngster as to the limitations, constraints and responsibilities that living in the material world implies. Overdone though, discipline makes the child frightened of all forms of authority (within or without) and unable to express its individuality.

Saturn is traditionally associated with the father and sometimes the mother. Certainly, Saturn seems to correlate with an internalised image of father and often with the physical father too. Where any parent or other authority-figure is meting out discipline they are acting in the role of Saturn. Discipline need not be negative. Saturn also represents the discovery that if you touch a fire your fingers will get burnt. Thus Saturn represents authority-figures in general, as well as our urge to develop self-discipline and self-control. Difficult Saturn contacts suggest lessons around authority issues; being able to accept the authority of others or being able to develop it within oneself.

Saturn contacts generally get better as an individual gets older and is better able to accept that living in the real world does involve living with fear, constraints and limitations, but that some of these are merely self-imposed. Saturn is the planet concerned with age and with the taking on of the responsibilities and duties that we associate with adulthood. Our Saturn placement and contacts usually have much to say about the way in which we deal with these duties and responsibilities.

URANUS

The urge to break free and be independent. The urge to rebel and to shock. Liberation. Sudden awakening. Freedom in truth. Radical change. Revolution. Deviation from the norm.

As with the other outer planets, Neptune and Pluto, the cycles of Uranus have great bearing on the psychological, economic and physical changes that occur on a world-wide basis. Uranus, spending seven years in a sign, is often considered to operate as a higher octave of Mercury. Certainly, the planet seems to symbolise the dawning change of collective ideas. Individuals who have Uranus contacting planets or personal points in their chart usually act, consciously or unconsciously, as the forerunners and trailblazers for these new ideas, through the medium of the planets involved. These are the individuals who may be considered to be unconventional or anarchic by their more Saturnian and orthodox peers.

Uranus heralds the latest idea, the newest invention and the most modern technology. Especially technology which offers the opportunity for a faster and radically different way of transmitting ideas; advanced electronics and computers for example. The changes, in collective terms anyway, seem to leap suddenly from nowhere and drastically alter our lives overnight. Uranus, like many inventions, cuts through both time and tradition. That Uranus also creates *resistance* is not surprising for the action of the planet is sudden, drastic, and tends to go too far. Uranus does nothing by halves and has no aptitude for co-operation and no respect for tradition or human feeling. Like all the outer planets, Uranus is non-personal in its action.

The Uranian principle challenges anything and everything that is Saturnian; that which is conventional, traditional and orthodox. The planet always opposes authority and age. It challenges anything that has become thwarted, repressed, oppressed or rigid. When Uranus touches a planet in a chart it urges those planetary principles to express themselves in the most contrary and deviant kind of way. Because society tends to be Saturnian, 'deviant' is often interpreted as something dirty, but the word merely means to take an alternative path. Certainly, the Uranian principle will always wish to go by a different route. Uranus symbolises the urge for rebellion. When it touches a planet in the chart it often creates a situation where the individual wants to rebel against expressing what that planet normally represents, or has represented in the past. And thus in challenging the status quo, the Uranian person may alienate themselves from society, but they will also act as the vehicle through which the inevitable change of ideas will occur. Thus, for example, individuals who have Uranus contacting the Moon may challenge the traditional role of mother. Uranus with Venus or Mars may describe those who challenge the traditional boy-meets-girl-equals-marriage kind of life scenario. Given that 'un' usually reverses the meaning of a word, Uranian keywords are often those that start with this prefix: unconventional, unusual, unlikely, unorthodox, unemotional.

Aspects to Uranus, especially hard aspects from the Sun or Moon, can be associated with the periodic orchestration of the most sweeping and drastic life-changes. Such changes can sometimes be seen to be a result of an inability to shift on a smaller day-to-day level, so that the inner impulse for movement gets built up. Extreme about-turns in life may seemingly be forced on the individual by some outside circumstance or they themselves may answer some inner call to overthrow the existing situation. In either case, such change is bound to meet with tremendous counter-pressure (usually of a Saturnian nature) from within the self or from without, from others who will be affected by those changes. Wherever Uranus goes, so too goes inflexibility, extremism and lack of co-operation, and on both sides.

Planets touched by Uranus seek excitement, freedom and independence. Thus Moon–Uranus contacts for example, very simplistically, can be associated with emotional independence, and domestic freedom. Venus–Uranus social excitement and freedom in relationships. Where there are challenging aspects, the individual will be forced to try to integrate, on the one hand, their need to give and receive emotional rapport, safety and protection (Moon) with, on the other, the need for independence, space, freedom and excitement.

Because the Uranian principle also seems to invoke the Saturnian one, Uranus sometimes freezes the development of what it touches for a time. People who have strong Uranus contacts are usually as fearful as they are excited by the prospect of change, which is why, when change happens it is often so extreme. The soft aspects suggest a facility for, and enjoyment of, change, freedom and excitement, and thus with these aspects extreme behaviour is much less likely, whereas the hard aspects suggest that the issues of being different, deviant, rebellious, exciting or in any other way 'Uranian' just have to be tested.

In early life strong Uranus contacts in the chart suggests that, with regard to the planet that is being contacted, there was probably not too much in the way of predictability and anchorage. Instead, some kind of sudden disruption, shock or, at least, inconsistency is indicated. The individual may have found this disruption exciting and liberating (as might be expected to a greater extent with the 'soft' aspects) or deeply unsettling, and often a mixture of the two. In any event, individuals with such contacts (and we nearly all have them to some planet) tend to expect and habitually precipitate disruption in adulthood.

Uranus is associated with shocks too. Any kind of shock may disturb but it will also excite and awaken. Shocks exhilarate and give rise to a feeling of vibrancy and being alive. Uranus is always the enemy of stagnation and always urges us to break free and cut through limitations, defences, laws, anything that binds us, whether these be self-imposed or imposed from the outside.

The purpose behind the Uranian impulse for drastic action is often concerned with awakening and liberating. The planet is also concerned with 'truth' and more especially with the quick, blinding intuitive flash of realisation which is so liberating because it just cuts through everything else. Uranus does tend to 'cut' through the expression of whatever planetary principle it touches in the chart. Whilst this can be very liberating and exciting, the Uranian principle of cutting through defences can go too far. At best, the Uranian principle cuts through the parental and social cords which hold us back, cuts through rigidity, fear and the addiction to social norms which stand in the way of change or independence, whether this independence be of thought or of action. At worst though, the Uranian principle forgets that we need a certain amount of holding back, a certain amount of safety and predictability in life, for this provides us with the anchorage and strength from which we can institute changes in our lives and in the world.

Perhaps *the* key word for Uranus is *radical*, for the planet is not only concerned with the advancement of liberal views but also with the most radical and drastic forms of actions. Action which strikes to the very root of something and seeks to revolutionise it.

NEPTUNE

Refinement, purification and cleansing. Infiltration. Deception. Sacrifice. Transcendence or escape. Ideals. Dreams, fantasies. Enchantment.

Neptune will tend to refine whatever energies it comes into contact with in the natal chart. It will seek to refine, purify and cleanse; to erase imperfections or defects. Planets touched by Neptune are rendered both purer and more difficult to get hold of. Neptune tends to remove coarseness or vulgarity from whatever planetary principle it touches. It will incline whatever that planet represents to greater delicacy, purity and subtlety.

The ability to discern and appreciate subtlety is one of the main gifts of the Neptunian principle. This is surely one of the reasons why those whose charts are strongly touched by this planet are often very creative or artistic. For the artist – whether in fine art, music or drama – is usually someone with a heightened perception of form, colour or sound.

But Neptune's association with refinement is not all good news. The more something has been refined, the further away it has been taken from its original state. We can think of refined sugar or flour, pleasing to the eye perhaps but rather synthetic. Already a reason for Neptune's reputation for falseness, deception and dishonesty becomes apparent. In lifting an experience, in heightening it, Neptune also takes us further away for that experience. Further away from reality. When something is taken away from us we can no longer see it clearly and we cannot get hold of it. Above all else, as all the textbooks will tell us, Neptune represents our urge to transcend and escape from ordinary reality. Whatever Neptune touches in the chart it will urge that part of us to go beyond the mundane, to exceed the limits and boundaries imposed upon us by living in the real world. Neptune will urge us to rise beyond earthly and material considerations. At best Neptune inspires us to go further, excel, surpass and exceed. This is presumably how Neptune's association with idealism has arisen. When Neptune touches a planet in our chart we are capable of being very idealistic in expressing that planet's energies. We often want to do so in the highest and purest way. So much so that there grows a vast chasm between the dream of what we want and the reality of what we have or can realistically hope to attain. We may then decide to make a great sacrifice, possibly become something of a martyr and do without altogether. Hence Neptune's reputation for loss.

When a planet is contacted by Neptune, we often give away whatever that planet represents. We become a victim or a martyr in respect of it. Victims and martyrs both sacrifice themselves; the only difference between the two may be that the martyrs sacrifice themselves in order to gain some sort of credit or because the sacrifice holds some sort of spiritual meaning.

Where Neptune is situated or what Neptune touches tends not to accept (possibly not even recognise) boundaries, it seems as if nothing will get in the way of the attainment of the wish, dream or desire. This is useful for bringing an ideal into reality, since where we are shackled or even more than routinely aware of earthly limitations then we will not aspire to anything. Non-acceptance of boundaries is useful because it opens up the possibility of that which might be magical, intangible and exceptional. It also opens up the possibility of anarchy, chaos and anything other than excellence. The disregard of boundaries works both ways. Where we have few boundaries we are open to experience and open to being seduced, as well as able to seduce others. It is the lack of boundaries that allows Neptune to seduce and it does so through infiltration.

An image for this is that of a room where there are evidently boundaries between the inside and the outside. There are walls and a ceiling and let's say the windows and doors are closed. If there is a gas leak outside, the gas will still manage to get inside the room. It will creep under the door, waft through cracks in the walls. However well the room appears to be sealed, the average room will be infiltrated by the gas. This seems to be how Neptune operates. Neptune is a significator of leaks, and leaks of all descriptions (including of course scandal and secrets) tend to be insidious and frightening. It is difficult to contain a leak. Perhaps only those things that are symbolised by Saturn can do so: walls, boundaries and defences.

When a planet touches Neptune, whatever that planet represents is always in danger of springing a leak. Mercury–Neptune may leak information: not the best person to tell your secrets to. With Sun–Neptune, the boundaries between the self and others are dissolved and the self and not-self leak into each other.

Neptune not only seeks to elevate the principles of what it touches, it tends to want more and more of that experience. Neptune is a significator for all forms of water, and where Neptune touches something in our chart we can feel perpetually thirsty with respect to what that planet symbolises. We may then feel dissatisfied or unwilling to accept things as they really are. Sun–Neptune, for example, often has a particular horror of being ordinary or mundane, and often yearns to be something special, 'higher'. Venus–Neptune will be thirsty for love, for the ideal and perfect relationship. The individual may then tend to go through life either idealising everyone or avoiding relationships altogether, always in search of some godlike figure.

Neptune likes glamour. Where Neptune touches a planet in our chart we want what that planet expresses to be expressed in the most glamorous way possible. A definition for glamour is: 'magic, enchantment, spell … a delusive or alluring charm'. Described in this way, the idea of glamour conjures up the world of fairy-tales, a world where there are kings and queens, princes and princesses. Spells and fairy godmothers and the like. Fairy-stories, fantasies, television, film, music, all these things distance us from the horrors of reality. They allow an escape route and Neptune is a significator for them all. But it seems clear that our fantasy life does more than merely offer an escape route.

Writing on the usefulness of fairy-stories for children Bruno Bettelheim writes in his book *The Uses of Enchantment*:

A child needs to understand what is going on within his conscious self so that he can also cope with that which goes on in his unconscious. He can achieve this understanding, and with it the ability to cope, not through rational comprehension of the nature and content of his unconscious, but by becoming familiar with it through spinning out daydreams – ruminating, rearranging, and fantasising about suitable story elements in response to unconscious pressures.

I suspect that what Bruno Bettelheim writes about children and fairy-stories equally applies to adults and their need for television, film, the Royal Family and so on. Like fairy-stories, these are vehicles for the constant struggle that we all wage to understand what is 'good' and 'bad' and 'right' and 'wrong'. Such vehicles mysteriously seem to help us make sense of our lives. Our dreams also help us make sense of our lives by connecting us to our unconscious. Perhaps they cleanse and purify us in some way.

The significator of the media is of course Neptune. Our own Royal Family (surely themselves an example of the collective need for enchantment) are really only turned into kings and queens and so on by the media. I have long wondered about the popularity of the so-called 'gutter-press' – the tabloids. What is it that makes them so popular? Surely it is that with these newspapers we are given a massive dose of Neptune; surely they sell because their stories are so far away from reality, *because* to a large extent they are false. Neptune refines by removing the subtle edges. Tabloid stories may be false but, like our dreams, they are based on a distortion of reality. Our day-dreams, the television, the tabloids all offer an escape route. They caricature real life, they often render it grotesque by inflating stories beyond all reality. Our dreams do that too, the message always coming in an exaggerated though often literal form. By presenting things in black and white terms our dreams enable us to perceive the salient points quickly.

As well as being a significator of our personal dreams, Neptune is also associated with the dreams and yearnings of the collective. People who have the planet highly emphasised in their charts by tight aspect to personal planets for example, are often in a position to embody these collective images and fantasies, and as such are often artists in some form. Through their particular medium, they speak for and to us all, and certainly to their particular generation who will have Neptune in roughly the same place in the horoscope.

It is the purpose of Neptune to show us that there is another side of reality, that perhaps reality itself is false and, more to the point, that nothing is quite as it seems. And perhaps in reflecting on Neptune we are also considering the 'uses of enchantment'.

PLUTO

Death, transformation, rebirth. Taboo. Survival. Obsession. Compulsion. Crisis. Rape. Paranoia.

In the choice of death, of course, the opposite lies concealed. Until we choose death, we cannot choose life. Until we can say no to life, we have not really said yes to it, but have been carried along by its collective stream. (James Hillman, *Suicide and the Soul*)

When Pluto contacts a planet or other point in the chart, it seems to *deepen* and *intensify* those things that that planet represents. With the hard aspects, where the expression of Pluto will seem at odds with the expression of the other planet, Pluto often seems to *bury* or even *kill* the other planet. Thus people with Moon–Pluto contacts, for example, have often seemingly 'buried' their feelings and feel quite cut off from them, sometimes for long periods.

In mythology Hades (Pluto) emerges from the underworld just long enough to abduct and rape the innocent Persephone, who is then fated to live in the underworld with him, whilst allowed to spend at least part of the year with her mother, Demeter. As Hadyn Paul says in his book *Phoenix Rising*, whilst this might appear as '… a tale of evil corruption, it is a symbol for a psychological process'. He goes on:

> For Persephone, it is the right time to be initiated into her own womanhood, to be forcibly taken away from her previous reality, which is now outgrown, and forced to experience and change to accommodate literally a new world. It is part of a process that has been inevitable from the time of her birth; and as always, Pluto performs the most suitable role of image and symbol as her initiator, or time-keeper of her life. It is an experience which is vital to development, and encapsulates a 'formula' suggesting that a penetration by the unconscious leads to greater light/insight which gives inner integration and self-unfoldment. Persephone emerges from her initiatory 'rape' as a more mature and conscious woman. Gone is the naive adolescent, and she greets her mother again from a perspective of rebirth and greater integration. The process will continue as she returns each year to Pluto's kingdom, because 'a real initiation never ends'; there can be a recognisable point where the process commences, but there is none where it finishes.

Often when a planet touches our Pluto we feel as if those things signified by that planet have indeed been subject to something rather ugly, have indeed been violated, invaded and taken by force, or that they might be in the future. We often feel persecuted with respect to planets touched by Pluto. Or at least this is often the experience with the conjunction and hard aspects. For example, the Moon–Pluto person often feels that their feelings have been violated in the past, intruded upon, trodden over with hobnail boots, and there is often tremendous fear of such invasion taking place again. Sun–Pluto often feels that their identity has been, or might be, stripped away from them. With Venus–Pluto or Mars–Pluto there can sometimes be a history of literal rape or the taking away by force of one's affection (Venus) or will (Mars).

We cannot live lightly on life with respect to those planets that touch our Pluto. It is through such contacts that we are able to gain a glimpse of the underworld, in the shape of our own unconscious and, I suspect, the uglier aspects of the collective unconscious. Such glimpses may not be pleasant but they transform our understanding of the planetary principle in question. Often when a planet is touched by Pluto there is a feeling of early violation but this is very quickly and deeply buried and may not resurface for many years until there is an appropriate transit. Before it resurfaces and there is an opportunity to integrate it fully, there is often a tremendous fear surrounding the planet concerned, a fear that presents itself through a compulsive and obsessive desire to keep something out. It is as if on some level we know we are going to be raped, and faintly remember it happening in the past perhaps, and thus fortify ourselves against it happening in the future. Wherever Pluto is we often try to close the door up tight.

The name Hades is usually taken to mean 'invisible' and in the myth it was Hades' helmet that made him so. Pluto comes from the word for 'riches' and it was he who received buried treasure. Perhaps the buried treasure attached to planets contacted by Pluto is potentially the depth of understanding that we might have with respect to that planet. We tend to have very dark images of the underworld because, naturally enough, we are frightened of those things we cannot see and do not understand. Those things that are hidden are always the most powerful, in the same way that the more unconscious aspects of our psyche are potentially the most dangerous, but alongside all the ugliness there is also usually buried treasure and this is the reward we receive for foraging into Pluto territory. In the myth, the underworld was not such a bad place; Hades was certainly happy enough to live there and left on only two occasions. In many myths, the underworld is more a place of *limbo* or retirement than a place of hell, but it came to be thought of as a place of justice where each soul received exactly what it deserved.

Planets contacted by Pluto often do operate from a position of 'limbo' for large periods of time (a definition of limbo is of a region intermediate between heaven and hell, especially for the unbaptised) or certainly in limbo with respect to their Pluto contacts.

The discovery of Pluto had a period of 'limbo' about it. Percival Lowell and others suspected as early as 1915 that Pluto existed, but it wasn't until fifteen years later, in 1930, that it was definitely discovered, and by a different man, Clyde Tombaugh. And that is very much how Pluto seems to operate in the chart: something is buried, hidden from view for perhaps years on end but will gradually work its way to the surface. Pluto is not only the significator of secrets and hidden things in general but is also responsible for the uncovering and surfacing of whatever had been buried. As a mole will always eventually come to the surface for air, so will Pluto issues eventually come to light. The further underground they are buried the longer it will take, the greater the effort to keep them concealed, the more devastating the consequence when they do surface, the greater the potential for self-transformation.

Some of the keywords for Pluto are transformation, death and rebirth – words that astrologers like myself reel off as if talking about breakfast cereal. The words are the right ones certainly, but they sound 'dead'; perhaps through over-use they have lost their meaning. But keywords are of little use in helping us to grapple with the meaning of Pluto in our charts, for this planet can only be understood, if at all, *from the inside*, and through personal experience. There really aren't words to conjure up the magnitude and depth of the issues that Pluto symbolises. Pluto issues are – to me, at any rate – ultimately quite unfathomable.

Focusing on the notion of 'death' for a moment, physical death of the self still seems, in my experience, to come largely within the domain of the grim reaper, Saturn, though Pluto is often very active in our charts when people close to us die, for such deaths also herald personal transformation for those left behind. Obviously there are many kinds of death other than the physical kind and any major transformation in our lives inevitably, involves the death of something, the stripping away of the superfluous, the death of inappropriate values, attitudes or ideas, the transformation from one state of being to another. It is this kind of death that Pluto is concerned with.

Stephen Arroyo associates Pluto with the idea of *taboo*. Apparently it was the late Richard Ideman who first coined this term. Personally I find that approaching Pluto from the notion of taboo is about the easiest and most useful way into the planet. Definitions of taboo include:

Set apart for or consecrated for special use or purpose; restricted to the use of a god, a king or a priest whilst prohibited to others.

A temporary or permanent prohibition from certain actions, food, or contact from others.

To put under a taboo: to give a sacred place or privileged character to a thing which restricts its use from ordinary use or treatment.

Thus there is a very strong 'forbidden fruit' quality about Pluto. The sacred aspect of the word taboo is interesting, for Pluto issues are not available for inspection in the shop window. Part of the reason why Pluto is so difficult to understand is that, as a rule, people are less likely to talk about or even understand the Pluto issues in their lives. Natal Pluto issues are much more likely to surface in a long-term therapeutic situation than in any one-off astrological consultation, although people do bring their Pluto transits to consultations of course. There is also something sacred about the major transformative experiences in our lives; they are not for sharing except with people we really trust.

What is taboo or sacred in one particular culture or particular period of time is not what is going to be taboo in another. Thus we can associate Pluto with collective Shadow issues; those things that our particular culture is unable to acknowledge or 'own'. When Pluto contacts a planet in our chart we are usually forced to acknowledge not only something that is a taboo for us personally but a particular taboo of our culture, through the medium of the planet that is being aspected. Sometimes this may threaten to ostracise us from society or so we believe, and that is another reason why we have a compulsive need to cover up our Pluto issues from ourselves as well as from others.

Whatever Pluto touches in the chart will often be touched by secrecy. Sun–Pluto is secretive about the self; with Venus–Pluto there are often issues around 'secret' love affairs or money secretly held somewhere; with Mars–Pluto there may be sexual secrets – and so on. A secret is a hidden or private piece of knowledge; those privy to it have more power than those who are not. Anything that is hidden, unseen, unknown or un-knowable inevitably carries much more power than those things that are out in the open. Frequently those areas are frightening to those who do not have access to them and potentially can be used as a weapon by those who do. But secret knowledge is not primarily kept secret for the purpose of committing injury but for the purpose of self-preservation and survival, and Pluto is always concerned with survival. If we have a planet linked to Pluto, we want whatever that planet represents to survive (*or at least to retain the power to kill itself*) and we are inclined to think that others want to rip it away from us, for as always Pluto inclines to paranoia. We often experience incredible feelings of power or powerlessness with respect to those planets touched by Pluto. What we do with that power will vary. Whilst it certainly is the power behind the most annihilating destruction it is also a power that can be used for the good.

Let us return to the notion of taboo. In our culture, rage, violence and any instinctual, primitive, uncivilised feelings are taboo, as are death and sex. All kinds of rape, all kinds of taking by force are also taboo. Certainly there is no 'would you mind, thank you very much' with Pluto. And neither should there be, for Pluto concerns itself with crisis and the fundamental issues of life, including birth and death. At such times, manners would be incongruous to the point of being hideous.

My favourite book on Pluto has nothing to do with astrology; it is James Hillman's analytical psychology book *Suicide and the Soul*, which concerns itself with death, suicide and transformation.

In his book, Hillman postulates that the urge to commit suicide is really an '*urge for hasty transformation*'. He says: 'This is not premature death as medicine might say, but the *late reaction of a delayed life which did not transform as it went along*' (my italics). When a planet is touched by Pluto it often feels that those things represented by that planet are trying to commit suicide, trying to sabotage themselves in pursuit of some kind of hasty transformation. Like Saturn, Pluto's father, Pluto often does give rise to a delayed reaction, a delayed but overwhelming transformation.

As Hillman says, transformation begins at the point where there is no hope but only despair. There are usually periods in life (triggered by transits) when planets contacted by Pluto do hit such a crisis point. But it is only when we reach rock bottom, when all hope has died, that transformation does occur. It is precisely at this point of 'death' that new life appears. When a planet touches Pluto, there is usually a tendency for whatever that planet signifies to go through periods of plummeting to the depths, interjected with periods of seeming limbo.

Pluto aspects are perhaps the most difficult ones to grapple with, but their exploration often yields great riches. As Hillman says: 'The death experience is needed to separate from the collective flow of life and to discover individuality.'

CHAPTER TWO

DIVIDING THE CIRCLE AND CALCULATING ASPECTS
(mostly for the novice)

Aspect — 'One of the ways a thing may be looked at or contemplated. A phase.'
(Oxford English Dictionary)

Like a surprising number of words and phrases in common usage, the word 'aspect' was, it would seem, first used astrologically. As astrologers we normally use the word to define the angular relationship, measured in degrees of longitude, between planets or other points along the ecliptic. Since we are usually dealing with geocentric (earth-centred) relationships there can also be aspects formed between the Sun and the Moon.

Technically speaking all the planets and points in the chart are 'in aspect' to each other. It is rather like a dozen or so people sitting around an elliptical table: each person is able to see every other, only from a different vantage point. But the planets, and other points of interest in the chart, unlike these seated people, are moving, and so the angular distance is being changed all the time. In other words aspects are always being formed and being dissolved as the planets move along their cycles. The horoscope is merely a map of a frozen moment in time, a picture of a dozen or so cycles captured at a particular moment.

Whilst it is important to remember that each planet is in aspect to every other, just as at a dinner party, one is more likely to talk to people seated in a certain relationship to oneself (seated next to or opposite, for instance), as astrologers we are used to thinking of some aspects as being more important than others, for example the conjunction, opposition, square, trine and sextile. More recently, it has become clear that semi-squares and sesquiquadrates are often equally as important.

The work of John Addey, David Hamblin and others has also show that dividing the circle by 5, 7, 9 or even higher numbers also yields highly significant information about an individual. However, except for mention of the quintile series, this book will mostly confine itself to the more discussed aspects and, more especially, those aspects that have been formed by the division of the 360 degree circle by multiples of two or three.

In the bad old days, the major aspects were generally described as being either 'good', or benefic, or 'bad', or malefic, in their nature. The more modern view shows that this view is, at best, extremely simplistic, and, at worst, absolute nonsense. More about this later. Suffice it to say that nowadays it is much more usual to describe aspects that have been arrived at by dividing the circle by a multiple of two (the opposition, square, semi-square and sesquiquadrate) as being 'hard' or challenging aspects and the trines and sextiles which has been derived from dividing the circle by a multiple of three as 'soft' or 'easy' aspects.

And there is also the conjunction, perhaps the most important aspect, which is not derived from dividing the circle at all, except perhaps by one. Here two planets are situated in the same place or very nearly so.

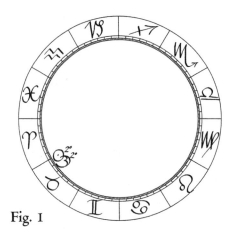

The Conjunction: Here both Sun and Moon occupy the same zodiacal sign and degree; 2 degrees of Taurus.

Fig. 1

THE HARD ASPECTS

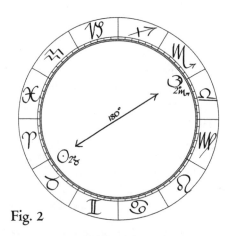

The Opposition: Here Sun and Moon are opposite each other in the circle. The Sun is at 2 degrees of Taurus whilst the Moon is at 2 degrees of Scorpio. The circle has been divided by two and the Sun and the Moon are six signs or 180 degrees apart.

Fig. 2

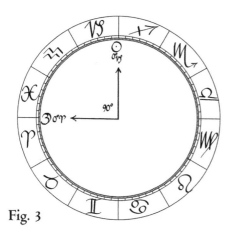

The Square: Here the Sun at 0 degrees of Capricorn and the Moon at 0 degrees of Aries are at right angles to each other. They are three signs or 90 degrees apart and form an exact square. The circle has been divided by four.

Fig. 3

The Semi-Square: Now the Sun at 0 degrees of Capricorn is 45 degrees away from the Moon at 15 degrees of Aquarius. The semi-square is literally half a square; half of 90 degrees.

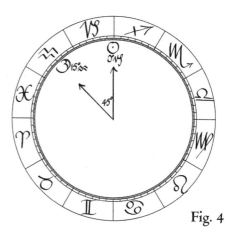

Fig. 4

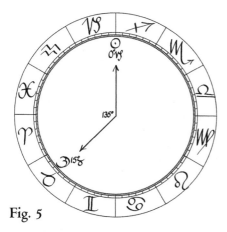

Fig. 5

The Sesquiquadrate: The Sun at 0 Capricorn is 135 degrees from the Moon at 15 of Taurus. With this aspect it can been seen that a square (90 degrees) has been added to a semi-square (45 degrees) to arrive at the sesqui-quadrate (135 degrees). With both the semi-square and the sesquiquadrate the circle has been divided by eight.

THE SOFT ASPECTS

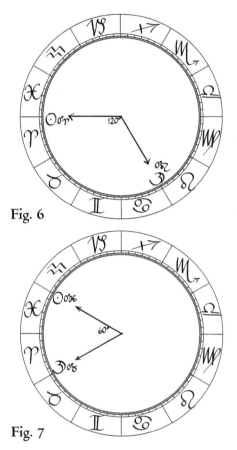

Fig. 6

Fig. 7

The soft aspects, the trine and sextile, are arrived at by dividing the circle by a multiple of three. In Fig. 6 the Sun at 0 degrees of Aries is 120 degrees from the Moon at 0 of Leo. They are four signs apart and form an exact trine. Fig. 7 illustrates a sextile. The Sun and Moon are two signs or 60 degrees apart. The 360 degree circle has been divided by six (2 x 3).

OTHER ASPECTS

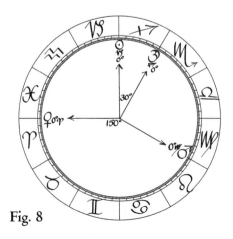

Fig. 8

The Quincunx and Semi-Sextile: Here Venus and Mars are 150 degrees or exactly five signs apart, creating a quincunx, whilst the Sun and Moon are exactly one sign or 30 degrees apart, creating an exact semi-sextile aspect.

The Quintile Series: Quintiles are derived from division of the circle by five (5 x 72 degrees = 360). Venus at 0 of Sagittarius is 72 degrees from Mars at 12 of Aquarius, forming an exact quintile. The Sun and Moon are separated by 144 degrees creating a bi-quintile. A separation of 36 degrees (half of the 72 degree aspect) may also be interpreted as part of the quintile series.

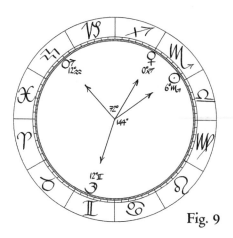

Fig. 9

FINDING THE ASPECTS

The safest but most laborious method of spotting the aspects is to count how many degrees there are between each planet and angle. To do this it is useful if the student has thoroughly grasped that:

— There are twelve signs in the zodiac
— Each sign is made up of 30 degrees of longitude
— There are 60 minutes in a degree
— Aspects are always measured by the shortest distance from planet to planet (or angle)

An **orb** is an allowance of so many degrees either side of what would be an exact aspect. One might call it an aspect's sphere of influence. For example, a planet at 14 degrees of Gemini would be 94 degrees from another planet at 18 of Virgo. Although an exact square is 90 degrees we might still count this 94 degree separation as a square aspect.

The subject of orbs in interpretation is discussed elsewhere but for the purposes of illustration, we will use the following arbitrary orbs: eight degrees for the conjunction, opposition, square and trine; four degrees for the sextile; and two degrees for every other aspect. We might then make a table that looks like this:

SYMBOL	ASPECT	EXACT	NO. OF SIGNS APART	WITH ORB
☌	Conjunction	0	0	8
⌄	Semi-sextile	30	I	28–32
∠	Semi-square	45		43–45
✳	Sextile	60	2	56–64
Q	Quintile	72		70–72
☐	Square	90	3	82–98
△	Trine	I20	4	II2–I28
⬚	Sesquiquadrate	I35		I33–I37
BQ	Bi-quintile	I44		I42–I46
⊼	Quincunx	I50	5	I48–I52
☍	Opposition	I80	6	I72–I88

Fig. 10

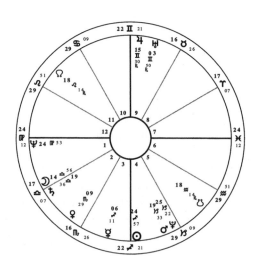

Fig. 11

Jane Austen 16 December 1775, 11.45pm LMT, Steventon, England, 51N05 1W20

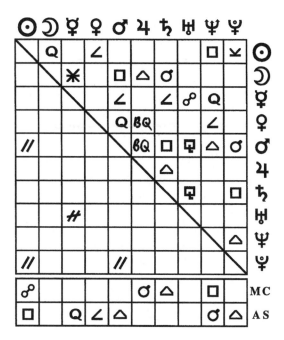

Fig. 12

Thus in Jane Austen's chart the Sun is at 25 degrees (we can round up 24 degrees and 57 minutes to 25 degrees for this purpose) of Sagittarius and the Moon is at 15 degrees of Libra. They are 70 degrees apart. From the table we can see there is a quintile aspect between the two planets. The Sun is 19 degrees from Mercury so there is no aspect formed between them. We can then do the same for every other possible interchange as shown in Fig. 12.

Aspects become much easier to spot when the elements and modes have become second nature, when the student has completely learnt whether the signs are cardinal, fixed or mutable and whether they are fire, earth, air or water. And this is because cardinal signs oppose and square cardinal signs; fixed signs oppose and square fixed signs; and the same with the mutable quadruplicity. Fire squares water and earth but opposes air; water squares fire and air but opposes earth – and so on. Fire sextiles air; earth sextiles water. Signs of the same element trine each other.

	FIRE	EARTH	AIR	WATER
CARDINAL	Aries	Capricorn	Libra	Cancer
FIXED	Leo	Taurus	Aquarius	Scorpio
MUTABLE	Sagittarius	Virgo	Gemini	Pisces

Thus, two planets in aspect in different cardinal signs, for example, would normally square or oppose each other. Two planets in aspect in different air signs would normally trine each other. I say normally because there are exceptions, and these occur in the case of disassociate aspects. Disassociate aspects are aspects which fall between elements and modes which would not normally be expected. For example: 27 degrees of Leo and 1 degree of Capricorn. Here there is a separation of 124 degrees and thus a trine aspect is formed, but it is a disassociate aspect because fire and earth do not usually trine each other; they are incompatible. Similarly, an example of disassociate square might be: 27 degrees of Libra to 2 degrees of Aquarius. Although both are air signs, there is a 95 degree separation here.

A disassociate aspect can only be formed between a planet at the end of a sign and one at the beginning of a sign and vice versa, as with Saturn and Uranus in the chart below. Counting avoids missing these aspects.

In interpretation, it is probably fair to say that disassociate squares are less stressful than ordinary squares and that disassociate trines are rather more dynamic than the more usual trines. Disassociate aspects of all kinds usually call for more delicacy and subtlety of interpretation.

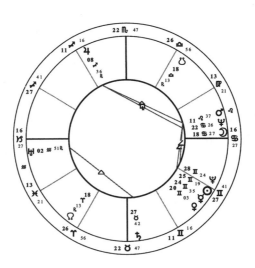

Fig. 13

Enoch Powell 16 June 1912, 9.50pm GMT, Stetchford, England, 52N29 1W54

CHAPTER THREE

THE MEANING OF ASPECTS

THE CONJUNCTION – DIVISION OF THE CIRCLE BY ONE

Astrologers of the past considered that planets were in conjunction if they merely occupied the same zodiacal sign. Nowadays an orb of 8 or 10 degrees is more usual and a conjunction may 'straddle' two signs. Some astrologers still believe the aspect to be so potent as to exert an influence over a much broader area.

The work of John Addey and Charles Harvey suggests that the meaning of a given aspect is at least partially derived from the meaning of the number necessary to form it – in other words, by the number that the 360 degree circle has had to be divided by in order to arrive at the given aspect.

In the case of the conjunction, the circle has only been divided by itself, by one. One is the number associated with the idea of unity and this is the core meaning of this major aspect, for planets in conjunction are always united. Their energies are merged, blended and always act together. As with all aspects, the nearer to exactitude that the conjunction is, the more potent will be its influence. When exact, it's rather like having two bells struck simultaneously: it's difficult to differentiate the sound of either one. In the same way, planets in conjunction tend to have problems in 'seeing' each other. In fact, if the conjunction is an exact one the two planets often don't appear to the individual to have separate identities. The differentiation may be seen by others but to the person concerned the two energies may appear as if they were one, almost as if a new planet has been formed. Thus planets in conjunction can have difficulties in separating and objectifying each other.

For example, someone with a Sun–Mercury conjunction would tend to identify very strongly with what might be called the 'rational' mind. They would identify with their ideas and opinions and with what they actually say. A person without the aspect would find it much easier to accept that they *have* thoughts, ideas, opinions but that they, as individuals, *are not* their thoughts. Their thoughts, and what they say, are just part of their whole person and may not necessarily reflect that whole person.

Thus the conjunction has a very subjective quality, and people who have one often don't recognise its overwhelming potency. Nevertheless it may be very obvious to everyone else. Sometimes it remains unrecognised because you assume that everyone else is built in exactly the same way and therefore you miss a unique characteristic of your own individuality. This is especially the case where conjunctions to the Sun and Moon are concerned, as any solar conjunctions, especially, will always affect one's personal identity and the way that is perceived. Conjunctions in general, and those affecting the Sun or Moon especially, are rather like having a mark on one's face: you can't see it without looking in the mirror. We can feel it but it's much more difficult to define if we cannot actually see it, unless someone else describes it to us. We need a mirror in order to see ourselves and as soon as we start thinking about mirrors, or other people, we are reaching outside of ourselves and beginning to talk about relationship, 'otherness' and the opposition aspect.

It is interesting to remember that at New Moon when the Sun and Moon are in conjunction one cannot actually see the Moon and this gives us a clue to this 'blind spot' quality of the conjunction.

People whose charts are dominated by conjunctions (either because they have many isolated or even one major or multiple conjunction) tend to be very self-driven and self-motivated individuals. They don't tend to look outside of themselves for self-definition or validation and therefore are less prone to self-doubt. Again, it's as if they look at themselves without the aid of a mirror. Clearly, this is a difficult task as we tend to define the self through meeting and interacting with others. Imagine an artist trying to paint a self-portrait having never seen their face in a mirror or photograph. I suspect the picture would differ greatly from the usual artist/sitter portraits and probably would not describe a very good likeness. At any rate, it would be a very subjective likeness, for the mirror, sitter or photograph allows the possibility of greater objectivity.

I have particularly noticed that New Moon people for example, seem less inclined to consult astrologers, therapists and the like. They may be strong in themselves, clear in their direction, certain of their goals but there can also be a certain lop-sidedness because it is through meeting the not-self that we are able to define ourselves and become more rounded individuals, more aware of the paradoxes within ourselves and in society.

The fact that the conjunction is the easiest aspect to spot in the horoscope immediately gives us a clue as to how obvious its effects are. Because so much energy is being concentrated into a small area of the chart, a conjunction will always provide the astrologer with an area to zoom in on, and especially so if personal planets are involved. It will be a focal point in the chart, rather like an open fire in the sitting room.

There is nothing inherently 'good' or 'bad', 'easy' or 'difficult' in the quality of the conjunction aspect; there just 'is'. Energies combined in this way are permanently wedded. The extent to which they are likely to get on depends largely on how well the energies blend together. The Moon and Venus for example, might be in conjunction without changing the fundamental soft and yielding quality of either. The Moon conjunct Saturn on the other hand might not feel so comfortable. If we take the idea that the energies of two planets in conjunction always act together, then we are saying that wherever one's capacity for nurturance and spontaneous emotional response goes (Moon), goes also caution, restraint, fear, control, duty, responsibility and so on (Saturn).

Because of the blending effect, planets in conjunction, and especially in multiple conjunction, can be quite difficult to interpret, requiring as they do careful synthesising of the energies involved. Usually an outermost planet seems to have a more powerful effect on an inner planet than vice versa. Since most conjunctions will also receive aspects from other planets or points in the charts, these will require very careful consideration.

A multiple conjunction involving three or more planets within 8 degrees or so is known as a stellium. Any pile-up of planets of this sort will reinforce all those things associated with the conjunction aspect. A stellium is obviously going to be an area of very real importance in the chart. A major focal point. Because the energies of all the planets linked in this way are going to be united, interpretation can often be quite difficult. There certainly is going to be great focus and concentration on the area concerned, but as with the conjunction generally, the stellium can act as a bit of a blind spot so that the individual can fail to realise how lop-sided they are in this area of life. Given that there is a real need to be able to find a way into a stellium it is often a good idea to try to isolate the strongest planet or a planet that seems to stick out for some reason.

In the example on page 40, one way in would be to isolate Mercury and Pluto as holding the key to the whole pile-up: Mercury, because it is the ruler of all the Gemini planets and in its own sign; Pluto because it is the heaviest body in the configuration. So we might expect a powerful communicator; someone who thinks or talks about taboo subjects; one who acts as a mouthpiece for the collective Shadow perhaps (in this case, racism); someone who identifies (Sun) with the rational mind (extreme emphasis on air sign Gemini plus Mercury); one who values knowledge; one who loves (Venus) language perhaps and sees language as beautiful. One who might be obsessed, possessed (Pluto) by an idea (Mercury) and the powerful communication of it. One could continue like this indefinitely but hopefully the reader gets the general idea. In the example given, the stellium falls in the 5th house but through rulership will actually affect most of the horoscope – all those houses which are ruled by Sun,

Mercury, Venus or Pluto. Psychologists might describe it as a 'complex'. If we also take any planets that might be in those houses into account and their aspects patterns, it can be seen that the stellium and the relationships it forms will virtually hold the key to the entire life. The stellium is to be found in the chart of the late British politician Enoch Powell, whose impassioned, and seemingly racist (though he predictably didn't see them in that light) speeches are well known to older generations. A powerful and controversial orator, Powell had strong opinions which were very forcibly expressed. He was something of an intellectual, if not a dry academic, and valued – arguably overvalued – the mind. He spoke about eight languages, including the 'dead' (Pluto) languages, ancient Greek and Latin. He worked in the intelligence service during the war, which is also resonant of Mercury–Pluto and the idea of secret information. Judging by an interview on *Desert Island Discs*, he felt most comfortable expressing his feelings of love in poetry. His preference was for powerful music (Venus–Pluto) – Wagner for example.

THE OPPOSITION – DIVISION OF THE CIRCLE BY TWO

The opposition is derived by dividing the circle by the number two. And as soon as we start considering two we are stepping into the realm of polarity, one of the building blocks not only of astrology but of just about every other philosophical, psychological and occult teaching. Our very existence is based (amongst other things) on the Law of Opposites, self and not-self, yin and yang, light and dark, male and female, conscious and unconscious, in and out, up and down, the list is inexhaustible. Inexhaustible because all things have an opposite. The interesting thing about opposites is that *things that are opposite are alike; they differ only in degree.*

As children we all learn that Jack Sprat could eat no fat and his wife could eat no lean. Like Jack Sprat and his wife, oppositions in the chart want opposite but related things. We often experience the opposition aspect as if we have both Jack and his wife inside of us, each wanting seemingly opposite things. Or perhaps a better image is that it is as if we are standing in the middle of our house and hear the front door and back door bell ring at exactly the same time. Which one do we answer? We can't be in two places at once. As part of the secret of dealing with an opposition is to become aware of and use both sides of it, the important point is that although we cannot attend to the front door and back door at the same time, we can answer both of them, if we just take it in turns. Otherwise we are leaving a stranger outside an unopened door and missing a valuable encounter. Even if the stranger is a foe as opposed to a friend, ignoring the enemy will not make it go away but is more likely to reinforce its determination to get in somehow.

Invariably, we become aware of and 'own' one half of an opposition some time before we become conscious of the other half. For some time one side of the opposition does remain like a stranger outside an unopened door. Usually the planet we accept is the one which is more in keeping with our image of ourselves. The stranger, the rejected planet, is usually the 'heavier' one and, in our view, the less socially acceptable planet. It doesn't always work like this and perhaps will vary according to many factors, not least the overall pattern of the chart, the sex of the individual, and the culture that they were raised in. Certainly in the West, we are more likely to disown Mars, Saturn or an outer planet than say the Moon or Venus. Reject an energy we may, but the psyche insists upon wholeness and thus insists that the energy of the rejected planet will intrude upon our lives in some way, and will intrude to the extent that we have disowned it. And so we meet this seemingly alien energy outside of ourselves in another person, group or object and thus become a 'victim' of it. This is of course what is meant by the term 'projection'.

We are offered the opportunity of becoming more conscious and 'owning' our rejected planet every time we meet it outside of ourselves in another person or group. Meet it we will, time and time again, until awareness dawns. This is not unjust or 'bad', for until we live out all sides of our nature we cannot become whole. In living out just one side of an opposition we are only using half the energy at our disposal.

Obviously, planets do not have to be in opposition aspect for us to reject them, and neither do we necessarily view them as 'negative' in their manifestation. When we fall in love we are invariably meeting an aspect of our chart in the beloved. Similarly, falling out of love usually involves the individual 'owning' the projected planet.

Following on from the idea that opposites are alike only differing in degree, signs by opposition are complementary to each other and serve, like political parties, to check each other's extremism. This is interesting when we consider that in politics both factions usually goad each other to greater extremism, the further right the Right go then the further left the Left go. It would be naive to believe that either party views the other as a necessary counterbalance to its own extremism, but nevertheless this is precisely what each becomes in terms of the decisions that are actually taken, if both parties are equally strong.

In Eastern philosophies, 'light' may be interpreted as being an absence of 'dark' and darkness as lacking light. Viewing a polarity in this way is perhaps more respectful and a great deal more positive in its approach to the whole idea of opposites. Conversely in our culture, the opposition is usually viewed as the bitter enemy which must be repressed at all costs. As many a cynical observer has noted, the more extreme the conflict, the more similar is the behaviour of both sides! This is not surprising if we consider that if we travel far enough in an easterly direction, we end up west of our starting-point and ultimately wind up in the same place.

Elements in opposition are compatible; that is, they can coexist with each other. Air signs oppose fire signs and air is the one element incapable of putting out fire. In fact it is not possible to start a fire without the presence of air. However, when we consider this word 'compatible' we might do well to consider also how quickly a gust of wind can turn a lighted match into a forest fire. Here, it is easy to see why oppositions have the reputation for *extremism*. And it tells us something about element compatibility. Air is compatible with fire, but from the standpoint of fire only!

Similarly, earth opposes water, and again they not only coexist happily enough but need each other. Earth needs water to make it fertile; too much and it is waterlogged, too little and it is barren. Opposite signs need each other to function at their optimum but for this to happen it is crucial that compromise, moderation and a spirit of 'give-and-take' prevail ... just the sort of ingredients required to sustain a long-term relationship. Not surprising perhaps then that the main difference in manifestation between the opposition and the other hard aspects is that it manifests particularly in the realm of relationship.

At its most negative, a chart strewn with oppositions can describe someone who tends to see-saw between extremes of behaviour or a person given to great indecision, perhaps leading to an inability to act and resultant dependence on others.

Oppositions foster *awareness*; they are designed to bring something to our attention through the medium of relationship. But a strong awareness of there being two (at least!) sides to every question can make us rather like a spectator at a tennis match, swinging our head first in one direction and then in the other. Being always pulled in two directions can have the effects of pushing us strongly in one direction; it can also stop us taking an extreme position; indeed it can stop us taking any kind of position at all. We may then attempt to steer a middle course. Sometimes this may be the most aware position, but sitting on the fence can be very difficult and uncomfortable. Perhaps it is as difficult as trying to keep a see-saw at a horizontal angle.

Basically we have to use both energies inherent in an opposition and use them in as integrated a way as possible. Some degree of swaying from side to side is probably not only unavoidable but may not be such a bad thing, for in this way we are given an opportunity to view the 'other side' of ourselves, given the opportunity of becoming a more rounded individual and of gaining insight and depth. At best the opposition can provide the means by which we can gain an awareness and appreciation not only of the paradoxes within ourselves but of the paradoxes that are present throughout all life.

The purpose of the aspect is to bring something to our attention and to increase awareness. Once we have gained that awareness, we can share it with others. The opposition is the aspect concerned with relationship, which not only provides it with the battleground for its problems but also the arena for its greatest growth.

THE TRINE – DIVISION OF THE CIRCLE BY THREE

The trine aspect occurs between two planets when they are 120 degrees apart from each other, and the 360 degree circle has been divided by three.

The major 'soft' aspect, the trine has traditionally been regarded as a very easy aspect and a most beneficial contact to have in one's chart. Certainly it is easy in the sense that it is descriptive of ease occurring between the planets or points concerned.

The idea of ease partly arises because the energies of two planets linked by trine aspect flow well together. Indeed they share the same element. Their directions may be different but they don't get in each other's way. Instead, they reinforce and support each other. They hold hands. Thus planets in trine describe those things we can do with a flowing kind of ease, almost as if doing them comes as second nature, and because they are so easy, we tend to enjoy doing them. To some extent our trines constitute innate talents. Our trines give us pleasure. They show what we delight in and what we enjoy; often what we find find aesthetically pleasing or spiritually uplifting; what we aspire to and what motivates us.

Trines describe motivation, perhaps because we seem to be motivated towards not only pursuing pleasure, ease and enjoyment but also a quality or 'being' rather than doing. When we are young, we may naturally think that a life of ease is what we aspire to, and perhaps seek to accomplish something in the first half of life in order that we might be able to live an easier existence when we are older. Ironically and ideally, as the years advance, we aspire less to the idea of ease and more to this state of 'being', of reflecting, of holding, and not uncommonly of wanting to connect with God in some sense (however we might interpret the idea of 'God'), which a psychologist might interpret as wanting to connect with our own inner core. In this latter regard one is reminded that the trine has been derived by division of the circle by three, the number associated in the Christian tradition with the Trinity, the Father, Son and Holy Ghost who, in some mysterious way, are all One.

As we will see when we come to the square aspect, tension is not only valuable but essential for growth and for our very existence. Clearly though, too much tension is very stressful and can undermine our psychological, physical and spiritual well-being, which is why some degree of ease, as indicated by our trine aspects, can be very healing. The stress of the hard aspects depletes our resources so that we can get to the point where our batteries are quite run down. Our trines allow us to recharge by doing something we have an easy talent for and enjoy doing. Trines are our lines of least resistance. People engage in all sorts of different activities in order to unwind, relax and generally let go, and the activities they choose may be described, amongst other factors, by trine aspects.

Our trines can be healing too because they enable us to *accept*. With the hard aspects, nothing is ever good enough, we exhaust ourselves either by pushing ourselves on and on or by feeling crushed, frustrated and defeated. Our trines help us to accept those things about ourselves and our accomplishments which may fall short of our aspirations. I better understood the healing qualities of the trine through going to an osteopath. Over the years I had been to several osteopaths when in crisis with back pain. I got the usual manipulative treatment, with the odd violent crunch here and there. A session would get me over the crisis situation but never seemed to have much long-term effect on my posture or the resulting problems. Then, I discovered a cranial osteopath whose manipulation was so subtle that I could hardly feel it. Anyway, he fixed my back. The point of the story is that his technique *allowed* my back to realign itself. He had been coming from a relatively trinal position. Previous osteopaths had been forcing the issue. Therapists in the psychological sense use trinal type energy too. A therapist may chose to force, push or challenge their clients sometimes, in which case they are using the energy of the square, but commonly it is trinal energy that is being utilised. For ideally, the therapist creates an atmosphere and rapport with their patient which *enables* and *facilitates* a healing process. As the therapist holds, contains, supports and, most of all, accepts the person who is their client, that person can come to accept themselves. And having gained that acceptance, they will be in a better position to deal with conflict and get on with the business of maturing, as shown by the hard aspects.

So trines facilitate acceptance and ease. But ease, even though it has its uses and is enjoyable, is not necessarily good, beneficial, fortunate or any of the other similar words that have been ascribed to the soft aspects in general and the trine in particular. Ease and enjoyment can heal, but are not usually productive of growth.

We do enjoy our trines but they are not necessarily 'good news' any more than squares are necessarily 'bad news'. What is good or bad depends very much on the vantage point of the observer and on what kind of energy might be required in a given situation.

Whilst planets whose energies naturally go well together are usually productive of character traits that everyone appreciates, some planets do not go so easily together, and this is where trines can be quite difficult. I know of a woman who has a watery grand trine involving Venus, Saturn and Pluto. This person could be said to have a talent for and be motivated (trine) by maintaining (trines always uphold the status quo) a powerful, deep (Pluto) lover (Venus) that stands the test of time (Saturn), by relationships that endure. Remembering that water tends to be dependent and that grand trines have a particularly compulsive quality, it is not perhaps so surprising that this individual kept her marriage going throughout her life (she accepted – trine – its inadequacies). But she associated love with denial, fear, deprivation and power, and because the planets were in trine aspect she did not question these associations. She found it easy to be harsh on her husband, and excessively strict and controlling with her children. She always justified her actions by telling them and herself that she was acting 'for their own good' and 'because she loved them'. It is hardly surprising therefore that her children inherited Venus–Saturn hard contacts. They felt unloved, unable to value themselves, and basically unacceptable as they were. Pages could be written about this configuration and the other chart factors which contributed to this behavioural pattern. The point here, though, is that the individual concerned had great difficulty in reversing, or even recognising the situation simply because the energy was of a trinal character. Psychological movement would have been much easier had the planets been linked by hard aspect because she would have been more doubtful of herself and less accepting of the situation.

We accept and don't question those things described by our trines. As we have seen, this can be very helpful. Some degree of acceptance and ease is needed in anyone's life, but we need the questioning and uncertainty provided by the hard aspects in order to grow. If we never question who we are or what we do we can easily become very complacent, and be rendered incapable of any kind of improvement.

A very passive aspect, the trine may provide some degree of motivation but it does not, unlike a hard aspect, actually force us to do anything. Instead, trines very much describe our lines of least resistance, in that we tend to fall back on them when things get tough. In this way trines which also contact more difficult aspects can drain off some of the stress and tension and thus can be very healing, softening, as they do, the blow of the harder aspect. Sometimes though, the reverse happens (this seems to happen especially when the trinal orb is very tight and the hard aspect orb is not) and the trine can actually prevent the individual getting to grips with the more difficult aspect, by making the person too ready to accept the difficult situation and too ready to justify their probably inappropriate way of dealing with it.

A chart strewn with trine aspects can easily describe someone who always takes the easy path, someone who 'gets away' with things. The person can be considered fortunate because things just seem to fall in their lap, in a way that leaves others speechless. Things tend to go well because, for one thing, in the trinal areas at any rate, we expect them to.

Often we don't recognise our trinal talents as being talents. When they are pointed out to us we tend to shrug them off, believing that anyone else could easily acquire the same skills. Curiously, we often spend much of our lives trying to do those things that we don't innately feel that good at (as shown by our hard aspects). Perhaps this is not so curious when we consider that mastering something that is difficult is much more fulfilling than engaging in those tasks that come more easily to us. Arguably, we also tend to value more highly those things we have worked hard for, whereas with our trinal talents and rewards, we have a much more *laissez-faire* attitude. Nevertheless, it can be very soothing and healing to involve ourselves at times, in the less stressful suggested by our trine aspects.

THE SQUARE – DIVISION OF THE CIRCLE BY FOUR

Derived by dividing the circle by four, the square differs from the opposition in several important respects.

For a start, unlike oppositions, squares occur between incompatible or antagonistic elements so some degree of tension is already implied and perhaps here is as good a place as any to consider the words 'tense' and 'tension'. The *Oxford English Dictionary* definitions are helpful and include:

The action of *stretching* or condition of being stretched; in various senses.

Nervous or emotional strain; intense suppressed excitement; a strained condition of feeling or mutual relations which is for the time outwardly calm, but is likely to result in a sudden collapse, or in an outburst of anger or violent *action* of some kind (my italics).

Thus like all hard aspects but perhaps more so than the opposition, the square is productive of tension and strain. It may not always feel very comfortable but tension is a useful condition. On a physical level, for example, it would not be possible for us to sit, stand or make any kind of bodily movement at all if it were not for the capacity of our bodies to tense their muscles.

Too much living in a highly pressurised state, too much tension in fact, can exhaust us, grind us down, make us old before our time, break and cripple us, to the extent that we can become incapable of doing anything at all. At that stage we are at the mercy of our squares, but more positively and as the *OED* tells us, it is tension that spurs us into action and it is tension that stretches us, that makes us grow, makes us become more of the person that we are.

When discussing the idea of 'polarity' and the opposition it was stated that polarities are alike, differing only in degree; thus 'up' is in polarity with 'down', 'right' is in polarity with 'left'. With the square aspect it is as if 'up' were confronting 'left'. Not only do planets in square aspect want something different, they work at cross purposes.

Unlike the opposition we usually recognise both sides of our squares; the problem is that the energies seem determined to get in each other's way. This creates tension and uncertainty and usually great resistance from each planet to the other. Because the energies get in each other's way, we get a very tense situation; we don't know what's going to happen next. There is often a feeling of uncertainty, and doubt as to whether we can cope. Like Saturn, square aspects are often productive of great *fear*. This fear and uncertainty can work out in several different ways. Firstly, in attempting to prove that we can deal with our squares we may go overboard. In attempting to prove the point we may become too pushy in the areas described by the planets involved and then run into all sorts of frustration and hindrances from the outside world. We often feel as if we are hitting our head against a brick wall with our squares. But proving that we can do something, bashing away and going on and on is great for strengthening character; it can also provide the energy out of which great things are made; our squares force us on.

Squares are useful too, because it is through meeting obstacles that we grow, either by refining our own position or by making it stronger, whatever is appropriate. That is why handling our squares, like handling Saturn, tends to get a bit easier as we get older. Grappling with squares is all part of the maturing process. People without squares in their charts often seem to mature later. Their early life does not confront them with challenges and so they may find it very difficult to summon up strength when circumstances demand it later in life, being used to taking the easier path: the path of least resistance.

Charles Harvey says of the number 4, from which the square is derived, that it is concerned with *matter* and with *manifestation*. With squares we are forced to grapple with the issues concerned, we have to actualise them and they do tend to manifest themselves in a very real, concrete way in our lives, both in terms of what happens to us and our behaviour, which of course can never be separated. Another reason why we notice squares, why they manifest so obviously, I think, is because as with all hard aspects there is an excess of energy; it tends to bubble over.

The word 'square' is commonly used in everyday parlance. We say that we are 'all square' when we don't owe each other anything, and when we say 'let's square something' we mean let's reconcile it. Fundamentally, squares are about reconciliation. How can we reconcile having X in our chart with also having Y? There is a conflict of interests. With an opposition, we could swing from one side to another; with squares we can't do that. If we were to put more weight on one side of a square than the other, a rectangle would result, which is not possible! We are stuck with our squares as they are; our only way to resolve the problem is by using the energies in as productive and as conscious a way as possible.

In its most negative form, the uncertainty of a square can render us incapable of 'doing' at all; we cannot find the way (there always is a way though) of reconciling X with Y in our charts. When this happens the energies get blocked in a kind of stalemate situation. This is particularly likely to happen with fixed squares and perhaps with Pluto contacts. This is dangerous because squares are *doing* aspects, and not to do implies that our squares have us rather than the other way round. The main problem and the main virtue of the square, as with all hard aspects, is the excess of energy created. Two people with fists up create more energy than two people holding hands. With our squares we have to find a suitable vessel in the material world for this excess of energy, otherwise it becomes self-destructive and maybe destructive of others too.

Constructively used, squares are the aspects which provide the energy for us to achieve the seemingly impossible. Squares create will and strength of character and force us to grow.

THE QUINTILE SERIES – DIVISION OF THE CIRCLE BY FIVE

The quintile is an aspect of 72 degrees and the bi-quintile 144 degrees. It is possible and totally in line with harmonic theory to continue dividing the circle by multiples of five, to arrive at the vigintile (18 degrees), the decile (36 degrees) and the tredecile (108 degrees). However, whilst these latter aspects do form part of the quintile series, only the very tightest orbs should be employed for them, in fact perhaps no orb at all beyond that of a couple of minutes.

The reader is strongly encouraged to look at the work of John Addey, Charles Harvey, David Hamblin and others, which has done much to throw light on the quintile series and the nature of 'fiveness'.

Hamblin has isolated and promoted the notion of 'style' as being descriptive of the quintile aspect, so that a quintile will say something not only about an individual's personal style but also about the style and technical quality of their creative work. With respect to fiveness, Hamblin quotes Leonard Bosnan (*The Meaning and Philosophy of Numbers*) which I would also like to do here:

> Five, according to its root meaning, is the number of *harvesting*, of *arranging the 'sheaves'* of the produced Substance, the hitherto potential substance which now becomes matter ... The number five represents that Cosmic process during which Matter is *qualified, separated into kinds*, and arranged, *like the harvest for use* (my italics).

This description of fiveness sounds to me very like Virgo, which is ruled by Mercury, the planet that a numerologist would normally attribute to the number five. In fact tentatively linking the ideas associated with Mercury to the quintile series is a good way of beginning to gain some understanding of this aspect.

The relationship between the *mind* and the quintile series has long been made, which also sounds very Mercurial. More precisely, John Addey links this aspect with the idea of *imposing one's mind on the world*.

If quintiles describe style, perhaps we can go one step further and say that a quintile aspect will describe how we might communicate or give form to our mental processes either orally, through the written word or through the use of our hands. Hamblin also points out that the quintile series is strongly emphasised in the charts of people who are preoccupied with making, forming, linking and arranging things.

In his book *Harmonics in Astrology*, John Addey suggests that the quintile series describes the *kind* of art a person is drawn to. He also links this series with the urge to power, 'the prelude of all creation, the desire to dominate some kind of material'. Knowledge is power, as is the idea that gives birth to some kind of creation. Addey also associates the number five with the character of a marriage. One aspect of marriage might also be considered Mercurial for it is about linkage and connection. If we take the word 'marry' in the widest and truest sense, it means to unite, and the quintile aspect is concerned with the impulse to unite an idea with some kind of material substance. As Addey says:

> Every artist (using that word to include every kind of human art – that of the sculptor, the town planner, the cook, the politician, the doctor) envisages an idea or ideal or formal principle and, wishing to express it, asks himself how he can make it a manifest reality.

The artist (again using this term in the widest possible sense) is also usually 'married' to his or her creative work. Bill Tierney says that quintiles 'seem to describe the potential of abilities normally considered exceptional or gifted, and abilities that are not necessarily developed or conditioned by experiences in the external environment'.

Because division of the circle by five, seven and nine does yield such exceptional, specific and rarified qualities, these aspects do not lend themselves very well to conventional 'cookbook' interpretations. By its very nature the 'cookbook' will tend to deal with the general, rather than the specific, those things common to all of humanity rather than the peculiarities and exceptional talents of the very few. Thus whilst there is David Hamblin's excellent book *Harmonic Charts* available, on the whole, the quintile, septile and novile aspects require more individual, refined and specific attention than is usually the case when examining 'ordinary' aspects.

Perhaps looking at some examples of quintiles might be useful here. Let's consider a Sun–Saturn quintile for instance. Here the individual might adopt a personal style of self-control, self-discipline, self-protectiveness and seriousness. Their creative gifts might involve planning and structuring. The mind might tend to work along quite ordered and systematic lines. The kind of psychology that might be associated with Sun–Saturn aspects, and in particular with the kind of hard aspect interpretations in the 'cookbook' section of this book, would not apply. If the quintile was describing anything about the father (and I believe it would still be doing so) it would describe him also as being rather self-controlled and serious and perhaps having creative gifts with respect to structuring and planning. In fact I know of someone who has this contact whose father designs shop layouts, gardens and the like – the former as a vocation, the latter as a hobby. He works out the layout, the overall structure, and decides what will go where. And the person with the aspect thinks a good deal and comments on *architecture*.

I have Jupiter in the 10th house bi-quintile Saturn in the 3rd. My work involves writing and generally communicating about astrology, which might be termed an old philosophy of time: Jupiter–Saturn. This is the way I impose my mind on the world, this is my *kind* of art and describes what I think about.

In our example (Fig. 11, page 38), Jane Austen has a lot of quintile aspects. Mercury quintiles the Ascendant, which is very fitting for a writer but perhaps we should not take this too seriously as her birth-time may not be that exact. However, she does certainly have Mercury quintile Neptune, which is ideal for imaginative thinking and creative writing. More striking though, is the fact that the Sun and Moon quintile each other as do Venus and Mars, which both also bi-quintile Jupiter.

If I was to see Venus, Mars and Jupiter linked in a chart by the usual hard or soft aspects I would expect the individual's love-life to be very interesting. The combination would be descriptive of a person who would just have to *have* a very full romantic and sexual life in real life. In fact, especially with the hard aspects, one might expect the individual frequently to be juggling with several partners at the same time, even in the eighteenth century when such behaviour might have been less acceptable. In fact, whilst she undoubtedly was very romantic and dreamed of the perfect romance, Jane Austen never married and, I think it's safe to say, never 'slept around' either. Reasons for this can be found quite easily in the chart; the Neptune rising in Virgo (ruler of the 7th house) semi-square Venus and Neptune squaring the Sagittarian Sun all speak of great romanticism and idealism. A romanticism that might render a person unable or unwilling to shatter their dreams by entering into anything less than the perfect union. Certainly this is not the chart of a woman who would marry for reasons of economic or social survival as women of the day and the lesser characters in her books did.

The Venus–Mars–Jupiter quintiles show very clearly in her creative work though. All her books concern themselves with romance and in particular, with the coming together of the young woman (Venus) with the young man (Mars). Members of the clergy (Jupiter) also inevitably crop up as suitors and potential marriage partners. Her own father (Sun in Sagittarius conjunct IC square Neptune plus Jupiter on the MC) was a rector.

The quintile between the Sun and Moon is also indicative of creative thinking which is concerned with the marrying of masculine and feminine principles.

John Addey has commented on what he sees as the 'obsessional' quality of the quintile, and this I take to mean the kind of obsession where the mind continually gravitates towards the same subject. With both Sun–Moon and Venus–Mars linked by quintile, perhaps one might say that Jane Austen was obsessed with thinking about relationship. Because the linkages are by quintile aspect though, this concern with relationship did not manifest in an exterior form in her life but instead described what dominated her thinking, the way she imposed her mind on the world, and the subject matter of her art.

THE SEXTILE – DIVISION OF THE CIRCLE BY SIX

In practice the sextile can be, and usually is, interpreted quite similarly to the trine, although the general idea of the sextile is that it is not quite so easy nor as passive as that aspect. Bill Tierney says that whilst squares 'push', and trines 'allow' or facilitate, sextiles 'coax', and I think this word 'coax' is exactly right for the sextile aspect.

Whereas trines are linked by the same element, sextiles fall between different but compatible elements. Fire signs sextile air signs and earth sextiles water. The linkage of different elements provides some degree of stimulation and renders the sextile much less passive than the trine aspect.

The number six is arrived at by multiplying two by three (or adding one to five) and the requirement of the number two also perhaps adds dynamism to this aspect.

In general, we have the ability to do those things that are represented by our sextile aspects, we have the *aptitude*, but need a little bit of a push. Not surprisingly therefore, sextiles are usually described as aspects of *opportunity*. The things denoted by our sextiles don't come quite so easily to us as those things denoted by our trines, and because of this, we tend to *value* our sextile talents more than our trinal ones.

The number six is often associated with Venus and there is a Venusian feeling to this aspect. The sextile is an aspect of enjoyment, pleasure and, I believe, valuation – particularly *intellectual valuation*.

Sextiles have also been linked to rhythm and repetition and thus with dancers and musicians, which also sounds rather Venusian. Certainly the sextile is an aspect of harmony and planets linked by this kind of contact tend to co-operate with each other. That's not quite the same as the 'hand-holding', non-questioning flavour of planets linked by trine aspect. Co-operation does involve some degree of effort.

THE SEMI-SQUARE AND SESQUIQUADRATE – DIVISION OF THE CIRCLE BY EIGHT

I am not exactly clear as to the exact difference between these aspects and the square but certainly they are not necessarily any weaker than that aspect. These are not 'minor' aspects. A tight semi-square or sesqui-quadrate will undoubtedly be far more important than a wide square aspect. For the sake of ease, for the rest of this section, reference will mostly only be made to semi-squares but the reader can take such discussion to include both semi-square and sequiquadrate aspects.

I have noticed one of the differences between squares and semi-squares through looking at the horoscopes for the times of accidents. These charts are often full of trines and oppositions but noticeably lacking in squares. Typically, earth is also the weakest element and Saturn is weakly placed for reasons that will become obvious. However, there is usually no lack of semi-square and sesquiquadrate aspects. There are many exceptions to this but these usually occur when the accident is not a *fait accompli* and there is perhaps an extreme fight for life or some other kind of exceptional struggle.

One might expect trines to feature prominently in accident charts because they allow the *unimpeded flow* of energy. I suggest that squares are less common because they *block, impede, hinder* and inhibit the free flow of energy. Thus in the case of the outbreak of a fire for example, squares in the chart might suggest that the fire would be less likely to get out of hand because it would meet with *resistance*. This illustrates very clearly I think that squares are not necessarily 'bad' news and neither are trines necessarily 'good' news. In this example, a multitude of trines would indicate good news *from the point of view of the fire* for it would be easy for it to grow and burn on without hindrance. Oppositions induce extremism and thus are common in accident charts, as are conjunctions (especially to the angles), because they give rise to a build-up of planetary energy.

According to Charles Harvey, semi-squares and sesquiquadrates 'can be remarkably productive of solid concrete results'. Personally I suspect that this is because these aspects do not have the uncertainty and hesitant quality of the square aspect. Because they are so purposeful, it is as if nothing can stand in the way of the concrete release of these aspects. They manifest and become actualised in a very obvious exterior way in the world. In other words, these aspects *precipitate events*. Squares do this too of course but whereas the energy of a square often gets blocked for a time because of the difficulty and uncertainty of integrating two energies that are at variance, semi-squares tend to *force* some kind of release.

From the point of view of an individual's psychology and early developmental history, in my experience the semi-squares and sesquiquadrates do differ from the other hard aspects. People do not usually relate so much to the psychology of planetary interchanges linked by these aspects. This could be because such psychology does not exist or because it is different, or as I believe to be the case, because it is *more deeply buried* in the unconscious. Unconscious aspects of our psyche are more likely to erupt violently in unexpected happenings in our lives. As soon as we become aware of something, the symbolism of our chart starts to get lived out in much less dramatic ways. As we become aware of the deeper facets of our nature we start to exercise more choice and have more control over our lives. I suggest that the reason why semi-squares and sesquiquadrates manifest so readily in terms of outward events is simply because of the greater unconsciousness of these aspects. To support this theory one might also cite the fact that astrologers themselves are only starting to become conscious of the importance of these aspects even though they have been known about for centuries. The same could of course be said of quintiles, which were discovered by Kepler in the early 1600s but largely ignored until recent years.

In any event, in practice, I think one can interpret semi-squares and sesquiquadrates in a similar way to squares.

In case the reader is in any doubt of the significance of these aspects, included is an example that should banish all such doubts for ever.

As we know, the planets (with the exception of the Moon) do not move a great deal on a day-to-day basis thus a chart for any kind of significant event should have major activity involving the angles, for the Ascendant and MC axis are totally personal to a given time and place.

The chart for the sinking of the ship the *Herald of Free Enterprise* which claimed so many lives in 1987 clearly shows this. Contrary to what was written earlier, it also has plenty of squares in it. This is perhaps because the event involved great uncertainty and struggle.

One of the central features of the day of the incident was the tight Mars–Pluto opposition which here falls across the 2nd and 8th houses. This is very consistent with violent death and a very intense fighting for survival. And of course hundreds of people were trapped in the ship and had to fight to get free. This fighting to get free is also described by the fact that the opposition links up with Uranus; thus the interchange is really a Mars–Uranus–Pluto one, a combination to be associated with sudden violence. The Mars–Pluto opposition is also consistent with the anger and impotent rage which would have been experienced by the survivors at the loss of their relatives, and the transformation that would have been enforced on their own lives. This is consistent too with the fighting of fierce battles with insurance companies about subsequent compensation. But why did the accident happen in Zeebrugge and at the particular time it did? The Mars–Pluto opposition would occur in these houses the world over at various times of the day. One of the answers of course is that this chart is also a transit chart of the company that owned the ship and a transit chart for the UK and the town of Zeebrugge.

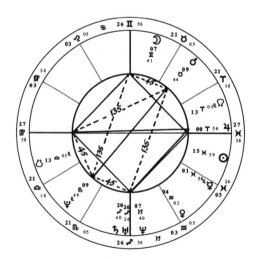

Fig. 14

Start of Voyage 6 March 1987, 6.38pm GMT, 51N19 3E12

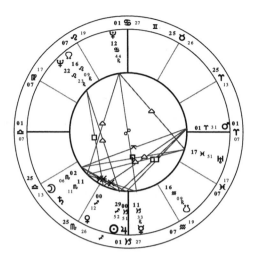

Fig. 15

Townsend Thoresen 22 December 1924, midnight GMT, 51N07 1E19

The map for the company, Townsend Thoresen, is included out of interest. Certainly the transits and general similarity of angles is very striking. However, providing one does use semi-squares and sesquiquadrates, the chart for the sinking on its own is staggering enough. Both Mars and Pluto contact the Ascendant and MC. Uranus, which also picks up the opposition, falls exactly on the IC squaring Jupiter. All very fitting for the sudden, violent, calamitous nature of the event.

Because the purpose of showing this chart is to illustrate the hard aspects and in particular the semi-squares and sesquiquadrate, only these aspects have been drawn in, but obviously there are many other significant factors in the chart. The signs and houses set and very clearly describe the stage whereupon the drama took place, and the exact quincunx aspect between the Moon and Neptune also contributes to describing that drama.

As a philosophical aside, it is surely significant that the name of the ship was the *Herald of Free Enterprise*. The company Townsend Thoresen lives in a building called Enterprise House and a lot of their ships have been given similar 'enterprising' names. The notion of *free enterprise* captures not only the spirit of Townsend Thoresen's own chart but the very strong political flavour of the UK at the time of the accident. It is left to the reader to speculate on what this might actually mean. Obviously, just as individuals will encounter incidents (and people) in their lives which will mirror more unconscious aspects of their psyche, so too will a nation or a company.

THE QUINCUNX AND SEMI-SEXTILE – DIVISION OF THE CIRCLE BY MULTIPLES OF TWELVE

The Quincunx

Signs in quincunx do not confront each other as with the opposition or get in each other's way as with the square; they are coming from such completely different places and heading in such different directions, they don't even see each other, rather like two planes on unrelated flight-paths. To become conscious of our quincunxes seems to take even more effort than to become aware of the other types of conflict in our charts. This is entirely speculation, but I don't think that this is because the material is more deeply buried as perhaps with the semi-squares and sesquiquadrate aspects, but because that material is really much less important and thus tends to get pushed into the background.

Whereas a square or opposition might be descriptive of major conflict to be resolved and thus by extension, major drama to be enacted in the life, the quincunx is more descriptive of some kind of additional irritation and stress. Imagine a person whose relationship is in a state of crisis and who is also just about to lose their job. The life is full of tremendous conflict. They come home and the kitchen is badly in need of decorating. The sight of it further undermines how they feel. It seems to me that the quincunx operates at the level of the shabby kitchen. There is a psychology behind this aspect and often a physical manifestation, but these issues tend to be a secondary importance. An individual usually chooses, indeed is forced, to deal with the central life issues as shown by the major aspects before they can turn their attention to the conflicts described by their quincunxes.

Charles Carter and many other astrologers have linked this aspect with illness and even death, mostly I think because the 6th and 8th houses quincunx the Ascendant. Personally, I can neither confirm nor deny this, but there is some logic to the idea. For surely, many health problems are caused by those things that continually produce stress and undermine us but are not so colossal that we are forced to deal with them. Thus I suspect that if quincunxes do sometimes give rise to health problems, those problems are not likely to be life-threatening but more in the nature of everyday constitutional weaknesses that both are caused by and create an underlying irritation in the life.

There seems to be a lack of rhythm and an awkwardness about the energy of a quincunx. A kind of disorganisation, which is probably why this aspect tends to feel niggly and uncomfortable. It's rather like a small piece of grit in a shoe: if you adjust your foot a bit, then it really isn't that bad.

As with any other difficult aspect, the purpose of the uncomfortableness of the quincunx is to bring something to our attention so that we can deal with it.

The main problem of the quincunx, as many astrologers have noted, is that it is too passive an aspect to deal, without considerable conscious effort anyway, with the conflict. In fact, it is not so much conflict as *friction*.

Signs in quincunx share neither mode nor element and at first glance seem to have nothing in common with each other. After all, what does Cancer have in common with Aquarius, Taurus with Sagittarius, Pisces with Leo? There are important exceptions to this rule as in the case of Taurus and Libra, which are both ruled by Venus, or Aries and Scorpio which share Mars as ruler. But most quincunxes don't seem to have much in common and I think this is the strength of this contact as well as the cause of the friction. If we look at a given sign and consider what it might most need to make it less lop-sided and more whole, it might well be the qualities of those signs with which it is in quincunx aspect. For example, one could make a case for saying that Pisces, which is so selfless, positively needs the egocentricity of Leo and vice versa. Aquarius needs to be softened by the familial, caring qualities of Cancer whilst that sign could do with some of the detachment of Aquarius. Signs in quincunx and also in semi-sextile keep each other's more extreme manifestations in check. Oppositions clearly do this too but they operate by pulling in the opposite direction, whereas the energy of a quincunx will come from a completely difference source. Thus quincunxes do not give rise to the extremism of the opposition aspect.

One thing I have noticed about quincunxes is the frequency with which they occur in synastry, not so much exact quincunxes by degree but certainly by *sign*. In close personal relationships and also in working partnerships sign quincunxes seem to me to be at least as common as oppositions and possibly more so. One partner's Sun sign is often quincunx to the other person's Sun or Ascendant sign. What this means is not clear to me but it may be related to the idea that the 8th and 6th houses are quincunx the Ascendant. The most significant relationships that we form usually involve the other person's planets falling in our 8th house or ours in theirs. And here I am particularly thinking of the personal planets or the Ascendant sign. This should not be surprising, for important relationships magically *transform* the person we are and involve the very deepest emotional interchanges. A fair number of these relationships are started at work (6th house) and certainly their success or failure has great bearing on our health and sense of well-being.

Perhaps too, quincunxes are common in synastry because of the idea that quincunx signs seem to have so little in common and thus potentially so much to offer each other.

Whilst quincunxes do sometimes provide new insights and information, more often they seem merely to add confirmation and perhaps a refinement of other factors already described in the horoscope. Thus my view of the aspect at the present time is that it can be considered to be of secondary rather than primary importance.

The Semi-Sextile

Charles Carter says he believes this aspect to be of 'negligible importance unless it is implicated in a larger formation', and I must say, I am inclined to share this view. Like quincunxes, semi-sextiles often support and confirm other information already in the chart, and this can often be seen particularly in progressions. Semi-sextiles also sometimes seem to act as linking factors. For example, if there were two completely separate aspects in a chart which were only linked by a semi-sextile aspect, then perhaps there would be a single complex of energy as opposed to two. Perhaps each 'sub-personality' as shown by the two major aspects would be better able to 'see' and integrate with the other more readily than if the semi-sextile were not present. And as Carter says 'it is plain that a strong emphasis on two consecutive signs should have a potentially harmonious value. This condition ought to make for a definite career as distinct from the scattered composition of some horoscopes, which indicates a diffusion of interests. It is a sort of integration by concentration.'

CHAPTER FOUR

INTERPRETING ASPECTS
IN PRACTICE

In practice, whenever trying to interpret an aspect configuration, worrying too much about the precise nature of the particular aspect is unnecessary, at least to begin with. In my view, instead of giving too much attention to whether the given aspect is an opposition, trine or square, it is more fruitful at the outset to concentrate on practising putting the given symbolism together.

The issues raised in a given planetary combination will be similar whatever the actual aspect happens to be even though they may *manifest* differently. A person with a Mars–Pluto contact for example, will still be concerned with survival, courage and winning whether the aspect is a trine, a square or a quintile, albeit in different ways.

Thus in the cookbook section, the individual aspects have not been dealt with, only the planetary combinations, for in my view, in a 'cookbook' of this sort which of necessity can only ever make generalisations, such distinctions would become rather contrived. However, this does mean that the reader obviously has to bear in mind the type of aspect under consideration when using the cookbook section, softening the text where trines and sextiles are concerned, and in all cases, bearing in mind that the descriptions of the combinations are really caricatures and often ugly distortions of what the true-life reality might be about.

The best way of interpreting an aspect, or indeed any other piece of astrological information, must be to work it out creatively for oneself, through long and careful deliberation. Books of potted interpretations can only ever provide food for thought.

There are different ways of attempting this kind of interpretation. One is the old, tried and tested keyword method, which personally, I rather like. An example may help. Let us assume the combination we are interested in is Saturn and Uranus. We can make a list of all the words or images we might associate with Saturn next to all the words or images we associate with Uranus. A shortened version might be:

Saturn	**Uranus**
old	new
control	rebellion
discipline	cold and hard
death	independence
delays	truth
time	awakening
tradition	deviation
structure	radical change
father	shocks
authority	liberation
responsibility	freedom
bones/skin	revolution
brakes	breaks
lead	uranium
caution	reform
fear	collective ideas
defences	sudden/unexpected
testing	deviation
denial	nonconformist
restriction	unconventionality

Although this may appear very simplistic, it is often a surprisingly productive exercise to attempt to try and fit the words together in an algebraic kind of way. Thus:

Cautious reform
Changing times
Breaks with authority
Unexpected brakes
Controlled change
Fear of change
Fear of truth
Denial of truth
Rebels in/with/against authority
Sudden death
New age
Broken bones
Cold skin
Freezing lead
Deviation from tradition
Breakdown of walls
Awakening to responsibility

Duty to liberate
Drastic discipline
Technological delays
Authoritarian radicals
Unconventional father

This is a particularly useful method if one has got 'stuck' in trying to interpret a combination. And it doesn't only have to be used for aspects but can be employed in every situation which calls for the marrying of astrological symbolism. For example the sign and house meanings can also be listed alongside. Despite its simplicity, this method can help to amplify our understanding of a given interchange, because the phrases dredge up a much deeper and wider understanding. The keyword method is a good way of reminding ourselves about what we already know about a given planetary combination.

A familiarity with mythology also helps to broaden and deepen understanding of how the planets relate to each other. Often there will be aspects of an individual's life-history which will exactly mirror a given myth. Sometimes this can be quite staggering.

However we reach our understanding, through keywords, mythology or by other means, we should perhaps be striving to *amplify* our understanding of the given symbolism. There is never a point at which we can say we do understand a chart or that we have got to the bottom of ourselves; the whole thing is an ongoing process. It is not enough to say that a person behaves in an X, Y or Z manner (even though as astrology students that is where we all have to start from), unless (ideally) we can also try to discover why we or the given individual is like this, what is at the root of the behaviour, what is the *purpose* of the interchange and in what *other ways* the individual might use the configuration. In a counselling situation, client and astrologer can work together to discover what choices are open to the client in the future after having discovered what have been the primary motivators in the past.

We all like to think that we have some measure of free will and indeed we have, should we choose to exercise it, but much of the time we are motivated by a whole spectrum of different influences of which we are but dimly aware. Without doubt many of these 'influences' can be linked to early childhood and family relationships. Thus much reference is made in the foregoing pages to the most likely childhood experiences that might accompany given planetary configurations. The future always has to be built on the past and our adult life is based on the foundation of our very earliest years. The early period of our lives is often the most difficult to get hold of (how can we, for example, know what it felt like to be born?) but it is often useful to try to trace our early history, for childhood experiences tend to be continually re-enacted in adulthood, and usually without our conscious consent. This is not to say that our childhood causes the experiences in our adult years. As astrologers we know that the earlier and the later experience is, as the astrologer Eve Jackson put it, 'embraced in a symbolism mapped before either occurrence'.

In other words we come into the world predisposed to react in a certain way and thus predisposed to hook certain life-experiences. It is not so much what happens to us in childhood that is important, so much as how we experience and process those happenings. Our early childhood is so important partly because we are so vulnerable at that early stage and partly because as Tad Mann might put it, when we are two days old, one day represents half of our life and therefore what happens in that one day carries enormous significance. When we are fifty years old, whatever happens in one day is much more likely to be experienced as a drop in the ocean.

Whatever the philosophy behind the situation, few psychologists would dispute that our early wounds (and joys) seem to reverberate throughout the rest of our life. Through the use of the birth-chart, it is possible to become much more conscious of those early wounds and the way they have resonated through the past and into the present, much more conscious of what really motivates us, much more aware of why we have made the kind of 'choices' that we have. In gaining this greater awareness we can increase our ability to exercise free choice in the future.

Thus the aspects in our chart, like all other chart factors, may be consciously pursued or unconsciously followed. Whilst we are fated to integrate the given planetary or angular combinations, we can choose to do so in a wide variety of different ways.

WEIGHTING

The most important point about interpreting a given aspect (and what makes astrological interpretation so challenging an art) is that any planetary configuration, indeed any factor in the chart, has to be examined, interpreted and understood not only in the context of the person's life but in the light of every other factor in the chart. Since the planets and points in the horoscope do not all carry the same weight, the astrologer is aided in his or her task of deciding what factors are the more significant ones and which might be considered to be of secondary importance. Aspects with wide orbs, for example, might not be heavily stressed in an interpretation but will usually confirm what is written elsewhere, or indeed will refine what is already more heavily stated. Briefly, the most important factors to be taken into account when assessing the relative importance of a given aspect might include:

— Angular planets. Planets tightly conjunct any of the four angles will be of exceptional importance. However, if the birth-time is not known with accuracy, such conjunctions should be treated with caution, for they may not exist! Other tight contacts to the angles are also very important, though not, I suggest, as much as conjunctions.

— Exactitude of aspects. Aspects which are exact or nearly so will always be highly significant.

— Aspects involving the Sun, Moon, Ascendant, Ascendant ruler (personally I believe that the Ascendant ruler is as important a factor in the chart as the Sun) and Sun ruler might be more heavily weighted than other aspects.

— The relative strength of the planet(s). A planet in its own sign or house will be purer in its manifestation and thus could be said to be stronger in its effect.

— 'Double Whammies'. An expression coined by Stephen Arroyo to describe a situation where a statement is written several times within the same configuration. For example, Princess Margaret has a Mercury–Mars square that illustrates this. Mars is in Gemini and the 3rd house (both ruled by Mercury) and Mercury is in Virgo and the 6th house (also ruled by Mercury). Since she has Aries rising, Mars is the chart ruler and so the feeling of the Mercury–Mars interchange is a very pure one.

ORBS

There is a certain amount of controversy as to which orbs should be used for the various aspects. It seems to me that when there is dissension of this kind in astrology it usually indicates that, at the present time at any rate, there is no 'right' answer. In the same way that a psychologist might devise a world of psychology which reflects *their* own psychology, their own experience, so surely will astrologers do the same with their subject and I suspect that is why there is disagreement on the subject of orbs and, indeed, dissension in other areas of astrology.

The Faculty of Astrological Studies suggests the following working model for orbs and this is probably as good as any:

Aspect	Orb	Aspect	Orb
Conjunction	8	Quintile	2
Opposition	8	Bi-quintile	2
Trine	8	Semi-Square	2
Square	8	Sesquiquadrate	2
Sextile	4	Semi-sextile	2
Quincunx	2		

This model also allows another two degrees for major aspects involving the Sun or Moon. If we are noting aspects of 22¹/₂ or 36 degrees then an orb of only 1 degree should probably be employed and in the case of an 18 degree aspect (which is a quarter of a quintile) one of no more than half a degree.

Whilst astrologers may not able to agree on an aspect's sphere of influence, all would probably accept the fact that there is not a point where an aspect *suddenly* ceases to become operative. As an aspect becomes more inexact so will its strength diminish.

John Addey in *Harmonics in Astrology* has much to say on the subject of orbs which is very apt. He calls for greater consistency in the orbs we allow various aspects and makes the proposition that orbs should diminish in direct proportion to the number which has been used to divide the circle. For example, if we allow an orb of 10 degrees for an opposition where the circle has been divided by two, then we should allow an orb of 5 degrees for the square where the circle has been divided by twice that number, by four.

Charts vary: some have half a dozen or so aspects with very tight orbs, some have aspects with mostly wide orbs, still others have hardly any aspects at all. Perhaps the question of orbs should be treated on an individual basis with respect to the chart under consideration. Where there are few aspects in the chart, wide orb aspects can usually be felt quite strongly by the individual.

But in most cases I suspect we should use much tighter orbs than are usually employed, especially with separating aspects. Aspects with tight orbs will always be of central importance in the life, no matter what the nature of those aspects may be. And by tight, I mean within 4 degrees for the conjunction and major hard aspects, about 3 degrees for the trine, 2 degrees for the sextile and 1 degree for everything else. In using wider orbs, we sometimes actually mix up aspects. For example, I have always thought that I could feel the trine in my chart between the Sun and Jupiter. In fact the trine is inexact by 6 degrees which might be considered rather wide. The *real* reason why I may be aware of the interchange between these two planets though, is probably because they are actually in tight *quintile* relationship with each other (72 + 36 + 18 = 126 degrees).

In practice people often vaguely feel aspects with quite large orbs (even as much as 10 or 12 degrees for the major aspects), but usually only if they either have few aspects in their chart *or if they concentrate on doing so*. Where there are many tight aspects we are not usually the slightest bit aware of those with wide orbs unless we are listening out for them. It's rather like listening to an orchestra: if you know a musician is playing the triangle, then you might just be able to hear it above the other instruments; but without that knowledge the sound of the triangle will be overwhelmed by the brass, woodwind, strings and so on.

Aspects with wide orbs can also be felt more strongly when they are 'pulled into' other configurations and sometimes by forming an exact midpoint. For example, Margaret Thatcher has a tight Jupiter–Pluto opposition in her chart, with Jupiter and Pluto both squaring Sun and Mars with 5 degree orbs. The Sun and Mars are usually 10 degrees apart and forming rather a wide conjunction, but their midpoint would be 14 degrees of Libra which exactly squares Jupiter–Pluto opposition. Thus the Sun–Mars conjunction could be interpreted as if it were an exact one and forming part of an exact T-square with Jupiter and Pluto.

In general, then, some flexibility is called for in deciding which orbs should be given to aspects, depending on the individual nature of the chart under consideration.

PLANETARY PROTOCOL

There is a general theory in astrology that planets can be weighted according to their relative distance from the Sun. Those that are farthest out are thought to have a much greater authority over the nearer planet than vice versa. For example, in an aspect between Venus and Saturn, Saturn would be interpreted as restricting, restraining or giving form to Venus. The heavier planet to some extent overwhelms the inner planet.

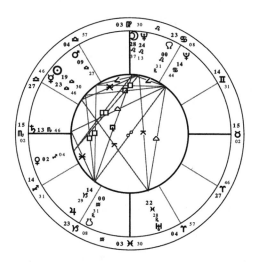

Fig. 16

Margaret Thatcher 13 October 1925, 9am GMT, Grantham, England, 52N55 0W59

Whilst there is some elegance to this idea and it is undoubtedly a useful one, personally I think it can be over-stated. In the case of Venus–Saturn for example, I believe that it could also be said that Venus will soften the Saturnian principles. In practice this might mean that the Venus–Saturn person may find it difficult to enforce discipline, for doing so might be seen to be at odds with being a popular and loving person. The Venus–Saturn person might find it difficult to discipline themselves because doing so may collide with other needs to be self-indulgent or have a full social life. In practice perhaps the extent to which one planet will tend to overwhelm another has to be *individually* weighted. Is Venus or Saturn the strongest planet in the chart? Are the Saturn signs, Capricorn and to a lesser extent Aquarius, more emphasised in the chart than the Venus signs, Libra and Taurus? Is either Venus or Saturn the more prominent planet by virtue of other aspects, their relative positions in the chart, or the signs or houses they are in?

APPLYING AND SEPARATING ASPECTS

An aspect which has not yet become exact is said to be an *applying* aspect whilst an aspect which has already been formed and is passing away is known as a *separating* aspect. In each case, it is the faster-moving planet which applies to or separates from the slower-moving planet.

If an aspect is applying then it will become exact *after* birth, sometime during the person's life, whereas if it is separating it will have been exact *before* the individual was born. Probably partly because of this, many astrologers, including the writer, believe that applying aspects are much stronger than separating ones.

A good way to test theories like this is to watch how people experience transits. This is a good way to understand how a given aspect feels too. If one has Pluto applying to the Sun for example, then during that transit one can get some idea of how it feels for people who have Sun–Pluto contacts all the time. Many people seem to experience transits according to the nature of the planet that is doing the transiting. Saturn transits for example are often felt as much, or even more, when they are separating from exactitude. And this is of course well in accord with the delaying quality associated with Saturn. Transits from Mars on the other hand, are often felt prematurely, whilst with Uranus transits there does not seem to be any rule as to when the major expression of the transit will be felt.

I am not sure how this helps with applying and separating aspects but it is possible that these too depend on the nature of the planets involved. It is possible also that applying aspects have more to do with action and experiences that might occur in the future whilst separating aspects may more describe the happenings that are behind the individual but still exerting an important influence. Thus separating aspects may describe '*effect*' whilst applying aspects may more describe '*cause*'. Thus perhaps it is easier to exercise free will with applying aspects, and perhaps people whose charts are more dominated by applying aspects lead more active lives in terms of outer events than those whose charts are dominated by separating aspects. John Addey felt that applying and separating aspects were certainly qualitatively different. According to *Recent Advances in Natal Astrology* he believed that the distinction between the two types of aspect, especially in psychological astrology, was at least as important as the distinction between soft and hard aspects. To applying aspects he gave the qualities of striving, restlessness and aggressiveness, and to separating aspects, stability, tranquillity and inertia. Personally I do believe that applying aspects are more active and striving in their nature than separating ones and I also believe that smaller orbs need to be applied to separating aspects than to applying ones.

ASPECTS IN DECLINATION

Whilst this book concerns itself with aspects measured in longtitude — that is, planets measured from 0 degrees Aries along the ecliptic — a planet, star or other body can have its position measured from a number of other vantage points. For example, a planet's position measured north or south of the celestial equator is known as its *declination*.

Two planets at the same degree north or south are described as being in *parallel* and where one body is opposite the other (Sun at 3 degrees north and Moon at 3 degrees south, for instance) they are said to be in *contra-parallel*. An orb of about 1 degree is usually employed.

In terms of interpretation, parallels can be viewed very similarly to conjunctions and contra-parallels can be interpreted similarly to oppositions. It is beyond the scope of this work to discuss these aspects in detail but they can be important and will do much to confirm factors already written in the horoscope in other ways.

In Jane Austen's chart, Sun, Mars and Pluto are listed in the aspect box as being in parallel aspect to each other (two forward slashes) and Mercury and Uranus are in contra-parallel (two forward slashes crossed).

CHAPTER FIVE

QUALITIES, ELEMENTS AND SIGNS IN ASPECT

In trying to understand a particular aspect, the interpreter has to understand not only the planetary combination but also of course the signs, houses and rulerships involved in the configuration. This is no easy matter but another way into thinking about aspects is to consider how the various *signs* may get on with each other and some attempt to do this has been made in this chapter.

To get a feel for the signs and for chart interpretation overall, the astrologer needs to have a fair understanding of how the elements and modes operate in a chart for these all affect the best way to weight a given aspect. There is a wealth of excellent material around about the elements and modes and there is no wish to repeat that here. However, I would like to highlight a few important points about the cardinal, fixed and mutable crosses and about elemental trines.

THE CARDINAL CROSS

Cardinal oppositions and squares tend to produce conflict which revolves mainly around the nitty gritty issues of personal and family life. How to go directly for what one wants for oneself (Aries) and yet meet the needs of one's partner and one's own need for partnership (Libra). On top of that is the need to carve out a place in society and to have some sort of career (Capricorn) and yet be able to make time for emotional, domestic and family life (Cancer). Possibly the requirements of having parents or being a parent.

The main gift of those with cardinal hard aspects is that when confronted with conflict, the individual usually at least attempts to deal with it. Often the individual comes unstuck though, because they attempt to deal with their problems by confronting them head-on, and often without sufficient planning and forethought.

All other things being equal, cardinal types have enormous drive, vitality, and what can only be described as 'get up and go'. Those whose charts are dominated by cardinal oppositions and squares will tend to live their lives in a permanent state of 'overdrive'. They may get up and go before they have really thought out where they should be going to. Thus they lead lives of continual frenzied activity, where they start things all the time but don't necessarily complete them (one would hope that Saturn or fixity might also be sufficiently strong in the chart to compensate for this).

There is little sense of personal limitation, coupled with a peculiar deafness to hearing of any restraints that might be imposed upon them from the outside world.

Classically, cardinal types get themselves into trouble with authority, insisting as they will on doing their own thing in their own way and at their own speed (a thousand miles an hour!). This insistence on doing things in their own way is especially a feature of Aries and is much more noticeable if Aries or Mars is present in the planetary picture, as is the general lack of poise, patience and calmness that cardinal aspects may be associated with.

The Cardinal Oppositions

Aries–Libra
I v. We. Me v. You. Me v. Us. What I want v. the social norm. Assertion v. compromise. Fighting v. co-operating. Independence v. relationship. Decision v. vacillation.

How can you do your own thing and yet do it with someone else? How can you enter into the spirit of give-and-take with a partner without sacrificing your own principles? How can you maintain your individuality, maintain your own position on things and yet co-operate, share and look at things from perspectives other than your own? The individual with this duo strong in their charts is fated to grapple with these questions.

This person is usually particularly concerned with relationship or, more specifically, with one-to-one encounters of all kinds.

Both signs can be associated with war and fighting and all the more so, in my view, when combined. Whilst the responsibility for combat is usually laid at Aries' door, Libra is concerned with fairness and justice, and justice can be seen as something that has to be fought for. Libra is also ruled by Venus, the significator of money and values. Most people will fight for what they value and the real reasons for warfare are often, at root, commercial ones. More commonly though, this opposition will fight out its differences in a marital context.

This combination can give rise to a strong awareness of the duality that runs through all things, including human beings and their relationships.

And at best the Aries–Libra individual knows how to temper self-interest with co-operation, knows how to be assertive without being aggressive. This polarity is concerned with learning how to be able to listen to, accept and allow other people to have different desires and needs without losing sight of one's own positions.

Cancer–Capricorn
Fluidity v. rigidity. Family v. career. Inner life v. public life. To yield or to discipline. Mother and father. Family v. the State.

This combination tends to be conservative, responsible and disciplined. Upholders of the family, and upholders of society and the status quo generally. There is usually respect for the past and an appreciation of roots. Cancer is sensitive, responsible and yielding whilst Capricorn has an awareness of the need for familial and societal boundaries, restraints and laws. Cancer says 'I love you because you are mine' whilst Capricorn says 'I love you if you keep within certain limits and obey the rules'. When equally and appropriately combined, perhaps we have arrived at an aspect of the 'ideal' parent. Certainly this opposition can be associated with parenting in the wider sense of the word. Cancer is a significator of the home and family and Capricorn a representative of society as whole and of the state. A political viewpoint might argue the effect of society upon the individual whilst a psychological viewpoint might be more interested in the idea that society is merely composed of families, and that it is through a child's early experience of parenting that its socialisation takes place. Those with this polarity strong are often concerned with these issues and, by implication, involved in social and political debate.

The Cardinal Squares

Aries–Cancer
Charles Carter describes this combination as the 'passionate pilgrim' and the 'stormy petrel'. Certainly this cardinal combination of Moon and Mars signs can get very 'steamed up' about things. Impetuous and impassioned, Aries–Cancer will often get particularly aroused when the family seems to be under threat, perhaps about housing issues or more personal matters on the domestic front. The conflict between the two signs concerns the fact that the Aries principle is independent, self-orientated and pioneering whereas Cancer is dependent, family-orientated and a homebody. There can be conflict over the desire to strike out on one's own and the pull of the family, mother, familiarity and past. The

resulting tension can feel very frustrating to the individual who has this pair strongly emphasised in the chart. Aries–Cancer is a good combination for any situation which requires fighting or trying to get away from the past, or fighting on behalf of the past. On behalf of conservation, history or tradition. Aries–Cancer can be found espousing causes for or against these issues. It is an ideal combination for anything that requires crusading on behalf of one's family or clan in the wider sense. Ideal too, for people who work at the frontline in housing: council estate managers, employees of housing co-ops and such like.

Aries–Capricorn

This is a very ambitious, go-getting combination. It has drive and initiative and is ideal for all entrepreneurial activities.

Sometimes the impatience to get to the top can result in the individual not minding whether they use fair means or foul to do so. This combination of Mars- and Saturn-ruled signs can incline to roughness and selfishness and a tendency to disregard feelings or principles. The presence of water, air or a strong Venus might do much to offset such tendencies though.

The desire to achieve something too quickly, in extreme cases, can yield someone who continually feels frustrated and thwarted by the rules and restrictions imposed by the outer world. This can spur the individual into making greater efforts or lead to them continually bucking against authority. It is a good combination for anyone who legitimately needs to wage war against government, tradition or the Establishment. Paradoxically it is also to be found emphasised in the charts of those who struggle to achieve high position within the established framework of society.

The combination is also to be found in people who are not ambitious in career terms but nevertheless set themselves goals which to others would seem very harsh. There is tremendous 'grit' with this combination which might come in useful in a variety of life-situations. It can sometimes be found in people who enjoy rock-climbing or mountaineering or in the charts of those who find themselves battling against the elements in other ways.

Cancer–Libra

An emphasis on these two signs in the chart suggests a strong concern with partnership and home and family issues. Sometime the square manifests as someone who enters into relationship primarily in order to build a family life. Often the requirements of the home, family and children are felt to be at odds with the need to have one-to-one interaction with another person.

Cancer is an obviously dependent sign because of its strong need for emotional security. Libra always wants a partner to reflect, share and do things with. Emphasis on these two signs can manifest as someone unable to 'stand on their own two feet' and generally cope on their own. This is certainly a very pliable, yielding and indecisive combination; these people are easily swayed on most things and especially with regard to the true nature of their feelings.

Conflict in relationships sometimes occurs because the Libran desire for equality is at variance with the Cancerian tendency in relationships to either mother or be mothered. Sometimes people with this combination find themselves in unhappy relationships from which they cannot seem to break away. They stay for 'the sake of the children' and also because they are unable to trust their own (usually fleeting) feelings as to the unfairness of the given situation or because the prospect of being on their own is too frightening.

Libra–Capricorn

People with an emphasis in their chart on these two signs usually come across as being very 'smooth' and not easily ruffled. They tend to be very civil and refined, with a cool, calm and collected attitude. The combination is ideal for anyone in public life or anywhere where an urbane kind of image is required, an image that will offend no one.

The type tends to care what others might think and is thus particularly sensitive to external opinion. There is often a strong need to be respected. Occasionally partnerships are entered into for largely prestigious reasons. More often the individual is challenged in life as to their ability to give time and attention to both the demands of their relationships and the demands of their career.

Whilst the Libran urge is for fairness, equality and compromise, Capricorn concerns itself with authority and discipline. Libra is vacillating whilst Capricorn is authoritative; thus the conflict between these signs is obvious for it is seemingly impossible to take both a paternalistic and democratic line on a given issue.

Whilst there can be something of an 'iron hand in a velvet glove' feeling about this combination, the type is usually very concerned with what is 'right' and 'wrong' in a given situation. Indeed, both these signs can be associated with 'law': the rules that govern society with Capricorn and the desire for fairness of Libra. Sometimes the concern with law and order manifests as an interest in and awareness of universal law, the law of cause and effect for example. Often the desire for order and skill at achieving it permeates the whole life, right down to the person's physical appearance and home environment.

The Fixed Cross

Those in whose chart fixed oppositions and square predominate are generally reliable, stable, determined and resistant to change. The problem of fixity is attachment: attachment to possessions and security (Taurus), to feelings, desires and the will (Scorpio), attachment to pride and individuality (Leo) and the ideas and principles (Aquarius).

As a rule the fixed signs have problems in 'letting go'. Persistent and reliable fixity may be, making for great strength and will-power, but it also makes for a lack of adaptability and an almost allergic reaction to change.

Fixed hard aspects usually require that something is let go of, in order for some sort of resolution to occur abut the fixed attitude to meeting challenge is to try and preserve and hold on to what is possesses. When confronting with a difficulty, fixity responds in one of two ways. It either decides to put up with the situation (and certainly this type can put up with situations that cardinality or mutability would find intolerable) or it chips away at the problem, slowly, carefully and determinedly.

The fixed type knows all about the difficulty that the immovable object has in moving the irresistible force. The fixed person has great will-power and enormous energy at its disposal once it gets going, but all too often fixity chooses to conserve energy rather than expend it. Little wonder that change comes rarely but usually quite drastically and explosively to the fixed type.

In relationship, fixity is, as everywhere else, very difficult to shift. The fixed type refuses to be pushed, pulled or coerced. The unyielding quality of fixity is both its greatest virtue and its greatest failing. Coupled with an awareness of where it's best to hold on and when its best to let go, fixity can provide the strength that makes the accomplishment of great things possible.

The Fixed Oppositions

Taurus–Scorpio
The builder v. the saboteur. Placidity v. Emotional storms. Security v. temptation. The status quo v. crisis. Sex v. taboos.

Both these signs are concerned with attachment and desire, and in particular with sex, money and power. Confrontations around these issues and feelings of rage, jealousy and envy are to be expected when this polarity is emphasised in the natal chart and more so if one or more oppositions are in evidence. Freudian psychology with its emphasis on sex and notion of oral and anal fixations, surely has its roots in this polarity.

Indeed, Freud himself had Scorpio rising with the Sun in Taurus. Scorpio is concerned with consummating deep psychic contact with others and with one's own soul; Taurus is more rooted in the physical, in security, in food and in the accumulation of possession. Taurus is concerned with sex more on the level of a fundamental enjoyment of the senses.

Leo–Aquarius
Individuality v. the Group. Personal distinction v. Joe Public. The autocrat v. the democrat. The artist v. the scientist. Proud ownership v. freedom.

Whilst Aquarius preaches being a democratic member of a group, Leo seeks to lead and be the monarch of all it surveys. Leo can feel that it doesn't exist without an audience (Aquarius). Those with this polarity strong in their charts tend to be proud, fixed and unconventional or at least they stick out by being different. They often cope with the autocrat/democrat dilemma by achieving a position of distinction or seniority in a situation which promotes Aquarian ideals of equal opportunities, democracy or freedom, or they become well known for their particular brand of originality or eccentricity. Perhaps the polarity is really concerned with love and friendship. Friends are people we take to our heart. Playing (Leo) is one of the first steps towards friendships and group relationships (Aquarius). Leo says 'I love you, I am proud of you, you are mine' whilst Aquarius says: 'Because I love you I will set you free.'

The Fixed Squares

Taurus–Leo
This is a solid and dependable combination, prone to stubbornness and inflexibility. Pride is also often a very marked feature. The 'solidness' can be physical as both these signs have an appreciation of the 'good life' (especially good wine and rich food!) and this becomes doubly so when found in the chart of an individual who has both signs strongly tenanted and more especially when there are squares between the two. There is usually a big appetite not only in culinary matters but also for physical comfort (if not luxury) on all levels. There can sometimes be health problems due to long-term over-consumption of rich foods. This is usually only the case when the individual is not engaged in some project that they can fully put their heart into. One would hope for a good emotional and sexual relationship too, for it is lack of these things that often leads the Leo–Taurus type to physical over-indulgence.

This is a good combination for occupation in the business or finance world as an awareness of the power of money and the worth of the security it can provide is usually well developed, coupled with a desire to appreciate all the good things that a large salary might provide. (After all, if you cross the Bull with the Lion you get Bullion!) One of the reasons this combination can be so successful in financial fields is that along with the steadiness and caution of Taurus there is also the ability to speculate. Leo is particularly fond of playing and not averse to gambling, and perhaps making large sums of money usually does involve a fair amount of risk-taking. Avarice and greed can be a problem with this combination, although, as always, the horoscope as a whole has to be carefully looked at. Certainly this combination is not particularly concerned with the principles underlying its actions nor their repercussions.

This combination is a very creative one; this needn't be in the business world but the creativity is likely to be in terms of *matter*, as Taurus is always concerned with *producing* something.

Taurus–Aquarius

Whereas Taurus is a sign concerned with conservatism, tradition, attachment and building a physically secure existence, Aquarius is deeply unconventional and detached. A radical concerned with friendship and group life. Thus the conflict between the two signs is easy to discern but often people with this square emphasised integrate the earthiness of Taurus and the idealism of Aquarius easily enough into their lives.

People with this combination often concern themselves with the material and physical problems of society. Possessive of their own freedom, they may be concerned with everybody else enjoying the same liberty of thought and action.

As Carter says, at best this combination stands for practical idealism. It is often found in unusual commercial situations, the more radical business enterprises and in particular in the charts of those that use or develop computers, for computers have revolutionised the material world.

This is also sometimes the combination of the person who seeks to live a simple, uncluttered life close to nature, sometimes in building a community life; the person who lives in an unconventional style but nevertheless in a way that is solid and secure. Thus it is the combination of the hippie, and the 'Good-Lifer' concerned with self-sufficiency.

One manifestation of Taurus–Aquarius is surely 'Friends of the Earth'. It is also common in the peace movement. Sometimes one can see this to a marked degree even in those who do not have this square but instead have a highly focal Uranus in Taurus in their chart.

There is often an intuitive understanding of the earth, and the type may be practical and inventive. Perhaps this is also the combination of the organic farmer, the person who wants to revolutionise the way the masses might be fed.

In all sorts of different ways, feeding groups of people on a large scale is also often a theme with this mix. This is the individual who does all the catering for their friends or the club to which they belong.

Leo–Scorpio

At best, Leo and Scorpio combine to produce a very warm and passionate kind of individual, though like other fixed combinations it can also produce great pride, jealousy, and stubbornness. Both signs like power and there is often a liking for status symbols. Scorpio, through its association with the 8th house, has long been associated with 'other people's money' and Leo with banking. Thus this combination is ideal for work in banks and large finance houses.

Part of the conflict of this combination occurs because the Leo part of the combination likes to be seen, to be recognised, to be noticed whilst the Scorpio part wishes to remain private. Nevertheless those with this combination strongly emphasised in their charts usually have a liking for the dramatic and they rarely lead a tranquil existence. The liking for the dramatic, vivid and colourful can find outlet in the entertainment industry or other creative arts.

The feelings go deep with the Leo–Scorpio person but they congeal easily and are not easy to dispel when things go wrong. This, coupled with the tremendous pride (especially sexual pride) of the type can give rise to bitterness and vengeful feelings which positively cry out for some kind of creative outlet if a real vendetta is to be avoided. This would be a wonderful combination for the mafia! Drama is often an excellent vehicle for release of this kind. The presence of air in the horoscope will do much to help the individual detach themselves from the given situation and be able to view things in greater perspective and proportion.

Scorpio–Aquarius

As Carter points out, a major conflict between these signs often revolves around the fact that Scorpio is deeply private, secretive and solitary whilst Aquarius is gregarious, friendly and concerned with being 'honest'.

Sometimes the individual gets around this conflict by following a quite radically different and unconventional life-style which is kept totally private whilst pursuing, at the same time, a more gregarious professional life. The person often holds what they see as highly unconventional views on Scorpio matters – sexual or occult issues or death – which they feel might alienate the larger populace were they to attempt to share them. Thus this is the person who becomes deeply involved with a small group of like-minded people.

Carter says that there may be a dislike of the human race. Certainly, the Aquarius–Scorpio person tends to be cynical about people's motives and is usually passionate about the few.

Both signs are often interested in psychology, although from different perspectives, and when this combination is strongly emphasised in a chart, an involvement in this subject or with therapy groups might be expected.

This fixed combination will often produce the very strongest ideas and feelings and the very deepest convictions. Although sometimes it can give rise to an individual who one moment feels passionately involved and interested in something and the next minute couldn't care less. It can also be a ruthless, cold and revolutionary combination. It is to be found in the individual who wants to transform the world (or at least a little patch of it), whether for good or ill.

Often the Scorpio–Aquarius person will not shrink from anything. The type is not concerned with social niceties and, depending on the situation of Venus, may be quite antisocial. At best, the penetrating insight and understanding of Scorpio combines with the humanitarianism and detached idealism of Aquarius to produce a person who is concerned with transformation in the highest sense of the word.

THE MUTABLE CROSS

When confronted with a problem, classic mutable-type behaviour deals with the situation by avoiding it altogether, for the type will usually do anything as long as it avoids confrontation.

The mutable signs (Gemini, Sagittarius, Virgo, Pisces) are all involved with ideas and the gathering of knowledge or ideals in some way and oppositions and squares between these signs usually result in an internal (and frequently external) war occurring between the individual's different ideals, ideas or beliefs.

Mutability is less concerned with power than either cardinality or fixity and as such is probably the least potentially dangerous of the three, although Gemini and Sagittarius (for obvious reasons) are usually prominent in the charts of accidents involving transport.

The joy of mutability is its adaptability and flexibility but the restlessness and constant desire for change can make the actual attainment of anything solid, permanent and secure quite difficult. This does not necessarily worry the mutable person for they are not concerned with achievement so much as being free to search and quest. Those in whose chart mutability predominates may not seem to know what they do want half the time and this can give rise to great discontent and dissatisfaction.

The mutual signs are best suited to situations which demand a flexible approach – areas such as education and communication (Gemini and Sagittarius) and service to others (Virgo and Pisces). They are most at home in occupations which not only allow for change and flexibility but positively need it.

Not being goal-directed, the mutable type is far more able to live from moment to moment than either the cardinal or the fixed and is at one with the notion of taking one day at a time. The major problems with mutability, especially with the T-square and grand cross, are a lack of consistency and a tendency to bend far too easily. At worst, people with dominant squares and oppositions between these signs may be aimless and vacillating. Mutability needs to learn to focus its energies a little. The scattering of thought as well as action often gives rise to difficulty in the individual being able to see things in perspective. Thus there is often a tendency to worry. There is also often great nervous tension and a tendency to live in a permanent state of flux. Hopefully the sign and house position of Mars may give drive and direction to the predominantly mutable person.

The Mutable Oppositions

Gemini–Sagittarius
Scattered pieces of information v. the whole picture. Reason v. intuition. Knowledge v. wisdom. School v. university. Short v. long journeys. Amorality v. morality.

This pair are both concerned with various aspects of education and travel, with the gathering, connection and spreading of information over long (Sagittarius) and short (Gemini) distances. Those with this opposition strongly emphasised in their charts are usually interested in everything; very talkative, restless and anxious to cover as much ground in their lives as possible. Gemini has the quality of the archetypal student who wants to know everything, whereas Sagittarius is the teacher who is supposed to have this knowledge. Gemini represents the young child, who is amoral and innocent and just asks 'why'; The Fool in the tarot pack perhaps. By contrast, Sagittarius is concerned with judgement, wisdom and morality. This pair can be associated with the idea of the 'eternal youth' – what Jungians call the *puer aeternus* and Charles Carter calls 'Peter Pan' – as the type is reluctant to outgrow adolescence, and tends to stay youthful in spirit and young at heart.

Virgo–Pisces
Discrimination v. universality. Order v. chaos. Criticism v. compassion. Perfection v. wholeness.

Those with this polarity emphasised are usually rather pliable and very concerned with service. At best, the discriminative and critical powers of Virgo combine with the humility, altruism and compassion of Pisces to give rise to a genuinely useful and giving kind of person. Virgo seeks to be of practical service to others whilst Pisces inclines to selflessness, sacrifice and devotion. Together, they can engender great humility and also great kindness – though there can also be a distinct tendency towards martyrdom. Those with this pair emphasised in the natal chart often do take on the role of victim, martyr or saviour. Rescuing others or asking to be rescued is a common theme in the relationship patterns of this type.

The dissension between the two signs occurs because of the Virgoan desire for purification and order and the Piscean inclination towards chaos. Virgo believes that if you examine an issue for long enough, you throw out what is extraneous, synthesise what is left, and then are bound to come up with the 'right' answer. Pisces, on the other hand, is not concerned with right answers but believes instead in relative values. Virgo is concerned with improvement of the self, of others, of society; Pisces merely surrenders to whoever or whatever. Pisces goes with the flow.

The Mutable Squares

Gemini–Virgo
Although these two signs are naturally in square to each other, they actually have a good deal in common. Virgo, whilst an earth sign is surely a rather airy earth sign, and here it confronts air itself. More to the point, both signs are ruled by Mercury and it is to this planet that the astrologer's eye must quickly point, as its position by sign, house and aspect will give clues as to the way in which the square might be utilised.

As mutable squares go, this one is particularly mutable, and individuals whose charts are dominated by it often have problems in making decisions in focusing their minds. Charles Carter says that one of its main weaknesses is *'lack of incentive'* and a tendency 'to find nothing worthwhile'. This certainly captures the spirit of this combination, which is especially prone to discontent and dissatisfaction. At worst, those with tight squares between Gemini and Virgo are critical, sulky, irritable and ever ready to find fault; what Carter calls a 'captious attitude'. On the other hand, the overdose of Mercury is likely to yield interest and talent with language and literature. Wide interests and great knowledge are also indicated. However, those whose charts are dominated by this square are prone to gathering more information than they are able to digest. The interests and activities of Gemini–Virgo are often very scattered and the tendency to know a little bit about everything can lead not only to a superficial understanding and a certain know-it-all quality but also to boredom and this pattern of 'finding nothing worthwhile'. It is to be hoped that the fire signs or the fiery planets are also fairly prominent in the chart for this element will lend direction, enthusiasm and faith.

Once aroused, and with a clear sense of direction, this is a splendid combination for all forms of study. It is good, too, for any work that requires the gathering, classifying and sorting of detailed information. Providing the work is interesting, Gemini–Virgo might be quite at home working in a bureaucratic system, compiling dictionaries, collating research data and so on. This is not to say that the type is particularly ordered – far from it, unless Saturn or Capricorn is also strong – but there is great dexterity with the handling of data. Gemini–Virgo tends to be dry, pragmatic, rational and realistic. It is also often a very witty combination, and good at anecdote. It is ideal for all forms of writing.

Gemini–Pisces

A very mild combination this and, like all mutable squares, quite a restless one. Gemini is a rational sign, concerned with ideas, facts and knowledge. Pisces is more concerned with ideals than ideas and is not concerned with facts so much as relative values and inner experience. Those with the square emphasised in the chart may experience a struggle between the objective reality of the outer world and the inner reality of their own experiences. Their special goal, therefore, may be bringing the two into alignment. Together, especially if Mercury is well placed in the chart, these signs can give rise to someone who is gifted at studying seemingly 'non-rational' subjects, gifted at understanding and expressing the un-quantifiable. It's an excellent combination for imaginative writing, especially poetry.

Charles Carter associates the combination with fears of solitude and possibly fears of insanity. Certainly some Gemini–Pisces people feel awash with the number of images and ideas that float through their mind. The type may be prone to trying to over-rationalise their feelings and those things they cannot understand – those things that perhaps no one really understands. There is a need to cover a lot of ground and sometimes a need to make everything 'fit' and feelings of anxiety when they don't. Thus there can be feelings of mental confusion. As Carter says, *talk* is a very good antidote for this combination, as is communicating through some sort of art form.

Virgo–Sagittarius

This Mercury–Jupiter pair usually has all the talkativeness and restlessness that one might expect from a mutable combination. Virgo is concerned with the minutiae of everyday life, which can feel very confining to the explorative roving side of Sagittarius, a sign that can never be bothered with detail. When squares between these signs are highly emphasised in an individual's chart, there can be a tendency for the individual to make 'mountains out of molehills'. A tendency, too, to exaggerate their own or others' imperfections and perhaps to be overly liberal with their criticisms.

Classically the type is critical and sceptical of others' beliefs and occasionally arrogant as to their own. This is a good combination for legitimately studying and analysing different beliefs and ideologies, and for working with areas to do with the philosophy of differing health treatments. It is also an excellent combination for all kinds of advisory work. Virgo–Sagittarius often works to bring their philosophy of life together with the need to serve, and thus it is ideally placed for occupations in the voluntary sector and in charitable organisations.

Sagittarius–Pisces

Big dreamers, Sagittarius–Pisces people are often found yearning and searching after some ideal. Great travellers in their imagination if not in reality, this must surely be the combination of space travel, fantasy fiction and Sci-fi; especially if Uranus is also strongly placed in the chart. Both signs share a dislike of being confined in any way and the war-cry of those with this combination might well be 'don't tie me down'. The Sagittarius–Pisces person would always want to keep the door open for the possibility that something magical and wonderful might happen.

There can be great restlessness and, as with all mutable combinations, a proneness to dissatisfaction and a kind of Mr Micawber attitude that something will turn up tomorrow. These people can be great drifters.

Pisces refines the Sagittarian exuberance, whilst Sagittarius gives 'spirit' to Pisces, and there is often a delightful mixture of naive wistfulness and perceptive insight with this combination which can be very broad-based in terms of both interests and understanding of others. There is certainly often a rather innocent, incredulous feeling to those with this combination prominently placed in their charts.

Easy-going and idealistic, the square between these signs is also often exaggerative and careless. Both signs are concerned with *beliefs* and when in square aspect there may be internal conflicts with the individual's political or religious convictions. Sometimes they seem to hold diametrically opposing beliefs and ideologies at the same time, and find great difficulty in being able to follow their ideas through with anything approaching objectivity or rationality. A strongly placed Mercury can do much to offset this tendency. Sometimes the individual finds their religious, political or other beliefs at odds with their environment and some kind of adjustment is necessitated.

TRINES IN FIRE

Trines in fire will increase an individual's ability to radiate warmth, enthusiasm and enjoyment of living as well as supporting the usual self-orientated, unthinking quality which can be associated with this element.

Fire trines tend to motivate people towards the future, towards looking ahead to something. There is an easy talent for being able to sniff out the future possibilities inherent in a situation, though without squares there may not be the impulse required to make those possibilities actually happen.

People with fire trines emphasised in the chart usually enjoy taking risks, or rather (and I think this may be more accurate), it doesn't occur to them that, in a given situation, there is any risk involved. Fire people don't see themselves as courageous because they are not aware that there is anything to be frightened of. The motivation for those with trines in fire is about action and excitement. People with these aspects seem to be motivated towards the idea of being actively involved in something, and retaining a feeling of being alive. There is usually an innate (and often unconscious) faith that nothing can go wrong or that they will be protected if it does, and their confidence in this usually ensures that they do indeed escape without harm.

The fire trine person enjoys drama, but on their own, fiery trines do not suggest that an individual makes such drama and action happen, more that they are confident and expectant of being entertained by others.

TRINES IN EARTH

Earth trines tend to protect in material matters. People with these trines are usually buffered with respect to money issues for example. Those with a grand trine, especially, are less likely to be forced to deal with poverty or fears as to where the next meal is coming from. This is because one of the primary motivations is usually concerned with being economically independent and physically secure. Earth trines uphold the status quo with respect to material life. They also increase pragmatism, realism and reliability, and add a social quality to the person. These aspects suggest that the individual enjoys, is talented at, or at least is certainly motivated towards actually *producing* something in the material world. People with earth emphasised in the chart are usually at home with their body and with the real world. They know when they are hungry, and how to feed and look after themselves and others. There is an understanding of money and a generally realistic and practical approach to living in a material world.

TRINES IN AIR

I always remember in one of the first astrology classes I ever taught, there was a student who came week after week, sat in the front row and whilst she looked interested enough she never took any notes or seemed to progress. She bought numerous books but only appeared to dip into them. Since she was a very pleasant, obviously bright kind of person and given that I was rather inexperienced at the time, I wondered what I was doing wrong. Was I boring her? Did she already know the material? But if so why didn't she *seem* to know it and why did she keep coming to the class? I was to discover later on that she had a grand trine in air and that she attended astrology classes all over town and did much the same thing. She attended these classes because she *enjoyed* learning situations, she was motivated by the notion of lots of mental stimulation and discussion.

The point I want to make is that air signs are not necessary learned, studious or intellectual; neither do they have a monopoly on thinking or 'intelligence' anymore than water has a monopoly over the feeling realm. The issue is really that the air signs, and more particularly trines in the air, suggest that the individual is able and feels confident about their ability to process information and ideas. These people enjoy learning. Air trines increase the easy ability to communicate, and will help an individual feel at home with, and dextrous in, a wide range of social situations. By themselves, air trines do not improve intellectual gifts but they certainly do increase interest and curiosity. Air trines do not force an individual towards pushing themselves into learning something, and thus, unless aided by other chart factors, air trines and especially airy grand trines, can actually yield someone with superficial knowledge and understanding. Air trine people feel contented with their intellectual gifts, and thus there is no felt need to work on developing them. This complacent quality can and usually will be nullified by other chart factors though — for example by 3rd and 9th house planetary placements or a Mercury that receives plenty of stressful (pushing and forcing) aspects.

Trines in Water

The strong presence of water in a chart is usually indicative of strong dependency needs. Water trines and especially water grand trines, suggest that the individual is able to get these dependency needs easily met (and therefore may not be forced to face them) in the outer world.

Water trines suggest a facility at being able to hold, support and protect others. They indicate that the individual is primarily motivated by the need for emotional security. Water trines will obviously increase the general watery quality of a chart and thus may suggest that the individual will have a certain sophistication with respect to their feelings; that is, they will know *how* they feel about something, whether they like it or not, and are less likely to be affected in this judgement by having to consider whether they are supposed or expected to like or dislike the object under question. Basically, it could be said that water trines increase the likelihood of the individual being in touch with the instinctual reactions to things, and they often confer an ability to experience how other people feel too. I think that it is important to say, though, that feelings are not the same as emotions, and the presence of water trines does not, in itself, mean that the individual actually *understands* their feelings, nor that they can necessarily *communicate* them. The talent of the watery trine lies in the fact that the individual is able to be immediately *in touch* with what they feel about something. Those with water emphasised in their charts do not necessarily have more or better 'feelings' than the other elements; the issue is that the individual is usually better able to *process* their feeling. Take, for example, a heated argument between a person with a lack of water and a person with plenty of water in their chart. The person without the water in their chart will be more likely to brood, shed tears, worry and get the whole episode out of proportion. The person who has the element emphasised in their chart will be able to take it all in their stride; they will be able to process the situation. And whereas the person who lacks water will wonder whether the disagreement spells the end of the relationship, this wouldn't even occur to the watery type, who will tend to uphold the status quo with respect to their emotional life and expect to be buffeted (and they usually are) with respect to their feelings. Because of their dexterity in this area, the person with water trines emphasised in their chart is less likely to helter-skelter with respect to their feelings, or at least will not be bothered by the fact that they do so. They are less likely to be subject to periodic and overwhelming 'passions' for people; rather, these types can accept, and stay with, the relationships they are actually in. As always, trines increase feelings of contentment as well as passivity.

PART TWO

A PLANETARY COOKBOOK

CHAPTER SIX

SUN ASPECTS

SUN–MOON

Wants/needs. Future/past. Mother/father. Character/personality.
Conscious/unconscious.

As discussed elsewhere, the Sun and Moon are especially significant in the
horoscope, and in view of their importance, this combination has been
dealt with differently to the other planetary combinations in the book in
that some attempt has been made to differentiate between the conjunction, the hard, and the soft aspects.

The Conjunction

There is probably some difference, as Dane Rudhar and others have
suggested, between cases where the Moon is applying to the Sun and
where it is separating, though myself I am not clear what the difference
might be. Technically speaking, when the Moon is behind the Sun it is a
balsamic Moon, but for the purpose of discussion here I have used the
term New Moon interchangeably with that of Sun–Moon conjunction.

Clearly, the conjunction between the Sun and the Moon will indicate
great emphasis on the sign, house and element in which it is found, thus
forming a major focal point in the chart, and as with all conjunctions,
aspects to the New Moon need to be examined very carefully.

As the Sun describes the future and where we are striving to go, while
the Moon represents our past and what we need in order to feel
comfortable with our lives, ourselves and other people, when these two
bodies are conjunct there is no disparity between needs and goals but
instead a great singleness of purpose, focus and direction. It could be said
that the person with this configuration has all their eggs in one basket; the
sign and house where the conjunction is to be found will describe just
what that basket looks like.

New Moon people often come from a background where the parental figures seem to have played a unified role and presented a united front to the child. Sometimes this is literally the case, as where one person or an institution, such as a boarding school or orphanage, has played both mother and father. More commonly though, the situation was one where both parental figures were coming from the same place in terms of attitudes, life-goals, or the way in which they responded to the child.

The repercussion of this can be that the child had nowhere to go to hear the voice of an alternative authority, and as adults, New Moon people don't tend to go to others for advice or to learn. They believe and want their own best authority to be themselves and seem to have no conscious dependency on others to help them define their goals or identity. For this reason, the New Moon type is less commonly found in the consulting rooms of astrologers, therapists and the like. As parents, New Moon types themselves often play both roles, sometimes not wishing to share the role of parenthood with another.

New Moon types tend to be very subjective; they have, or seem to have, great identification with themselves, with their own totality. It is often not so easy for them to identify with other people or to register that others have different needs. This is an aspect to be associated with great *insularity*.

Because there is a fusion of the so-called masculine and feminine principles in the chart, one might expect the individual with this conjunction to be something of an androgyne, and at best this is what occurs. More commonly though, New Moon people are confused about their sexuality, especially when young. New Moon boys are often surrounded by women in childhood and also feel overwhelmed by the feminine within themselves. For girls, masculine figures, and sometimes a very patriarchal background, can be equally overwhelming. This need not be problematical; the confusion, where it occurs, is surely a result of society's inclination to polarise the masculine and feminine principles and, more dangerous still, to confuse them with actual men and women, with a resultant demand that everyone conform to particular roles.

Men with this conjunction often look rather lunar, being large, well-covered and round-faced, and tending to identify with their mother more than their father. I have known few women with this conjunction so am not in a position to comment but it may be that women with this conjunction tend to identify with their fathers more than their mothers in a similar way.

New Moon types are usually very sensitive and recognise the importance of their need to give and receive care and nurturance but, because of their insularity, can be slow to register other people's needs. This contrasts sharply with the Full Moon type who is always highly aware of the other person and tends to pick up every subtle nuance that occurs between people and around them.

The pull of the family is strong with all Sun–Moon contacts and often with the conjunction it results in difficulty for the person in 'leaving the nest'. This can be the signature of the teenager who opts to stay living at home and is still to be found there aged 45! More usually though, it's the symbolic issue of throwing off the family history, ideas and attitudes which is paramount. The Moon represents our history and when fortified by the Sun, the pull of the past is very strong and there are usually very deeply rooted and largely unconscious habits. At New Moon, there is no Moon to be seen, it is the darkest night of the month, and this can be taken to symbolise the fact that New Moon people are often thoroughly dominated by (but unaware of) the unconscious processes operating within themselves and in society. By definition, we are all unaware of our unconscious, that is why it is unconscious, but New Moon people are often reluctant to accept the concept of its existence as a valid one anyway, and when they do they feel overwhelmed by it.

Often it can be seen in retrospect that the goal of the conjunction person is to affect the future by concentrating on the past; to bring the past into consciousness, to illuminate that which has gone before. An example of this and the one-pointedness of the New Moon type is to be found in Karl Marx, who had a Sun–Moon conjunction in Taurus in the 2nd house. His philosophy of ownership, or the lack of it, as being the foundation of all societies is a very clear one; to him there are those who own 'the means of production' and those who don't. Marx saw this notion in very black and white terms and was able to put it across with great conviction. Like Marx, the classic New Moon type does not compromise but just goes their own way, seemingly positive and assertive, though often passively so, depending on the sign involved. For this reason the New Moon person has some of the qualities of Aries and like this sign can be associated with pioneering, and with starting things. The conjunction person is one who is usually in at the beginning, even if they are not the actual initiator themselves – though they often are. This is the type who might say, 'I can do anything, for I am myself,' although obviously the sign the conjunction falls in will modify this, as will any aspects to the conjunction. But even introvert types will usually seem quite strong and inflexible. Decisive, focused, strong in themselves, and clear about their goals.

The Opposition

The Full Moon type contrasts sharply with the New Moon person, tending to be indecisive and not very focused. There is a strong need for relationship which, coupled with the inner insecurity of the type often leads the person to look outside themselves to someone or something for fulfilment. The Full Moon type is to be found in the consulting rooms of therapists and astrologers and in all other relationship situations. Relationship is the *raison d'être* for the opposition person and the type has the skill and understanding to know how to use the one-to-one encounter to further its own need for self-definition and clarification of goals. The advantage of this is that the Full Moon person has great capacity for objectivity and awareness. They possess self-awareness of others and an awareness that there are always many different possibilities. They have an appreciation, too, of the ambiguities and paradoxes within the self and throughout life generally. But whilst it makes for a more rounded individual, the opposition can make the achievement of goals difficult, for if one is always conscious of other possibilities and different ways of looking at things it is not going to be so easy to have the kind of conviction to push something through. One can imagine the impact Marx might have had, or rather not had, if his approach had been, 'It could be like this, but on the other hand it could be like that … what do you think?' Leaving aside the influence on politics of the collective unconscious, we could say that Marxism might not have happened had Marx had a Sun–Moon opposition instead of a conjunction.

Unlike the New Moon person too, the Full Moon type often comes from a background where they perceived the parent figures as playing very different roles; perhaps one was an extreme introvert and the other excessively extrovert, or one was always to be found at home and engaged in the domestic life, whilst the other was always out in the world; there can be many variations on the theme but the issue is that in some form the parents seemed to be each coming from a very different place in terms of their attitudes to life and responses to the child.

Sometimes the parents split up and live apart; this needn't create special problems for most children but often does for the Full Moon child who, feeling close and wanting to stay close to both parents, finds the practical difficulties of coming and going between two places emotionally trying and productive of great inner insecurity. Often there is warring between the parental figures, and the problem for the child can be in deciding which of these two very different people is going to provide a role model. Whatever the actual situation the child often feels a bit like piggy in the middle. Well into adult life the individual can be found striving to integrate both these different people into their psyche. The Full Moon child, like the Full Moon adult, is extremely sensitive and as a child can be prone to temper tantrums. These tantrums may be seen as a cry for attention, a demand to be seen as well as a symptom for the youngster's insecurity. Sometimes too, and this happens with the square as well, one or both parent figures were not expressing their true feelings and it falls on the child to do it for them.

The Square

The square shares many of the same issues as the opposition, though I think it is often more restless. The individual usually has to work very hard to achieve real emotional security in life and a real sense of who they are. Often there is some feeling of conflict between the individual's wish to adapt to their environment and those within it and their desire to go out for what they want in a creative way. It could be said that with all hard aspects between the Sun and Moon there is a split between what the individual wants (Sun) and what they need (Moon) and the goal is in some way to integrate these two factors. When the individual is able to define their goals there often seems as if there is some practical obstacle that gets in the way of their being able to bring them to fruition. Sometimes it is their own habitual behaviour patterns that get in the way, as in the case of a man I know who decided he wanted to be a greengrocer but eventually gave up because he couldn't get up in the morning to go to market to buy his stock. All his life he had got up late, and he didn't, or couldn't, allow himself to break the habit of doing so. Sometimes the family or the domestic situation blocks the path of the person trying to get ahead and break free of the shackles of the past, as in the case where the young person is just off to college and someone at home falls ill and demands to be taken care of. Basically, the person's ability to be clear about and to express what they want is challenged at each step of the way with these contacts, but the family and the pull of the past will only interfere with the future if we allow it to.

Those with the square often have a very real need to achieve something in life, something they and their family can be proud of. Often as children those with the square didn't feel that their parents were proud of their accomplishments and this feeling of lack can be a spur towards them pushing themselves forward in life, or the reason for them not being able to do so. Eventually the Sun–Moon square learns that it is immaterial whether their parents were actually proud of them or not; it is more the case that they came into the world programmed to pick up these cues, programmed to feel that they should be someone different to who they were.

The early family life is more likely to have been difficult with the square aspect than with the opposition, with the parental figures not so much seeming to be opposites, but people who are continually in conflict and disposed to getting in each other's way. Frequently the child feels in the way, too, of one or both of the parents. Sometimes the child feels that they are the cause of the conflict in the home and can then become shy of spontaneous self-expression, believing that whatever they say will make matters worse, though usually when things are this oppressive,

Saturn is also involved. Messy family break-ups are common with the square aspects; with one parent, by accident or design, opting out of parenthood altogether, or, as with the opposition, the child being caught in the middle of the difficulties cause by the logistics of having a relationship with both parents. Unlike the opposition, however, the child often does not consciously want a relationship with both parents, and sometimes one parent blocks the possibility of a relationship with the other one. Sometimes with these aspects, the home life is no more traumatic than anyone else's but the family relationships and domestic situation are very dynamic, with lots of happenings and moving around, and whilst some may find this exciting, and Sun–Moon may find it exciting too, it tends also to produce feelings of great insecurity to those with these contacts.

Classically, we all work through the difficulties in our parents' relationship through our own relationships in adult life, repeating the patterns and hopefully learning from them and putting them to more creative use. This is nowhere more the case than in the lives of those who have difficult Sun–Moon aspects.

As with all hard Sun–Moon aspects, the challenge for those with the square is to try to integrate all the seemingly conflicting needs around personal goals, and the present, past and future home and family situations.

The Trine and Sextile

Those with the easy aspects tend to feel quite comfortable with themselves and their life. There is not the same feeling of split between the conscious and unconscious sides of the personality and no conflict between past and future. The parental relationship was usually stable and there was an early feeling of security around the home life. This needn't imply that the home life or parental relationship was happy or otherwise, merely that there was a resistance to upsetting the apple cart.

Those with the easy aspects usually find it quite easy to express themselves and in particular their feelings. More negatively, those with the trine, especially, can be rather self-satisfied and complacent because they don't tend to question themselves or their lives in the way that those with the hard aspects do. On occasion the trine can actually be a problem, for if the individual is too self-accepting there can be difficulty in working through some of the other more difficult areas in the chart. On the other hand, the easy aspects can indicate enough good feeling about the self to enable the individual to cope with some of the more stressful elements of their life.

SUN–MERCURY

Self-knowledge. Independent thinker. Strong opinions. Importance of knowledge.

Since the Sun and Mercury can never be more than 28 degrees of longitude apart from each other, the only aspect possible in the natal chart between these two bodies is clearly the conjunction.

There is a tradition, I think an Arabic one, that when a planet is within 5 degrees of the Sun it is 'combust' or 'burnt' by the Sun and when within 30 minutes of the Sun, in extreme combustion, it is known as casimi. A casimi Mercury is thought by some authorities to describe superior intellect and a combust Mercury to be descriptive of a mind that is in some way debilitated. Personally, I can neither deny nor affirm the casimi tradition and it has to be said that cases where Mercury is *that* close to the Sun aren't common enough for a case to be proven either way. People I have known with Mercury casimi seem to me to be just like anyone else as far as brain-power goes. In my view, the Sun, when conjunct Mercury, far from burning out Mercury, gives it power and force.

Basically, Sun–Mercury people extend their ego over their opinions; they identify more strongly with what might be called the 'rational' mind. This is a person who *identifies* with their thoughts, ideas and with what they actually say. Those with this combination want what they say to be important and to be recognised as such: a kind of 'I am what I say, I am what I think' philosophy.

For Sun–Mercury, knowledge is important, something to be proud of, something to be expressed with power, authority and confidence. At best the individual's goal in life is to be a genuine authority in some area and not just believe that they are. Depending on the sign and aspects to the conjunction, those with this combination can often express their ideas with confidence and enthusiasm. This conjunction describes an opportunity for the individual to think for themselves, to form their own ideas, to be a real independent thinker.

The main problem with the conjunction can be the inability of the individual to perceive any viewpoint other than their own. Everybody's opinions are subjective. The problem with Sun–Mercury is that the individual can fail to realise that their opinions are not, and never can be, entirely impartial, nor the ultimate answer, and that other people do have completely different but perfectly valid ideas.

One can do no better than quote John Addey in *Selected Writings*:

Mr Carter has pointed out in his *Aspects* that this contact tends to be too mentally fixed, to incline on its worst side towards obstinacy, opinionatedness and pomposity and to be somewhat blinded by its pride and personal feelings generally. The student might consider how this tendency will affect the Mercurial faculties: the powers of observation, the sight, the memory, the speech, the adaptability and the rest. ... One might compare this contact with the story of Icarus who flew too near the Sun on the wings made by his ingenious father, and also with the story of Bellerophon who did something similar on the winged steed Pegasus, and being thrown for his presumption was obliged to wander through the world blind and lame.

Given that the Sun and Mercury are so close to each other in the sky, we can take this to mean that we are all, being merely mortal, owners of purely subjective knowledge, a mere armoury of opinions based on insufficient information, incapable of perceiving any situation from all angles and in its entirety.

It is easy to see how the combust idea arose for potentially the Sun–Mercury individual can have something of a blind spot about their ideas; at best an independent thinker, at worst an overly subjective thinker whose viewpoint is so narrow that when disagreed with they construe the difference of opinion as a personal attack.

The sign placement of the conjunction is obviously crucial, as are aspects to it. A square from Saturn to the conjunction might describe someone who, far from being overly sure of their ideas, feels very unsure about them and about their ability to communicate them. The conjunction in this instance would be more likely to indicate that the person desperately wants what they think and say to be important. Similarly, the possible opinionatedness and obstinacy is more likely to be a negative feature of the fixed signs and less likely with water and air, with the exception of the fixed sign Aquarius.

Sun–Mercury types usually appreciate the importance of brothers and sisters and others in the immediate environment. Unless the conjunction is picked up by Saturn or Pluto, Sun–Mercury people may well come from large families, raised in an atmosphere where there were lots of comings and goings and plenty of chat. Sometimes the father is a talkative type. The presence of a largish family may, in part, explain the Sun–Mercury easy gift for conversation and smalltalk. The type is interested and interesting, curious about everything, anxious to know and keen to learn.

Assuming the conjunction is a tight one and that it falls in an appropriate sign, Sun–Mercury types share Sun in Gemini characteristics, usually being chatty, expressive (often talking with their hands) and inquisitive people, with a tendency to touch their listener every now and then to make sure they're still listening, and a penchant for asking you forty questions the minute you walk in the door. Usually Sun–Mercury types have a healthy ability to think and talk about themselves and their goals.

The conjunction is favoured for all occupations and activities of a Mercurial nature: all forms of communication, education, agency work, transport and anything which involves the connecting of people, places and ideas.

SUN–VENUS

Importance of relationship. Importance of popularity. Malleability. Self-love. The loving heart. The loving father. The pursuit of peace.

Since the Sun and Venus can never be more than 48 degrees apart, the only aspects that can be formed between these planets (in the natal chart at any rate) are the conjunction, semi-sextile, and semi-square. In this section I am mostly writing about the conjunction and certainly feel quite unable to comment on the effects, if any, that might be felt with the semi-sextile aspect.

Sun–Venus people above all want to love and be loved; they tend to identify, rightly or wrongly, with the notion of being a loving and affectionate kind of person. And they want to be seen in that light, recognised as a person who is amiable, popular and tender-hearted. Usually Sun–Venus, ever wanting to please and be popular, *is* popular, especially with women. To be a loving person, and to be recognised as such, may be the most important thing in the world to the Sun–Venus type, although obviously the rest of the chart needs to be very carefully examined. The need for personal popularity can be so strong that the individual finds it very difficult to confront unpleasant issues, or to show themselves in an unpleasant light. They may find it difficult to push themselves forward, for doing so might 'make waves' and Sun–Venus would rather not risk that.

Typically, the type wants to believe the best about any given situation and those within it and will tend to gloss over those things that are less than perfect, either about themselves or about others that they are in relationship with. This can make the type rather short-sighted, seeing only what it wants to see. More positively though, Sun–Venus can be very accepting of others and very good at 'making allowances'. A charitable combination this and, at best, one that can be associated with a genuinely loving heart. Because of this tendency to take the charitable view, the type can put up with people and situations that others might find quite unacceptable. Sun–Venus would balk at squashing a fly, let alone another's ego.

The Sun–Venus individual is usually ever willing to compromise, to share and to give of themselves. They can appear weak and get crushed under pressure because of the emphasis that is placed on achieving harmony in relationship, avoiding pain and maintaining popularity. Like Libra, peace at any price can be a problem. It is not a good combination for leadership, or for the upholding of principles or for standing firm in any way, for it is just far too malleable.

Not surprisingly, relationship is of primary importance to the Sun–Venus person. They type of relationship that is so important, will be indicated by the sign and house positions of the two planets. The problem with a tight conjunction can be a tendency to view the self only in terms of the love, valuing and approbation that is being received (or perceived as being received) from others. In other words it is sometimes difficult for the Sun–Venus person to get any clear handle on themselves outside of whatever interpersonal feedback they happen to be receiving at any given time.

The father, or at least this one aspect of the father, was probably also like this. He might be experienced by the individual as refined and artistic, often someone disliking anything harsh or crass; certainly a charitable and loving kind of man. He, too, may have tended to avoid confrontation and been rendered ineffectual as a father-figure, or as a man, by his addiction to popularity and his insistence on trying to keep his marriage, and/or other situations, as sweet as possible. Nevertheless, children with this conjunction often feel that they are Daddy's little girl or boy.

One of the key phrases that could be ascribed to Sun–Venus is 'self-love' and an understanding and a dialogue with this concept seems to be a major task for those with a tight contact between these planets. The accomplishment of self-love may not be an easy task if the conjunction is forming hard aspects to other planets, as will often be the case. Though easy aspects or even hard ones from a planet such as Jupiter might well describe vanity. As always, the Sun describes what we are striving to become, not what we already are, and with this combination the hero's task involves discovering self-love and an awareness that one can never truly love anyone else until one loves, and is at peace with, oneself. Often the Sun–Venus person does not seem at peace with themselves though, and whatever the rest of the chart says about self-valuation, the conjunction especially does suggest that the individual is happy enough with certain aspects of themselves – self-satisfied even. The long-term goal of the Sun–Venus type is often the pursuit of peace. Complete inner and outer peace.

There is usually refinement and artistic appreciation, if not talent with this combination. Beauty is all-important to the individual and often the spirits can be lifted by a glimpse of a beautiful face, or the beauty of the landscape or the sound of harmonious music – anything that is pleasing to the senses. There is usually a leaning towards the arts and the individual will be proud of any artistic talent that they might have. A love of music especially is often very marked with all aspects. Both the semi-square and semi-sextile are common in the charts of singers, although not, I think, the conjunction.

There is usually also a very strong valuing of the feminine with both sexes. On the whole, the conjunction, if not the other aspects, is passive, if not lethargic. Agreeable and pleasant, with a fondness for the easy life and an inclination to avoid harshness of all kinds. Like Moon–Venus (though rather less so) there can be a liking for sweets and rich foods. Typically the Sun–Venus individual is extravagant and has a liking for ease, comfort and even luxury. Money is usually important to the Sun–Venus person, if only because they want to avoid the rigours of work, live an easy life and be able to indulge themselves and others. On its own though, this combination is probably far too passive, too easy-going and too fond of socialising to go out and earn a fortune – in the competitive business world anyway. Other areas of the chart may say differently of course.

As always, the element that a combination falls in is very important. Falling in airy signs, Sun–Venus is often particularly fair, just and reasonable. In water, the combination can be very compassionate and caring. Earth is usually exceptionally supportive (and self-indulgent) and may have business acumen. Fire is especially warm and loving in its response to others.

SUN–MARS

At war with self. Fighting Father. Pride in winning. Importance of daring. Importance of courage.

Strong contacts between these planets usually give rise to great 'personality'. People with this contact are usually real individualists, tending to be leaders rather than followers, participants as opposed to bystanders. The Sun–Mars type, unless there are strong indications to the contrary, has bags of energy, wants to be actively doing something and hates just sitting around waiting for something to happen; and with this outlook on life, inevitably events just gravitate towards them.

Those with Sun–Mars contacts tend to be very focused; they know what they want and the shortest route towards attaining it, and when Sun–Mars wants something, it usually wants it very badly, and it wants it *now*. Sometimes this can be a contributory factor in the charts of those who engage in criminal activities (and especially with those who get caught!) for to take by force can be perceived as the quickest means towards getting something.

There is usually great ambition and competitiveness here too, and, like Aries, a desperate desire to get 'there' (wherever 'there' is) *first*. The Sun–Mars type thinks it's important to achieve, important to 'do'; they are proud of their courage, daring and ability to accomplish. Unless fixity or Saturn is strong, however, the Sun–Mars person may not achieve as much as they would like, for the combination can be so impetuous and impulsive, so prone to jumping into things headfirst, that it runs the risk of making some very bad mistakes. Usually though, the impetuosity of Sun–Mars is tempered by other factors in the chart, tempered too by time, age and experience.

In any event there is tremendous 'fight' with this combination, especially with the hard aspects, combined with lots of drive and leadership potential. This is the person who just wants to win, win, win and having won the battle, wants to find new fields to conquer. Sun–Mars types are not scared to stick up for what they want or for what is theirs and a good way of using the aspect is for the individual to fight battles on behalf of others less able to do so.

This combination tends not to have a very good track record when it comes to the cultivation of poise, calm and equanimity. Ever ready to roll up its sleeves for action, Sun–Mars doesn't usually have a good reputation for sorting problems our peaceably or amicably, unless of course Venus or Libra is also strong in the chart.

This combination is very useful for those employed as trouble-shooters in some capacity, and for those engaged in 'getting things going'. Sun–Mars usually has a very healthy and honest regard for self-interest, though sometimes there can be a fine line between healthy self-interest and a total disregard for the needs of others, which can be a more negative manifestation of this combination. One can hardly associate this combination with a milk-and-water temperament; indeed those with strong contacts between these planets tend to ride roughshod over more gentle types. There is a danger too of assuming that everyone else is equally capable and operating from a similar position of self-interest.

Basically, Sun–Mars, like Moon–Mars, is at its best when it has a cause, a legitimate vehicle for its honest zeal, courage and get-up-and-go – somewhere where its flair for action and speedy decision-making can be utilised. This is the born fighter of *something*. At worst, without a vessel for its excessive fervour, it can wind up just spoiling for a fight.

Like Ascendant–Mars, Sun–Mars will often be found walking into walls, lampposts and other potentially dangerous or violent situations. Like Ascendant–Mars, too, the type will often be seen with knocks, cuts and grazes, especially to the head. It can be a good combination for a soldier or anyone who potentially has a fight on their hands. Robin Hood might have had a Sun–Mars contact, as may many people fighting against social injustice. This combination is also ideal for any kind of sport and especially combative or competitive sport; tennis, boxing, squash, situations which allow the individual to compete not only with others but also with themselves and their own past best. Occasionally those with Mars aspects strong in their charts, including those with Sun–Mars contacts, can be found in situations where they are not actively competing, but even so, it can be found that the individual is actually very competitive indeed, choosing not to compete only because coming second would be too horrible to contemplate.

It could be said that the Sun–Mars person is at war with themselves, and frequently they are; at war too, with an early father-figure, either the person himself or the things he stood for. This anger with the father can fuel the individual to accomplish all sorts of exceptional feats; it also quite often fuels a lifetime battle with the entire male species and at the same time an identification with it. Dad himself is often a belligerent sort, always spoiling for a fight, and the child may have grown up defending themselves against him. Often he was someone with a strong, pervasive, unchecked sexuality, and it can be this that the young child finds particularly threatening even though they may have no name for what they are experiencing. Sometimes there was competition between father and child. At others, the father-figure embodies the quality of Mars by working in a Martian trade, with tools and metals – the soldier, the surgeon, the butcher, the man who often has blood on his hands, and these occupations can provide ways in which Sun–Mars themselves are able to utilise this combination.

Typically, there may have been times in the life of the father where the question of his courage was raised, as in cases where the father went to war for example. Frequently, too, the Sun–Mars individual can be found to be fighting the father's battles for him. For example, I have known two cases where individuals with Sun conjunct Mars, far from having warrior fathers, had fathers who were conscientious objects during the war. In the one case the father stayed at home farming and slaughtering his own pigs. He was still displaying Sun–Mars behaviour inasmuch as he was sticking out for what he thought was right and he was fighting the system. In some communities, as was the case here, choosing not to fight during war-time might take as much courage, if not more, than actually going to war. The repercussions of his choice though, were that his daughter, the Sun–Mars child, often found herself in battles at school as both she and her father were accused of cowardice by some of the other villagers and especially by her schoolfellows.

Calling a Sun–Mars type a coward is a bit like waving a red rag at a bull; it could easily end in bloodshed! Those with the square aspects are often uncertain as to their capacity for courage, are fearful that they might indeed be cowards, or interpreted as such, and classically they put themselves into situations which require that they be bold and fearless just to prove themselves, albeit often unconsciously. Those with the opposition aspect are perhaps even more likely to end up in one-to-one battles, especially when young, when they often see others as being argumentative or aggressive rather than themselves. Those with the conjunction merely identify with the Martian characteristics of courage, daring and zeal but often have a blind spot as to the extent of their assertiveness. They keyword for Sun–Mars is, I think, *courage*, and whilst we associate the word with bravery, valour and boldness, the word literally means, 'to put heart into'. The word comes from 'cor' meaning heart.

Curiously, a connection between Sun–Mars hard aspects and potential heart attack has been noted by many astrologers, including Carter and Ebertin. Before the reader with this combination starts worrying themselves into cardiac disease, it should be pointed out that all Sun contacts potentially can give rise to cardiac problems: Sun–Venus, a fatty, sluggish heart; Sun–Jupiter, an enlarged heart; Sun–Saturn and Sun–Uranus, heart blockage or problems with rhythm – and so on. Many millions of people with contacts between these planets, including Sun–Mars, do not have any such problems. Nevertheless, by progression and transit, if not by natal aspect, I have found this correlation, especially with the opposition, to have much validity. It is easy to see a justification for making the connection, for we can associate Sun–Mars with 'overdrive', with living life in the fast lane, never stopping until forced to do so, so that the heart, like the rest of their psyche, just gets overworked and overstretched. Sun–Mars can just put too much 'heart' into things and needs to find a little corner of their lives where they can just allow things to take their course rather than forever forcing issues, a little corner where the quality of just 'being' rather than always 'doing' can be valued. Conversely though, health problems are perhaps more likely to occur for Sun–Mars when they have not got a project on the boil which they can put their heart and teeth into. Without a suitable vehicle for their talents, Sun–Mars people feel very angry and frustrated with life and with themselves, and this can be very stressful for the body especially later in life. These feelings need not be interpreted negatively of course, for it can be this anger that spurs Sun–Mars types into leaping into action and doing something about those situations that make them angry.

An example of a Sun–Mars conjunction can be found in the chart of the Duchess of York. For someone in her position she appears to have tremendous daring. She is also very much her own person and has not seemingly adapted herself to the media image of what a princess should be. Because she is so authentically herself, she is popular anyway and even has another common Sun conjunct Mars characteristic – red hair.

As both the Sun and Mars are significators of inner male figures, it might be expected that women with this combination, as well as hopefully living it out for themselves, are likely to be attracted to others, especially men, who display Mars-type behaviour: figures, perhaps in the forces; pioneers, types who go out for what they want; those who dare to take risks.

SUN–JUPITER

The Explorer, Quester, Visionary, Opportunist. Large-hearted. Big goals. Self-enlargement. Identification with God.

Whatever the actual contact, this combination inclines to buoyancy, optimism and confidence. With the soft aspects this takes the form of a gentle, almost complacent contentment with one's lot and optimistic expectations of the future. The hard aspects are more likely to yield over-confidence and a more obvious exuberance, and the conjunction might come from either or both positions at different times. Generosity is also usually a very marked feature of this combination and not only in the material sense. On the whole, Sun–Jupiter people are well-intentioned about their own motives and charitable in their interpretation of the motives of others. Perhaps here we can glimpse the potential arrogance of the type, for at worst, the charitable viewpoint can be seen as patronising and condescending, as in the person who does not view their fellow mortals as equals but as individuals who are in some way inferior to them and to whom therefore they should be generous and make allowances.

Perhaps Sun–Jupiter identifies with God, embracing not only the positive manifestations of the divine but all the arrogant assumptions that such an identification must imply. So the behaviour of the Sun–Jupiter type (and especially those with the hard aspects) may sometimes be viewed by others as patronising and paternalistic. Sun–Jupiter may feel deflated by this response, not easily understanding why its bountifulness and benevolence should be greeted so ungraciously.

Sun–Jupiter does get quite easily deflated – but only for a very short time. Physically, the planet Jupiter is rather like a big balloon, being as it is very large and very light. Sun–Jupiter shares this buoyancy and sometimes hooks the impulse that we all have with balloons – to prick them with a pin. Jupiter exaggerates the solar principle of pride with this combination so that those who have it can be very proud, puffing themselves up like peacocks and reminding us of the old adage that pride comes before a fall.

At worst, the hard aspects especially can suffer from inflation and grandiosity, a state in which the individual has unrealistically high expectations of and opinions about the self, a large but fragile ego. Here, the individual thinks that, like God, they can do anything, be all things to all people, and that nothing can possibly go wrong. There can seem to be just too much faith in life and in the self. 'Seem' may be the operative word, as Sun–Jupiter is often not as confident as it appears; if it were it would not take such pains to cultivate this overly confident manner.

Sun–Jupiter people are great visionaries, intuitively seeing their place in the overall scheme of things and having the gift of being able to see any situation in terms of bigger and better future possibilities. Their big goals can seem very over the top at the outset but it's surprising how often people with these contacts make their vision a reality (though usually fixity of Saturn will be strong in the chart too) and it's their innate faith in life and in themselves that enable them to do so. The Sun–Jupiter type is a gambler at heart and likes taking risks, indeed, has little awareness of the possibility of danger or failure, believing perhaps that their project has the divine seal of approval and as such is protected from disaster. Their love of adventure and obvious belief in what they are doing, coupled with the confidence as to the likely successful outcome of events, is infectious and imbues others with confidence. A modern-day Sun–Jupiter type can be seen in the TV character 'Sergeant Bilko', though I have no idea of the actor's chart or that of the programme.

There is enormous capacity for leadership with this combination and, more specifically, a positive attitude to authority and especially to taking it! Margaret Thatcher, who has a square between these planets (as part of a T-square with Sun, Mars and Pluto) is a good example.

Those with Sun–Jupiter strong believe in growth and freedom, and ideally will be concerned with growth and freedom for everyone. This often leads to an interest in politics, though this is not a particularly democratic combination, for Sun–Jupiter types want to do things in their own way and are not so hot on the humility and self-effacement that the true democratic process requires.

If the rest of the chart is in accord, all contacts between these planets seem to incline the individual (or project come to that) to success and ever-increasing prominence in their field. But lest the reader is thinking that Sun–Jupiter is blessed with the Midas touch in its dealings, it should be pointed out that things *can* go wrong (especially with the hard aspects) and sometimes do so ... and disastrously. What can be so infuriating about Sun–Jupiter is that even when things do go wrong, they somehow seem to mange to get away without shouldering too much of the blame or the responsibility, even when there might be substantial charges of negligence and carelessness. The popularity of the classic Sun–Jupiter type will be merely dented, and the individual will have the happy knack of being able to view the episode philosophically, as part of the large scheme of things. Never was there a type more able to pick themselves up, brush themselves off and start all over again.

Because of its recklessness and carelessness and misplaced belief in Divine protection, hard contacts between these planets can be quite accident-prone, especially if Mars or Uranus is plugging into the combination. An example of this is the chart for the Townsend Thoresen company, owner of the fated *Herald of Free Enterprise* which sank claiming many lives in 1987 (see pages 58–9). Those with the soft aspects *are* usually lucky but do not tend to overextend themselves or behave as carelessly as those with the hard aspects and sometimes the conjunction do. Those with the hard aspects just *have* to try their luck – and push their luck.

Innately this is the contact of the explorer and the quester. This type just wants to grow and wants space to do so. Sun–Jupiter types forever seek to broaden themselves, to embrace more and more of life, and the type is unlikely to get themselves into a rut or into behaving in any kind of mean or petty way; their vision is the grand vision and they are not going to be bothered with little details or any but the most major obstacles. Not surprisingly, Sun–Jupiter types are usually great travellers in the physical sense and, like Sagittarius, usually seek to explore mentally as well as physically. Often there is interest and involvement in such fields as law, education and religion. Sun–Jupiter tends to be very concerned with meaning, as well as with the future, and these areas provide scope for this kind of exploration.

The combination is also useful for situations where the individual can legitimately 'play God' as in advice-giving occupations. It's good for the stage too, for drama provides many opportunities for exaggeration, caricature and self-promotion. Nevertheless, whilst one might associate a Sun–Jupiter contact (especially the conjunction and hard aspects) with a larger-than-life personality, the combination can equally occur in the charts of more introverted individuals, who would find life in the spotlight quite unbearable. Introvert or extrovert, Sun–Jupiter people will all share a basic ongoing need to enlarge and expand themselves and their horizons.

A glutton for experience, Sun–Jupiter hard aspects can suffer from spells of dissatisfaction (especially falling in mutable signs) believing that the grass is greener everywhere else than on the little patch one happens to be standing on. This dissatisfaction is of course the very spur that is required to prompt individuals towards making major changes in themselves, their lives and the world. Conversely though, when times are really hard, Sun–Jupiter types usually know how to make the best of a difficult situation, how to look on the bright side and how to imbue others with optimism. Sometimes this optimism can get out of hand, as where the individual refuses to 'come down', refuses to face, indeed can't bear to face, the harsher reality of the situation. There is much of the

Divine Child in Sun–Jupiter, and to bring that child down to earth would be to make it merely mortal.

Those with these contacts strong may not necessarily belong to any formal church but they usually have very strong beliefs. These may or may not be of a religious character though the hard contacts between these planets have long been associated with 'religious difficulties'. Certainly the father often seems to have, to the child at any rate, religious problems. That is, the beliefs and especially the moral code of the father may be experienced as getting in the way of the child going where it wants to go. That can be the problem for those with these contacts too, the individual often being faced with a challenge of some sort in terms of integrating their life-goals with their belief system. The tendency to moralise can also be another issue for the type. The father himself may have been seen as a moraliser. He is also often a greater traveller, a restless figure who wants plenty of space and refuses to be confined. This might mean that he is not around a great deal but can also give rise to an image of him as some kind of explorer. Sometimes he is experienced as a Godlike figure, too big to get hold of, too far away to touch. With the soft aspects, perhaps the feeling is more of a generous, philosophical type of man. In any event, it would seem that the father-figure's beliefs are those that are internalised and have to be integrated and processed by those individuals with these contacts.

SUN–SATURN

Self-denial, self-discipline, self-control, self-defence. Importance of authority. Illumination of fears. Importance of time.

When Saturn touches a planet in the natal chart the individual tends to crave those things that that planet represents. This is usually because of some felt lack in that area. Taking the solar keyword 'important' for example, it can be seen that Sun–Saturn people often yearn to be considered important because they believe and fear that they are really rather insignificant, and these feelings often start early on in childhood.

A young child assumes as its right that it is the most important person in the whole world. Indeed, few parents do consider anyone or anything more important than their child. Sun–Saturn children often do not feel this strong sense of personal importance, do not experience the knowledge that the world revolves around them and them alone. For some reason the child's uniqueness and individuality was not recognised, accepted or reinforced. Commonly, early traces of exhibitionism and feelings of self-importance and behaviour describing that self-importance would have been 'sat on' in childhood. Possibility the child was not really seen in its own right but viewed as a parental satellite. Commonly the parents or other caretakers were not appreciated as individuals by their own parents, and therefore tended to look to the infant for their own reinforcement. So, in the classic scenario, the identity of Sun–Saturn is quite tightly controlled.

The Sun–Saturn child is particularly likely to be overlooked by the father-figure, whose time is usually felt to be in rather short supply – and it is time that is really necessary to recognise and nurture the unique individuality of the growing youngster. So perhaps through no fault of his own, Sun–Saturn's father was weak as a parental figure. In such circumstances, the mother often takes on the mantle of Saturn and becomes a strict disciplinarian, or at least someone who has a strong idea about what sort of 'character' the child is going to have. Whilst the child may not have been seen and recognised as a unique individual, conversely it is often very closely watched. Sun–Saturn are usually brought up with caretakers who have very strong opinions about what the child's 'character' should be and the child is kept under strict control and surveillance to ensure that its development runs along the prescribed lines. So the youngster picks up a very early message that it has to be a certain type of individual. Hence the real self is denied.

Things don't always work out in this way, but whatever the 'cause', Sun–Saturn's main problem is usually that of identity. Indeed, it could be said that the purpose of having a Sun–Saturn contact (especially the conjunction and hard aspects) is that of individuals building for themselves a true sense of self, a real identity that has been worked for, understood and accepted the hard way, by the individuals themselves. The early feeling of being overlooked (sometimes a similar feeling to Sun in the 12th house) usually results in individuals, unconsciously if not consciously, desperately wanting to be seen, to be recognised, to be noticed and above all, to feel important. Sun–Saturn types are often 'fame freaks', but whilst desperate to be seen, at the same time are often rather embarrassed about putting themselves forward. The type would love fame, glory and recognition beyond anything, indeed needs that kind of external reinforcement, but because thinking of themselves as something 'special' was not allowed when young, Sun–Saturn individuals often find it difficult owning this need to be seen and heard and can be quite self-conscious about putting themselves in the spotlight. It is rather like being in a classroom where the teacher asks who would like their picture put up on the wall: there is usually at least one person whose hand is half up, half asking to be chosen. The person wants their picture on the board but doesn't want to be seen to be wanting it, because on some level they believe that the picture isn't good enough or that they aren't good enough to be in the spotlight in that way. More to the point, the Sun–Saturn person may think the picture is good enough but certainly doesn't want anyone else to think they think it is – the classic 'inferiority complex'.

Disappointed with authority figures in the past, Sun–Saturn hard aspects often have difficulty with what might be called 'seizing authority' although there is often a craving to do so. They type may well give off to others an impression that they believe they are their own best authority but in actuality they are unlikely to believe this until the fear of their own omnipotence has been faced. The other side of the paradox has to be faced too, the fear of one's own insignificance. Part of the mission of those with these contacts is to find real authority inside. In later life, the Sun–Saturn type genuinely tends to trust no authority other than their own. Having learned about most things the hard way, Sun–Saturn becomes their own best authority, very self-determined and reliant on no one.

The type wants to be in a position of authority, a position of respon-sibility in order to be held in good esteem. They may, as in the classroom, have difficulty in putting themselves in that position, either overdoing and pushing forwards too much or shrinking back and half-expecting and hoping that others will put them in that central, so desirable position. The Sun–Saturn type dares not risk being judged on their own merits (and they assume they are being judged and so they are – by themselves) so they try to do something that will be meaningful in the world. They try to build the identity by doing something they can be proud of, perhaps by creating something tangible in the world (remembering that Saturn is always concerned with that which is tangible and concrete) or by making some unique contribution to humanity, something that will stand the test of time and that can bear testament to the individual's value in the world and to themselves. Sun–Saturn longs to be a hero.

Whatever Sun–Saturn's achievements are, the type is never likely to think that they are good enough, and thus the individual can be found driving themselves on and on. In many ways this is the good news about Sun–Saturn contacts, for whereas Sun–Jupiter, for example, will tend to be careless and fairly happy with what has been produced, Sun–Saturn may feel less than comfortable and in driving themselves on and on, can get quite near to achieving that much-sought-after excellence. If Sun–Saturn's achievements do fall short of their aspirations, it doesn't matter too much, for growth still takes place, for with every test the individual faces (and Sun–Saturn are always testing themselves) the person gains much in the way of confidence and self-knowledge. Ideally they will gain recognition for their efforts too, some sort of positive rein-forcement that will help to heal their wound. Conversely though, and at worst, the deep lack of confidence of the Sun–Saturn type can also mean that they fail to deliver the goods, for this person cannot bear for something they are producing to be merely mediocre and so at worst can sometimes be found 'bunking out'. If Sun–Saturn is unable to acknowledge their fear of failure, the fear can become a reality. When the person relies too heavily on receiving 'strokes' from others, on receiving external reinforcement, the door is opened to personal weakness, for the individual can be controlled by this dependence on the good opinions of others. And when this happens, personal integrity flies out the window; there is indeed a denial of the self.

The Sun always urges us to illuminate whatever part of the chart it touches, and with Sun–Saturn the individual needs to illuminate their fears. Becoming conscious of the issues is, as always, the first step on the path to cure. When Sun–Saturns are unaware of their own psychology this can have dire consequences, for they tend to feel so inadequate themselves that they set about making sure no one else is ever good enough either by controlling other people or situations. Inevitably, the people they control the most are their own children. Hence we perpetuate the sins of our fathers. There can also be a kind of vicious circle created where Sun–Saturn, ever self-reliant and self-determined, never lets anyone penetrate them sufficiently and so denies the possibility of being truly valued and recognised as the unique human being that each one of us is. Sun–Saturn usually has very strong defences. These may have been required when the individual was young, but in adult life, and if taken to extremes, these defences can serve to trap and isolate the person they once merely protected.

The Sun–Saturn type is usually a serious person, tending to take themselves very seriously and to take all that happens around them rather personally. This is especially the case in early life when the individual's sense of identity is gleaned from whatever external reinforcement is available. But the individual usually finds a true sense of identity in time, and usually gains considerable confidence too. Not the seemingly endless but actually rather fragile self-confidence of Sun–Jupiter but a confidence borne out of a realistic appraisal of oneself and one's limitations. It's true that Sun–Saturn people can limit themselves, keeping their goals within too cautious bounds, but if these goals are tested and accomplished, then greater confidence can ensue. As always, Saturn denies in the short term but not necessarily for ever.

Sun–Saturn may, as I have suggested, take itself rather seriously but these contacts are quite common in the charts of comedians, who amongst other things have to have a good sense of timing. Exampled include Lucille Ball and Eric Morecambe. I have found that the conjunction aspect is common in the charts of clowns. Amongst other things, clowns are protecting themselves by wearing masks. For most of us, our skin is our physical defence, the barrier between us and the outside world. In wearing a mask, a clown is wearing a double defence, a double fortification and barrier. And more than all comedians, clowns are saying laugh *at* me. There is a bitter irony in the message of 'don't take me seriously' from the person who takes themselves so very seriously. Part of the Sun–Saturn defence system often involves hiding behind a mask, a defence system of some sort, for this type is often frightened of the nakedness that real exposure would bring.

With both Sun–Saturn and Moon–Saturn contacts the individual often has difficulty in being the 'right age'. People with these contacts rarely behave in keeping with their chronological years, either being too responsible and serious whilst young, perhaps in response to what was felt was required by the parents, or displaying juvenile behaviour when much older. Perhaps this comes about because of the general experience of a denial of childhood. Childhood serves as an apprenticeship for adulthood; with these Saturn contacts it is as if the apprenticeship was never served, and true maturation comes with difficulty. Also I suspect for the average Sun–Saturn type, life really does get better with age, and greater light-heartedness is bound to follow as the inner child is allowed to emerge.

SUN–URANUS

Reformer, rebel, radical, anarchist, innovator and revolutionary. Insistence on freedom and independence. Importance of truth. Pride in uniqueness and originality. Change meets resistance.

Usually those with the conjunction and hard aspects especially, exhibit a very strong urge to be unique, to be different from others. More common still, is a very marked, strongly *independent* spirit. Sometimes though, those with Sun–Uranus contacts may on one level want above all else to be 'different', but on another level may desire to conform. Hard contacts, particularly, between these planets can describe a situation where the individual feels that they are odd, eccentric, different and alienated in some way and what they would most like would be to fit in. On the one hand being 'different' might have afforded them some recognition, some attention within the family. On another level, it may have made them feel like an outsider. Carter talks of the combination as being prone to taking 'the wrong end of the stick'. Sometimes, I suspect this touchiness has arisen because the individual feels sensitive about being laughed at or pointed out as different, for some reason.

Whatever the personal history there seems to be a strong urge to break free from it, to wage a revolutionary war against whatever traditions and values one was born into.

Frequently, Sun–Uranus types cannot bear to think of themselves as being anything like, or in any way associated with, some authority-figure or regime they encountered when young. Commonly, the rebellion is against an early father-figure but sometimes it is against one's country or the political atmosphere in which one was raised, or some other collective influence. This marked urge to rebel and be 'different' is of course much less marked in the charts of those with the soft aspects, who, happy in the knowledge that they are unique, feel less propelled into having to go out into the world and prove it.

The main problem with the hard aspects is that the person *will* insist on doing things *in their own way* sometimes because they have met tremendous resistance to their attempts to do so in the past. Co-operation can be difficult to achieve with this combination, though a strongly placed Venus will do much to offset this tendency. If you want to come to an arrangement with a typical Sun–Uranus person it's best to be entirely honest (the type cannot bear being 'handled') and be prepared to give plenty of space and freedom. Telling a Sun–Uranus type what to do, or what is best, will seldom have the desired result. Even if they have the same idea themselves, they will often take a contrary line. This difficulty in co-operating may arise because the person fears that their spirit will in some way be crushed, that they might lose their individuality if they bend.

It can also mean that the individual may sometimes find themselves out in the cold, alienated, an outsider and a loner. Sometimes this alienation occurs because the individual is merely expressing views that are very ahead of their time or too advanced for the people they are with. In any event their views will often meet with great resistance from others. Sometimes, the resistance occurs not so much because of the nature of the individual's views as because of their manner of expressing them. Because they tend to expect resistance, Sun–Uranus people may express them-selves in a rather tense and forceful way. The condition of Mercury and Venus may do much to modify this. Additionally, those with Sun–Uranus conjunctions or hard aspects can be incredibly perverse, unpredictable, stubborn and wilful. Not uncommonly, their stubbornness elicits the same kind of entrenched stubborn reaction from others.

The extreme Sun–Uranus type may also be very *inconsistent*, inflexibly supporting and pursuing a particular course of action one day, and advocating the opposite course only days later. More frustrating still, the type will be seemingly unaware of their turnaround in outlook. Sun–Uranus views can be very extreme, and expressed in the most uncompro-mising fashion. But this is, in itself, an extreme interpretation. Sun–Uranus usually only exhibits this kind of extreme behaviour and rev-olutionary, anarchist tendencies when either the contact is angular or Aquarius is also strongly emphasised in the chart.

Sometimes the situation in which the Sun–Uranus individual finds themselves is one in which compromises cannot or should not be made anyway. Sun–Uranus will think along these lines in any case. For example, I have known several fiercely anti-apartheid white South Africans with Sun–Uranus contacts. They are making a strong statement, not only about apartheid but about themselves – the statement being: we are different from the regime that we have come from. Behind that statement may lurk the fear that they may indeed be tarred with the same brush or that they may be viewed by others in that light. Their background also sets them apart as being 'different'.

Basically those with Sun–Uranus hard aspects often have a problem with *change*. It may seem that the Sun–Uranus individual wants to introduce changes all over the place, which is often the case in the outer world. But on a more personal level, Sun–Uranus is, I suggest, very frightened of change. On a day-to-day level, Sun–Uranus finds it very difficult to move on – all the more so if mutability or air is weak in the chart, so that when change does occur it is often drastic and seems to come from the outside world and not through choices made by the individual. Such dramatic and drastic changes can be viewed as the result of a release of a built-up need for reform, alteration and movement. On all levels, *change creates resistance*. Sun–Uranus people may be stubbornly reluctant (or sometimes unable for practical or sociological reasons) to change themselves of their own lives. Not only is there fear and resistance coming from inside themselves but also there is an expectation of resistance from other people. Commonly Sun–Uranus people are frightened that others mean to change them, and indeed all of us are changed by contact with other people and new situations. We need a fairly strong ego in order to be flexible enough to accommodate change and it often takes Sun–Uranus some years to develop a strong inner core and self-image. I have known several blind people with hard Sun–Uranus squares. For them, even the most minor changes in their environment can mean the difference between being able to move around or having to be rooted to the one spot, or at best only being able to proceed with extreme caution.

The Sun–Uranus tendency towards always taking a contrary line from the mainstream, to generally putting 'a spanner in the works' of whatever is going on, need not be viewed negatively, for surely it is the purpose of those with this combination to get themselves into positions where these qualities are required. It is the purpose of this combination to implement change. The Sun–Uranus individual can be superb at breathing new life into any situation where change is needed. Any situation where things have become stultified, rigid or taken for granted. Many people who work with computers or other forms of advanced technology have strong Sun–Uranus contacts and such technology does strongly challenge previous ways of working. Computers challenge Saturnian boundaries, for, like many inventions, they save time. They also meet with resistance in many office situations. The Sun–Uranus mission is not only to challenge outmoded traditions but to help others find the freedom to discover their own uniqueness and pride in the truth. Frequently, the Sun–Uranus individual acts as a trailblazer and spokesperson for progress and this is how these contacts might best be utilised. Sun–Uranus can be inflexible and self-willed but then they often get themselves into situations where these qualities are *required* in order that change does take place.

Sun–Uranus types can make wonderful reformers. They have little respect for authority and therefore do not feel constrained by it. Instead, they have great talent for cutting across tradition and conservatism. This type does not accept things merely because they have always been done in a certain way or because the voice of some authority states that this is how they are going to be done in the future.

Even so, in implementing changes, those with Sun–Uranus hard aspects can go overboard. Instead of just wanting to make a few changes here and there, Sun–Uranus may take a really radical line, and want to pull out all the roots as well, which may or may not be appropriate. Not surprising therefore, that the extreme Sun–Uranus type will often meet with great resistance from others who are likely to be affected by the upheaval.

Sometimes the root of this behaviour can be that the individual wants to pull up and rebel against their own roots, and especially against what is experienced as the father's roots.

It is not uncommon to find the father of the Sun–Uranus individual (and I have found this particularly with the conjunction) to have been something of a bully and an authoritarian. Hardly surprising therefore that the individual often wants to be as different from this early father or other authority-figure as possible. Ironically, in their insistence on following a different path, their insistence on deviating from the norm, Sun–Uranus can exhibit the same fascist tendencies as that early authority-figure or regime did. Not infrequently the father 'cut out' in the some way with these aspects, even if it was only behaving in an impersonal and aloof manner. Commonly, he found it difficult to integrate his desire for space and freedom with the responsibilities demanded of him by fatherhood. Maybe he literally deserted the family. Perhaps he was not so much missing as inconsistent and the child either did not know if and when he or she would see him or did not know how he was likely to behave. Sometimes he is just very different, for some reason, from other fathers. This might make him very exciting or productive of a deep inner insecurity.

Being a radical usually means that in large sectors of one's community, one is likely to be an outsider. This doesn't seem to worry Sun–Uranus in the way it would other types. Perhaps Sun–Uranus does not want to join the club, for it often turns its nose up at the rest of humanity and announces itself, by default, to be much more worthy. Choosing not to toe the line with the rest of the family or the rest of society, leaves Sun–Uranus unfettered and free, though sometimes also out in the cold.

Whilst compassion is not part of its armoury, the Sun–Uranus person can often be found championing the cause of the underdog. The underdog is usually also ostracised from society and Sun–Uranus, amongst other things, can identify with the brand of alienation. With their insistence on their own personal freedom, it's hardly surprising either that this combination will also often be active in the charts of those that support causes that campaign for freedom and civil rights.

Those with the easy contacts between these planets are less likely to exhibit the extreme stubbornness, perversity and wilfulness of the hard contacts and sometimes the conjunction. Neither will they give rise to individuals with the potential to change the world. The soft aspects incline to a more gentle unconventionality. The person feels different, is motivated by being so, and is happy about it. Those with the square aspects are often not that certain about whether they are really all that different, or whether they really want to be. Both the conjunction and square aspects can give rise to a very taut kind of nervous tension and also a need to dramatise the self in the most drastic and unusual ways. The individual may feel a bit like the strings on a violin that have been strung too tight. Bordering on genius perhaps or bordering on hysteria.

Sigmund Freud, whose early work was with so-called 'hysterical' patients and whose revolutionary ideas have stood the test of time, was born with a Sun–Uranus conjunction. The psychiatrist, R. D. Laing has a tight square between these planets and is well known for being a rebel in his field and for his radical approaches to mental illness. He speaks much of alienation in his work. The actress Vanessa Redgrave has Sun in Aquarius square Uranus conjunct MC. She is perhaps as much known for her radical views as for her electrifying performances on stage. Another radical, Germaine Greer, also has the same square.

SUN–NEPTUNE

Self-deception. Glamorising self. Father as victim. Loss of ego. Escaping from the self. Mediumship. Identification with the victim or the Saviour. Importance of a vision. Pride in compassion.

Whatever the aspect, the Sun–Neptune person often yearns to live some kind of ideal life, often yearns to be someone 'special', to touch the Divine in some way in their lives. This is often a wistful quality about individuals with tight contacts between these planets. Charles Carter captures it perfectly when he describes it as: 'delicacy or remoteness from what is ordinary, tangible and concrete'.

Neptune always seeks to heighten whatever it touches in the horoscope. But in heightening an experience, the planet takes us further away from the reality of the given situation. When Neptune touches the Sun, it's as if the individual wants to heighten as well as glamorise their experience of themselves, and it follows that there is often a feeling of dissatisfaction, loss or confusion about the self.

The pitfall in wanting to be someone special, especially with the hard aspects, is immediately apparent. If a person always wants to be something out of the ordinary, it can be very difficult to accept that which is 'ordinary' about oneself, or one's life. It is hardly surprising therefore that this combination is associated with self-doubt and discontent. The person is always thirsty for more, thirsty to *be* more. Frequently then, the individual spins fantasies around themselves and their motives. Sun–Neptune contacts, with good reason, have a reputation for self-deception. At its most extreme, this combination can certainly be associated with delusions about oneself and one's motives. At worst, the Sun–Neptune person can distort anything in order to be able to cling to a fantasy about their own identity or about the nature of a particular situation.

All individuals need a fairly strong and firm ego in order to be able to shine light onto the rest of the self. For those with Sun–Neptune contacts, the development of this strong ego can be elusive in early life. People with these contacts are often searching for the spirit in some way in their lives, and in searching for the spirit, perhaps they are really searching for the self.

A parent of the Sun–Neptune person, usually the father, is often psychologically 'missing' in childhood, usually physically present unless the 4th house is implicated but not available as a flesh and blood person for the child and developing ego to relate to. Despite this, it is common for Sun–Neptune to idealise their father (especially those with the hard aspects) and it is often some time before awareness dawns as to that parent's real inaccessibility. When it does dawn, or in other situations, the Sun–Neptune person will often see themselves as a victim of their father. The individual often has an image of him which, in early life, is far removed from the reality of how he is or was. The image may distort favourably or unfavourably, but, for whatever reason, the image seems a very necessary one for the development of the individual. The fantasy image of the father replaces his physical presence – and perhaps this is necessarily so.

On a more literal level, the Sun–Neptune person is often at a loss to describe the father-figure, to get hold of him in any identifiable way.

Similarly for many years Sun–Neptune often has difficulty in getting hold of themselves. The father may work at sea and be literally oceans apart from the child. Or he might be a Doer of Good Works, often a clergyman or something like that, a saviour to others but still seldom at home. He might embody Neptune by being an artist or something of a mystic but can just as easily be a businessman, a road sweeper or an alcoholic. The issue is much more that the child recognises him as wishing to pursue a particular vision or dream and more especially of escaping from or transcending a more mundane kind of life. This might be experienced in a multitude of different ways by the child. The youngster may weave romantic dreams around him, or may merely feel all at sea, not knowing quite who or where he is.

Sometimes it will seem to the child that the dream or the escape route, whatever it was, was more important to the father than his child was. Often he is experienced as pursuing, successfully or not, that which might be termed 'spiritual'. In any event a situation is often set up where the father acts as a model for pursing a Neptunian way of life, one that involves pursuing a vision or elevating oneself beyond ordinary reality. Often, though, he can be seen merely as a victim. Perhaps he is a man of great talent or potential, who nevertheless finds himself trapped in the mundane would and often burdened by various hardships and responsibilities. He is often addicted to pursuing the spirit in some way, and on a low level he may merely be inaccessible by virtue of addition to drink or drugs.

The possibilities are endless but the most common development background I have found with Sun–Neptune contacts is that there are no boundaries set in childhood, no rules, and often a lack of authority-figures (Saturn in the chart may do much to reverse this situation though) and this may explain why individuals with the hard aspects, especially, between these planets, seem to have no sense of what is 'right', normal or possible in life. People with these aspects get so disillusioned, often because they do not know what to expect in life, from themselves or from a given situation. There is difficulty in deciding if the job, the relationship, the home, whatever, really is that awful or quite acceptable really. It is as if the Sun–Neptune person has difficulty in arriving at a yardstick for judging the reality of their life. The lack of yardstick, the lack of life-rules, can be extremely useful or very disorientating. If there is no concept of what is 'normal' or 'acceptable' then clearly anything is possible; there is no need to accept the standards set by the rest of humanity. If the standards, the ideals, for life and for the self, are set too high though, then whatever the real life-situation under discussion is like, it is not likely ever to be good enough. This can be very useful too. Whilst the main problem for those with the hard aspects between these planets is often about accepting things as they are, it is through *not* accepting things that the impulse to change and improve a situation is born. The Sun–Neptune person often does have very high standards about themselves and how the world should be. They want to excel and surpass ordinary reality, and the challenge is to make this happen rather than let disillusionment lead to the desire to escape from it all or to the mistaken belief that things are acceptable when they are clearly not. People with Sun–Neptune contacts, like those with Sun in Pisces, are often so sensitive and aware of all the harshness and suffering in the world that it is often little wonder that they feel like escaping from it at times.

Those with the hard aspects and conjunction are often prone to feeling dissatisfied with their lot. And it is sometimes difficult for them to decide to go in a particular direction, to team up with a certain person, or go for a particular type of work, because either the expectations are too high or the individual feels that if they accept this opportunity then they will close the door to other future possibilities. In accepting reality, the Sun–Neptune person often feels they will be selling themselves short of fulfilling some kind of vision they have of themselves or their life, whereas sometimes it is through accepting the reality of a situation and working with it that the individual can actually make their dreams come true.

In my view, most of the difficulties and much of the potential of these aspects is bound up with issues of self-acceptance of one sort or another, though such issues can manifest in a wide variety of different ways. Sometimes the Sun–Neptune person is too ready to accept a situation and too passive to do anything about it. And at others, and often at the same time, there is an inability to accept either the self or the situation; thus there is outer acceptance but inner unacceptance.

The Sun contributes to the notion of the ego, our self-opinion, the person we know ourselves to be. When contacting Neptune there is often no clear identity and little differentiation between oneself and others. The Sun–Neptune person, or indeed anyone with Neptune strongly placed in the chart, can almost be anyone they choose. The boundaries between the self and every other person seems amorphous with these aspects. Like a chameleon, the type can take on the colouring of whoever they are with or whatever situation they are in. This lack of clarity about the self can give rise to self-doubt and discouragement. It's not just that a sense of identity can be elusive for the Sun–Neptune type; early on, too, there can be difficulty in deciding who they *want* to be. There is a yearning to be someone, and someone glamorous and special – but who and what?

Because the Sun–Neptune type is so thirsty for some sort of identity and so sublimely unaware of boundaries, the type can often be found 'borrowing' an identity from someone else and indeed can be found living their lives vicariously through others. Because there are few boundaries between self and not-self, the individual with these aspects can *infiltrate* people and situations. Sometimes the Sun–Neptune person, so wanting an identity themselves, attempts to get close to another, not from any feelings of affection, although those may be there too, but because the individual wants to become like the object of their devotion. The devotee always seeks to become like the guru. Basically perhaps, the Sun–Neptune person wants to merge with others, merge with the universe and ultimately I suppose merge with God. It works both ways of course; Sun–Neptune people are themselves 'open' to others and can easily be seduced.

As always the lack of boundaries can be useful for bringing an ideal into reality. Others who may be shackled or even simply more aware of earthly limitations may not aspire to anything, and the Sun–Neptune person usually does aspire even if they find it difficult to actualise their aspirations. The Sun–Neptune non-acceptance of boundaries and the total disregard for rules can be very useful because it opens up the possibility of that which might be magical, intangible and exceptional, but lack of boundaries can also open up the possibility of anarchy and chaos. As Carter says, the Sun–Neptune person can 'blind themselves to existing obstacles, facts and conditions'.

The lack of boundaries and ability to infiltrate can be seen very clearly in relationship situations. The Sun–Neptune person can sidle up and talk to anyone regardless of the boundaries set by society or built into a given situation. This is the person who becomes friendly with the local priest, the pop-star round the corner, the maestro violinist. Many people with these contacts also become involved with and idealise a father-figure at some time in their lives. Such involvement is necessary, for it is in the service of the individuation process. And sometimes the involvement is less with a person and more with an image of God, or with someone who appears to be in touch with God. These people can be very 'guru-prone'. The Sun–Neptune person in early life is often looking for a redeemer, whilst in later life they may find themselves playing this role for another.

Sometimes the Sun–Neptune person gets friendly with someone who is something of a 'celebrity', a guru in their field, basically because the individual is attracted to glamour and hopes it will rub off on them in some way. In mixing with people who to Sun–Neptune are in some way 'special', the individual may find out what is and is not appropriate for them. But they are bound also to become disillusioned. Classically the type idealises something or someone and then finds that everyone is rather ordinary really and every situation has its sordid side. And when the object of devotion, the particular pursued dream, falls from grace, the Sun–Neptune person feels lost and disappointed. Given that the Sun–Neptune person often believes that other people's lives are more important, special, wonderful or glamorous than their own, getting disillusioned in this way may be precisely what is required. It is only through becoming disillusioned that these individuals are forced to accept things as they really are. Unfortunately the typical Sun–Neptune person often seems as if they want rescuing and so people take pains to buffer them from such disillusionment. Whilst sometimes this might be appropriate, often it isn't. Sometimes the Sun–Neptune person has to see themselves as victim (if only of their own dreams) before they can propel themselves into the role of saviour.

People with this combination can, and often do, identify with either end of the victim-martyr spectrum. It is only by discovering this and that both ends are actually two sides of the same coin that the individual with these aspects is often able to build some sense of identity for themselves. For they can choose which end of the spectrum – if either – they wish to live out and in what way. Rather than living out someone else's dream, living vicariously through another, the Sun–Neptune person needs to pursue their own vision. Often the Sun–Neptune person does have something of a 'saviour complex'. Sometimes this is embodied in the individual's choice of vocation and especially so if the 6th or 10th houses are involved by placement or rulership. Sometimes they form relationships with people who may be interpreted as saviours by the rest of society. Sometimes Sun–Neptune people adopt children and this too is more likely if the 5th house is implicated. Sun–Neptune knows what it feels like to be lost and adrift and is exceptionally good at stepping in to heal any breach of this kind.

I think that it is fair to say that there is a great deal of kindliness, compassion and sensitivity with all aspects between these planets, although the motives for the self-sacrifice are not always as altruistic as they may seem. Nevertheless the Sun–Neptune person often has a rare understanding of the importance of compassion and can take pride in this fact. As Carter says of these aspects: 'Sympathy, kindliness, and love of animals are very pronounced. They are nearly always "good sorts".'

Because of their lack of boundaries the Sun–Neptune person often seems 'fated' to embody the Neptune principle in some way, for all of society. Such embodying may involve taking on the role of saviour, martyr or victim but it might also be embodied in a multitude of other different ways. Because the boundaries are weak between self and others, the Sun–Neptune person is often adept at acting as *medium* for the thoughts and feelings of others, indeed the identity of others. Whilst some have obvious mediumistic gifts (or believe they do) in a literal sense, others act as a medium through some sort of artistic or creative work. The actor who gets inside their characters. The musician or artist who describes the feelings of us all. Such art-forms do call for a loss of ego. For example, the gifted actor is one whose own identity cannot be gleaned as something separate from the part that he or she is playing.

Both the problems and the gifts of the Sun–Neptune person revolve around their innate mysticism. They have a tremendous openness to the intangibles of life and understanding of the non-rational. The type is often not as attached to the world or their own ego as the rest of humanity. The urge both to escape from the self and to find the self is often very strong, as is the urge to transcend ordinary life. This may present problems, but it is usually *by* 'losing' the self in some project, by devoting the self to something that the individual personally finds very important, that they can, paradoxically, actually find some sense of their own identity.

Involvement in some form of artistic expression is very good for the Sun–Neptune person, for they then have a medium through which they can objectify their own psyche and explore the reality of the world whilst at the same time escaping from its harshness. Examples of Sun–Neptune contacts abound in almost all creative fields, drama, music, writing and fine art. In the case of drama and writing, the Sun–Neptune person often has the rare gift of being able to get inside a character, let the audience inside that character, and convey that person's complexities with rare accuracy and insight. Examples include: Elizabeth Taylor (Sun, Mercury, Mars in Pisces opposite Neptune) and Alan Bennett (trine,), Jane Austen (square), Mozart (opposition). Charles Carter links this combination with astrologers and again, one aspect of astrology (and psychology) can be linked to the idea of infiltrating another person, being a medium for the psyche of another.

Astrology can also of course, be considered a form of mysticism. Perhaps the most obvious example of Sun–Neptune can be found in the chart of Carl Jung, who made use of astrology in his work. His analytical psychology, with its stress on the 'individuation process' (the conscious realisation of one's *unique* psychological reality), the lack of rules within the analytical situation, the use of dreams, fairy-tales and art as a means of exploring the psyche, is a testament to Sun–Neptune. Moreover, Jung stressed that complexes and conflict were not only acceptable but the source of human creativity. Jung himself has become something of a guru, an idealised father-figure, and he himself saw Freud in a similar light for a time. And the analyst, like the actor, also, to some extent lives their life vicariously; for they suffer on behalf of another. Sun–Neptune also finds expression in the way in which analysts suffer on behalf of, and sympathetically with, their clients.

SUN–PLUTO

Hidden self. Importance of power. Illuminating taboos. Powerful father. Transforming pride. Obsession with self.

Perhaps one thing that can be said of those with Sun–Pluto contacts, especially the conjunction and the square aspects, is that the individual seems to take pains to *hide* themselves. This isn't always that obvious or necessarily a conscious decision. Nevertheless, it is possible to 'know' a Sun–Pluto person for years without ever seeming to get beyond first base in terms of understanding their inner dynamics. It's not that feelings of closeness are necessarily absent – in fact they will often be very strong – but the individuality of the Sun–Pluto person is often hard to get hold of, as are, quite often, the actual facts and feelings about their early life. At times, the self-protectiveness of the Sun–Pluto combination can make Sun–Saturn self-defensiveness seem like child's play.

These people often have a very powerful presence and can sometimes exert an extraordinarily magnetic hold over people, whilst at the same time remaining essentially impenetrable themselves, letting little in and still less out. They are often quite powerful in their own way and yet seemingly unaware of this power or overwhelmed by it. Often, in earlier life at any rate, the individual finds it difficult to own this power and use it in a direct and extrovert manner. There is often an intense self-awareness with these contacts, it is as if these people cannot get away from themselves, cannot step outside of the self in order to objectify who that person might be. Thus it is as if the Sun–Pluto person assumes that others will be as aware of them as they are aware of themselves and this can give rise to a kind of paranoia. Coupled with this the individual often seems to want to hide from themselves.

Whilst these contacts can be found in, on the one hand, extremely extrovert and obviously powerful people, it can often be found in those who seem much more introverted and defensive and quite unable to radiate the person they are. It is as if they have dug a hole and crawled into it themselves. Extroverted and powerful or seemingly the reverse, the Sun–Pluto individual still seems to be taking pains to hide the real self. It is as if people with these contacts feel as if they have no hiding-place and thus must make an effort to create one. Like Moon–Pluto people, Sun–Pluto types seem to need their privacy and often seem to fear invasion. For the Sun–Pluto person it often seems as if they fear that their very identity is under threat. Sometimes there is something in the early history which colludes with the individual forming such a view.

It is by no means invariable, but some people who have tight contacts between these planets have colossal family histories, with regard to those things that society usually deems only fit to be buried. Such history may include the usual Pluto taboos: sexual abuse, violence, criminality and madness, whatever we actually mean by that term. The child is taken down into the underworld and exposed to the shadier sides of human life at an early age. This is not always the case in reality, so much as the feelings attached to the coverings up of what the parents may view as previous shady happenings.

One might expect the father image of Sun–Pluto to be something of a heavy and domineering character, but he is rarely described in those terms although he is certainly usually experienced as the dominant figure in the home. Unlike Sun–Saturn and Sun–Neptune the personal father was usually very much around with these contacts, sometimes to the extent that there seemed to be nowhere to hide from him. He is often experienced as a suspicious kind of person, something of a policeman figure (and I have seen several Sun–Pluto people whose fathers literally were policemen), a censor of all he surveys. He often seems, to the Sun–Pluto child at any rate, as if he knows everything, not only the petty misdemeanours that they have committed in the past but even their vague intention or desire to do so in the future. Sometimes he will have embodied the Pluto principle through his work, which might have involved him being exposed to the darker sides of society and human nature generally, to the 'taboos' of society: violence, death, abuse, madness; those elements of life that society and individuals discard, bury or ignore. The possibilities are many: the policeman, mortician, psychologist, dustman, plumber, sewage worker; anyone whose trade involves society's secrets or psychological or physical refuse.

In any event, the paternal relationship is usually the dominant one. Whatever the relationship, the father often exerts a very strong hold on the Sun–Pluto person. His death, for example, usually strikes to the very core of the person. He is not easily forgotten and will continue to inhabit a very sacred place in the psyche of Sun–Pluto. There will often have been very intense power struggles with him in youth, but, most positively, this only serves to make the father-child relationship a very real and potent one where real transformation of feelings may have occurred. Both sexes with these contacts tend to have few relationships with men. It is as if the presence of the father is so strong in the unconscious that it leaves little room for other powerful masculine figures.

Quite often it happens that Sun–Pluto's father is so aware of his own darker side, and that of human nature generally, that he takes superhuman steps to protect the child from them, to ensure that the child will not be exposed to the things the father may have done 'wrong' in the past or the skeletons in the family cupboard. The 'heaviness' that the Sun–Pluto person seems to absorb from the father is often guilt. The child then is exposed to the seamier side of life and yet is counselled (by demonstration at least) as to how 'bad' such things are. Basically the child is often not allowed to acknowledge, let alone accept, their own darker side, and sometimes that of the father. In such a situation, the child does not know what to do with what it then sees as its own ugly thoughts and impulses and either buries these deeply within the unconscious or else feels totally overwhelmed by them. In the latter case, the individual cannot separate themselves from, and indeed identifies with, Plutonian images, identifies themselves as being a devil, an antichrist, or a beast of some kind. In some way, the Sun–Pluto person seems fated to 'carry' such material for all of society, and it can take years for the Sun–Pluto person to understand that they are neither responsible for, nor the embodiment of, the world's power to destroy. Rather, it is their journey to be exposed to those things (or those people) that the rest of the collective rejects, and hopefully to penetrate and transform them.

Many with these contacts, especially the opposition, will endeavour to disown their Pluto and thus will meet the energy in a much exaggerated form by becoming its victim, perhaps by forming relationships with people who are extremely powerful, dominant or even brutal, or by suffering disablement or some kind of handicap. People with Sun–Pluto contacts often have superhuman will-power and sometimes it is as if life propels them into situations where they are forced to develop it.

Many people with Sun–Pluto contacts bury those aspects of their psyche which to them seem to be too 'taboo' to acknowledge until such time that their ego and their sense of themselves is strong enough to be able to integrate such material.

The challenge for those with Sun–Pluto contacts is to be able to integrate the light and dark sides of the self without being overwhelmed by either end of the spectrum at the expense of the other.

Until the Sun–Pluto person has contacted their own inner power they can have a very poor self-image indeed. The young Sun–Pluto person often identifies with the notion of being a destroyer of some kind (or being in some way 'deformed'), so it is little wonder that those with the hard contacts often have strong suicidal impulses. All the rage, jealousy, violence and annihilating impulses just become tuned in on the self. This is perhaps an extreme example, but the attempt to commit suicide can be seen on less dramatic levels and usually takes the form of some kind of *sabotage*.

Sun–Pluto types who have not found some niche where they can legitimately give themselves permission to exercise power, will often seek to sabotage the position of those in authority; their own ego can feel too vulnerable to cope with the threat of more powerful personalities than their own. People with these contacts will often become, or attempt to become, close to people in positions of power. At the outset they are attracted to such power but less conscious types can sometimes be seen to demolish that person's position, usually through setting up a situation which will facilitate some kind of exposé. This often works so subtly that it can be missed, but it works the other way round too. Just when Sun–Pluto looks about to achieve, just about to succeed in some way, perhaps capture the spotlight or have access to power, something or someone seems to sabotage their efforts. Sometimes I suspect that the Sun–Pluto individual cannot quite bring themselves to the point of success for risk of incurring the rage of a jealous father, even if that father is dead or unavailable. Often the individual with these aspects has picked up powerful and yet quite subliminal messages in childhood, warning against ambitions to usurp the father's powerful position and authority. Perhaps on some level, the child has picked up the notion that the father would rather see him dead than successful, although outwardly there could be no greater champion of the child's success. It's as if unconsciously the father-figure wants the Sun–Pluto offspring to stay in the underworld. So usurping the father's power becomes, unconsciously, the forbidden fruit that gets projected onto any suitable authority-figures.

This kind of 'sabotage' occurs for other reasons too. When the Sun contacts any of the outer planets, the individual seems to expect extra-ordinary things of the self. Perhaps with Sun–Pluto contacts, the individual, on some level, expects so much of themselves that they will sabotage the given project if the achievement is going to be anything less than record-breaking. With the hard contacts, the compulsion to be the best can be both crippling and killing.

In the section on the planet Pluto, I quoted James Hillman who suggests that the impulse to suicide represents 'the urge for a hasty trans-formation'. Sun–Pluto people often do want to 'kill' themselves or their efforts. Whilst on one level I often think this is a response to an internal father image, on another level, perhaps this is, as Hillman says, an unconscious response to an urge for hasty transformation. Sun–Pluto people can put so much energy into an outer event that something has to ensure that their powers of perception are tuned inwards on the self and the sabotaging of a project sometimes ensures that this will happen. Basically, perhaps the Sun–Pluto person is supposed to spend periods of time in the underworld.

There is often an *impatience* about Pluto contacts, and with Sun–Pluto this often takes the form of a wish to transform the self into a kind of Wonder Woman or Superman overnight, to kill off all the 'baddies', and either purify the self or save the world. Whilst the Sun–Pluto person man indeed need to 'kill' and bury an aspect of themselves before their own creative treasures and true sense of individuality can be tapped, the thing that usually has to go and gets continually tested in the life is the individual's *pride*. Sun–Pluto types often seem to need to allow themselves to fail occasionally, to be something less than perfect. Instead of trying to kill off the psyche's less acceptable side, the average Sun–Pluto person needs to try to accept their imperfections and cultivate some humility, especially towards themselves. The Sun–Pluto person, whilst they have a poor self-image, paradoxically, can have such a high opinion of themselves that they imagine they are responsible for everything and that they have the means and the power (if only they could dredge it up from somewhere) to manipulate everything and everyone to their view. It can take a Sun–Pluto person quite a time to realise that they are a *channel* for collective power rather than the owner of it.

This combination is undoubtedly very manipulative. Whilst this word has disparaging connotations, implying as it does the use of underhand methods to make people and circumstances bend to one's own will, it really means 'to handle with dexterity' and thus needn't necessarily be viewed negatively at all. Manipulation may be precisely what is required in a given set of circumstances. Nevertheless, manifesting at its most negative level, Sun–Pluto manipulation can indeed be very insidious. These people have a tremendous capacity to entrap others into a corner from which they cannot possibly escape.

Often people with these contacts become interested in psychology. At best, those with Sun–Pluto contacts will actively seek to become self-aware, will seek to delve into the recesses of who they are.

This combination is ideal for any kind of work that involves plumbing (either psychological or physical) and for work which involves assisting others in their transformative processes. Many with these contacts work with others who are physically or mentally disabled in some way, and this combination is common in psychologists and therapists. It is good for any situation where the individual can legitimately and consciously not only wield power but assist others to transform their lives.

Pluto always refuses to treat life lightly. When coupled with the Sun it is as if the individual just cannot deal with themselves or with life on a superficial basis. If they attempt to do so, some crisis will hurtle them back into the underworld. In many differing ways, the Sun–Pluto person usually has innocence and naivety forcibly removed from them at an early age, and there really is no going back afterwards. Part of the purpose of Sun–Pluto interchanges seems to be concerned with *illuminating those things that are hidden*, bringing what is buried out into the light of day where it can be acknowledged and valued, turning the spotlight on society's taboos and thus transforming the collective's attitude to them.

Examples of Sun–Pluto include: Elisabeth Kubler-Ross, Mick Jagger (both conjunctions); Alfred Adler, whose psychology was especially concerned with *power* (a square); and Carl Jung (a quintile).

CHAPTER SEVEN

MOON ASPECTS

MOON–MERCURY

Common sense. Sympathetic response. Rationalising feelings. The accommodating mind. Fleeting opinions. Keeping a diary.

The Moon–Mercury combination is often associated with *common sense*. The *Oxford English Dictionary* defines this term as: 'Good, sound practical sense; combined tact and readiness in dealing with the everyday affairs of life, general sagacity.' Perhaps what one might describe as shrewdness.

At best, this combination suggests that the cool, detached communicative and reasoning skills of Mercury are softened by the sympathetic, protective and caring qualities of the Moon to produce a very responsive and thoughtful companion and a person able to accommodate many different viewpoints and ideas. Indeed, this is a very accommodating combination in all ways. Mercury is concerned with facts. When coupled with the Moon it might be hoped that hard facts will be tempered with consideration of what is actually useful to the matter in hand, with the memory of past experience and with a consideration of the feelings involved in the current situation. This is surely common sense. And these skills can certainly be expected from the soft aspects and often from the conjunction and hard aspects too. But with the hard aspects and sometimes the conjunction, the individual may have to work to arrive at this common-sense viewpoint.

At worst, feelings, emotional bias, considering what's best for the family and remembering what happened to Auntie Maud way back in 1923, distort the individual's capacity to look at the facts of the current situation and arrive at the most reasonable solution. Listening is often another major issue with Moon–Mercury. Some Moon–Mercury individuals are exceptionally skilled at listening; others (or perhaps the same people at different times) seem to find it impossible. For some, the habit of endlessly talking gets in the way of remaining silent long enough to absorb properly what the other person is saying. And then the Moon–Mercury person will bring all the history of their family and domestic life to the conversation – experience which may or may not be relevant to what is being discussed. Basically, the Moon–Mercury individual can be a difficult person to have a discussion with in areas where solutions or decisions are being sought, because the Moon–Mercury mind tends to be unfocused. This is particularly the case with the hard aspects and in very mutable charts. The unfocused quality can also lead to learning difficulties as the Moon–Mercury student often finds it difficult to lift the salient information out of a lesson and ends up with masses of notes and no feeling as to what, out of it all, is really relevant. In extreme cases, there is no selective hearing. The individual absorbs all the information and then suffers from factual indigestion. The lack of focus can also lead to a particularly woolly way of communicating and singular difficulty for the person in getting to the point. The listener waits and waits – and waits, only to discover that there *is* no point! But perhaps I am being unkind to a combination which, in the main, is a very kind, sympathetic and sensitive one.

Moon–Mercury is also a very useful combination for communicative situations which do not require special emphasis in any particular place; situations that do not require there to be a point. The Moon–Mercury person is often wonderful at telling anecdotal stories, stories where nothing much may happen, certainly nothing dramatic; no crisis, nor even necessarily a clear beginning, middle or end; but instead, a poignant, acutely observed narrative dealing with the minutiae of everyday life or perhaps some small incident.

This capacity for acute observation of the daily round, the daily happenings between people and their feelings, is, I believe, one of the great potential talents of Moon–Mercury for it is out of such observations that real understanding is born. The Moon–Mercury narrative is also often very funny, drawn as it is from real life. Whimsical too. Many comedians have both the Moon and Mercury prominent in their charts, even if they do not actually have an aspect between the two bodies. Much comedy is based on acute observation of everyday life. One might also associate both the comedian and the Moon–Mercury combination with public speaking and performing and sometimes this duo yields talent in these areas. For when Moon–Mercury is able to communicate their own feelings and experience through speech or writing, a real rapport with an audience can be built up. If the listening skills are well developed, there can also be a gift for mimicry.

The classic Moon–Mercury person likes to *chat* and usually has a wide acquaintanceship with which to do so. Doubtless there is a tendency towards large telephone bills too! There is often a need to discuss feelings and the everyday trials and tribulations of domestic life. The ups and downs in the family, the goings on with the neighbours.

People with this combination tend to have sisters rather than brothers and sometimes take on the role of mother to their siblings, inasmuch as they are the person who is there to give a sympathetic response. Commonly this role and that of 'agent' is continued in the individual's local community.

Sometimes Moon–Mercury's accommodating nature can be just *too* accommodating and then the individual's feelings, views and opinions just shift and change as new information or feelings tip the scales in a different direction. This combination can be one of fleeting moods and fleeting opinions. Little is hard and fast or cut and dried to this type. At best, this can mean that the Moon–Mercury type is aware of their feelings and can easily communicate them, for feelings are changeable things. On the other hand, Moon–Mercury can be so emotionally tied to their opinions that a truly rational viewpoint becomes elusive and insecurity of opinion results. The ideas shift to fit a change in mood. This can also mean that how the Moon–Mercury person feels about you from one day to the next can vary greatly. Bringing the rational thinking process and instinctual 'gut' feelings into alignment can prove a real challenge to those with the hard aspects.

How the Moon–Mercury combination manifests, will, as with all combinations, depend largely on which planet of the two is stronger – if indeed either is. Where the Moon is stronger, and especially with the challenging aspects, the individual can find it hard to be rational and objective. Where Mercury is stronger, the individual can get caught up with over-rationalising their feelings. Both manifestations can often be found in the same individual at differing times.

Nevertheless, individuals with this combination prominent in their charts are usually able to communicate their ideas and opinions with sensitivity. Whatever the Moon–Mercury person may lack in clarity or sharpness of expression can more than be made up for, all things being equal, by the roundness of understanding and soft way of communicating that this type is so particularly gifted with.

This is an ideal combination for the journal keeping, for the daily recording of everyday feelings, events and the individual's responses to those events. Perhaps the most well-known diarist of this century in Anne Frank. Her chart has Mercury in Gemini quintile a Moon–Neptune conjunction. The Mercury is also semi-square the Ascendant.

The chart for the television soap opera *Coronation Street* also owes much to Moon–Mercury. The Moon is the chart ruler and is both semi-square Mars and square Mercury. Moon–Mercury–Mars; what better significators could there possibility be for *gossip*. And where would *Coronation Street* be if it were not for gossip!

MOON–VENUS

Lovers of peace. Co-operative behaviour. Sensitivity to fairness. Loving mother. The beautiful home. Valuing women.

Both these planets are very soft and yielding in their nature and thus when coupled together will usually give rise to someone who is very willing to co-operate. Because of this soft, pliable nature, any other bodies plugging into the Moon–Venus relationship will need to be very carefully evaluated.

Anyway, assuming that such a complication does not occur, this combination usually makes for great *adaptability*. Indeed, the problem with the hard aspects and the conjunction between the Moon and Venus is usually that the person tends to be *over-adaptive*. Individuals with either the conjunction or hard aspects between these planets are very sensitive and tend to get hurt and feel rejected far too easily. They thus get very frightened of hurting others and will often go to great lengths to avoid difficult situations and confrontations. These people find it difficult to take and to give criticism. Thus, in some cases, if other factors in the chart concur, they will do anything to please. I have noticed that Moon–Venus children (and adult students for that matter), having handed in a piece of schoolwork, only hear criticism when it is returned. The teacher may in fact, heap praise on the work but might, as well, suggest one minor adjustment that could be made in the future. Only the criticism will be heard. This can propel people with these contacts to do everything as beautifully as possible. In any event, individuals with these contacts seem to get hurt and 'bruise' very easily.

These people are usually very peace-loving and are often staunch pacifists, though this, and their sensitivity is sometimes covered up under a gruff exterior, particularly if Mars or Saturn is involved. The need for fairness and over-sensitivity to what is or isn't fair often does, paradoxically, propel the individual into combative situations though; and once again, a hard aspect to Mars makes this move likely.

Contacts between these planets can be associated with a loving and caring parental figure, usually the mother. She is normally experienced as a very popular person and is sometimes seen as having a great deal of grace and charm. Usually she is also experienced as being rather passive and apt to cave in under pressure. Thus the Moon–Venus individual learns how they can get what they want from this parental figure and, by extension, how to get their own way in adult life through diplomatic means. These people can charm the birds out of the trees and seem to find it difficult (unless Mars is strongly emphasised in the chart) to say what they want in a direct manner.

People with these contacts come into the world programmed with the notion of an unconditionally loving mother. Usually they have inherited this image from their own mother – an image that no mere mortal could ever live up to. Nevertheless, the Moon–Venus person often tries to live up to it in their own life, or looks to others to do it for them.

For some reason, people with the hard aspects between these planets often do feel unloved or abandoned in early life, even though such abandonment or rejection seldom occurs without the input of heavier planets – although with the hard aspects there can sometimes be a history of physical affection being lacking, depending on the signs involved. Similarly people with these contacts are often very fearful for their loved ones and over-sensitive to the possibility of things going 'wrong'.

Sometimes the mother-figure, or the family history, embodies Venus by being very creative or artistic. There are endless possibilities. Usually though, unless Saturn or the outer planets are also plugging into the con-figuration, people with Moon–Venus contacts have a mother who was exceptionally good at feeding their needs – possibly even too good. Indiv-iduals with these contacts can be so sensitive to rejection and criticism because they have never had to deal with it in the past. Sometimes the mother-figure with these aspects was herself very needy for love and looked to her Moon–Venus child for a good part of the affection in her life, sometimes, so much so that she never quite manages to let her offspring go. Some people with these contacts experienced their mother as someone who gave up her social, romantic and sexual life in order to become a mother. Others experience their mother as putting her sexual needs or creative work above that of mothering and feeling guilty about that. Typically, in such cases, the father's maternal responsibilities don't enter into the matter, which reinforces the notion that woman equals mother and mothering.

Because the upbringing was usually a very traditional one with these aspects, there is often a difficulty in being able to see women outside the context of the mother role, or at least outside the context of caring, protecting and nurturing. This may or may not create problems depending on the life-situation and other needs in the individual's chart and may be dealt with in a wide variety of different ways.

People who campaign for women *not* to be seen exclusively in the role of wife and mother often have this combination emphasised in their charts. The notion of seeing women only in the context of the mother role is not only the experience of childhood, but is projected out into the world. Women with this combination often feel constrained to take on traditional female roles. The rest of the chart and in particular the relative strengths of Saturn and Uranus will say something about what they are likely to feel about this pressure, how appropriate it is for them and how they will deal with it. Typically, girls with this combination are brought up expecting to wear pretty dresses, ribbons and go to ballet classes and the like. Boys are cautioned against being 'too rough'. Such upbringings may have been in accord with the child's wishes or deeply at variance with them, depending on the chart overall. As always, the possibilities are endless but for both sexes one can usually say that the individual was brought up, in some way, *strongly valuing the feminine*. For some, especially those born in the 1940s and 1950s and before, this means a mother who had very traditional notions of the place of women. For others, and especially those born more recently, valuing women means their emphatically not being confined to traditionally demarcated roles, and for nearly everyone it suggests a need to establish what words like 'womanhood' and 'feminine' actually mean for them.

Whatever the background was in terms of care, or the role of women, it will often be one where the individual was spoilt on a material level, perhaps cosseted and given lots of food. Depending on the overall tenor of the chart, this may be to compensate for guilty feelings on the part of the mother-figure. In reality there may or may not have been any real lack of affection. Commonly, the issue is that the mother herself had an inflated notion of 'supermothering' and felt guilty about not living up to this. Thus the Moon–Venus child with hard aspects especially, sometimes inherits the feeling that they should be given more. In some cases, the more the mother-figure 'feeds' and cares for the child, the more hungry it feels, for it is picking up the mother's guilt. Some men with these contacts feel that their mother would have preferred to have had a girl, and this can have a whole host of different repercussions. In any event, whatever the reason, the Moon–Venus child is the one given lots of sweets, treats and toys in childhood. This may explain why, whatever the financial background, the Moon–Venus person often seems accustomed to, and to expect, an easy material life. Those with the hard aspects often overstretch themselves financially, and in extreme cases to the point of getting into real trouble. The presence of a strong Saturn may, however, do much to curb such tendencies. Like Sun–Venus, this combination is often a very self-indulgent and generous one. Occasionally aspects between these planets can provide the motivation behind criminal activities, for with such aspects the individual may be motivated towards achieving an easy, non-challenging, peaceful and materially buffered life-style.

In relationships, for those with hard aspects between these planets the two images of woman and lover are at variance and there is a need to integrate them. With heterosexual men this can mean that they hook up with women who fall into a very extreme archetypal mould, either being very maternal or femme fatale types. Whichever woman they hook they often want the other. The journey is of course about integrating the two sides of the feminine within themselves and amplifying their understanding of this side of their psyche.

Gay and lesbian relationships are common with these contacts, for often individuals with this interchange not only feel so overwhelmed by the feminine within themselves but feel too vulnerable to expose themselves to battling with the differences of the opposite sex.

Aspects between these planets are ideal for any occupation or activities concerned with nurturing and caring, and for activities that involve catering, gardening or interior decor. If other chart factors concur, this combination often makes for an excellent cook. Whatever the actual aspect, people with this combination usually just *love* their food and are usually very sensitive to how it is presented. In particular, the Moon–Venus type often has a sweet tooth. Leaping to the biscuit barrel for comfort is a common behavioural trait. In some cases this can reflect the overly 'sweet' and even gushy behaviour of the type.

This combination is a romantic and sentimental one. These people often value the past and often love history and even merely poring over photograph albums.

The joy or this combination is the fact that, whatever the aspect, the desire to protect, care for, hold and love is usually very well developed, as is the desire for such nurturance. If other factors concur, these people are naturally warm, friendly, generous and hospitable, and very responsive, sympathetic and diplomatic. They are particularly sensitive to beauty and have a strong urge to create a pleasing home. Often there is a strong appreciation of such things as flowers as well as the more usual music and dance.

This is also an ideal combination for interior design. These people are usually very concerned with taste on all levels and especially with respect to their home. The need for a harmonious domestic environment tends to be very marked and a family atmosphere is usually also very highly valued.

If the combination is strongly emphasised though, it is usually in the individual's best interest to cultivate some 'Mars' characteristics. In particular, the ability to assert themselves in a direct and honest way and the ability to maintain their own position in the face of pressure to yield. Because of the overly passive nature of these contacts and the tendency to avoid difficult situations, the individual often actually meets Mars-type energy from without. For it is easy to get angry with Moon–Venus types for seeming so weak and passive at times, so ready to accept peace at any price. Often Moon–Venus people meet Mars from without by forming relationships with people who have this planet highly emphasised in their charts.

Examples of this contact include Mahatma Gandhi (who has the square, also picking up Mars and Jupiter), surely one of the greatest pacifists of the twentieth century, and Vanessa Redgrave (opposition with Saturn conjuncting Venus). Whilst Vanessa Redgrave's various causes owe much to the Uranian aspects in her chart and her angular Mars, her involvement with anti-apartheid, for example, clearly shows concern with *unfairness*. Many of her roles also reflect this opposition.

MOON–MARS

Fierce protection. Quick nurturing response. Sensitivity to discord. Angry feelings. Emotional conflict. Sexual feelers.

Rather like Sun–Mars, those with hard aspects between the Moon and Mars have a very strong need to 'do', to act, to roll up their sleeves and get on with the project in hand. Commonly there is much activity around the domestic scene, and the home is often not so much a place to retreat from where the individual may recharge their batteries, as the reason for those batteries getting run down in the first place. Typically, there are lots of comings and goings and snatched meals. The individual may find this exhilarating or exhausting depending upon the nature of the aspect, the overall feel of the chart and the condition of the 4th house in particular.

Usually there is plenty of emotional action in the individual's life, together with internal emotional conflict. Often the individual finds it difficult to integrate their need to take one course of action in order to feed one emotional need whilst having to take a different course of action in order to feed some different, seemingly conflicting emotional need. For example, safety, home, familiarity versus independence and sexual excitement. Sometimes there is emotional action in the life, as in arguments and plates flying around. Frequently though, the individual will have come from such an atmosphere and may take pains not to repeat it. All Moon–Mars contacts give rise to people who are very sensitive to any kind of conflict as well as any kind of threat.

Although Moon–Mars combinations may be associated with 'touchy' behaviour and sometimes a tendency to fly off the handle very easily, people with the hard aspects especially, often find it difficult to express their anger. Whilst this may result in them going overboard in attempting to make their position abundantly clear, it may also sometimes result in the individual being unable to express their anger, perhaps through fear of the consequences. The fixed signs are especially prone to hold on to their rage and then just letting rip every once in a while, whilst the mutable signs tend to express their anger through irritability and carping behaviour.

Some Moon–Mars people speak of an early home life (and this is especially the case with the opposition, I have found) where the parents or other family figures 'never argued' but nevertheless were extremely angry with each other. Typically the Moon–Mars child would have picked up on all the unexpressed rage and, like a sponge, absorbed it.

Charles Carter describes the Moon–Mars type as usually kind-hearted, sympathetic and keen to help. Certainly people with this combination are nearly always very *protective*.

Basically, people with these contacts have to integrate their need to assert themselves with their need to feel safe. On the whole the Moon–Mars person is a very good individual to have on your side, for they will seek to take care of you. With the hard aspects though, the individual may sometimes act like a mother whose children are about to be snatched away from her or accused of something. The problem with the hard aspects especially is, as always, the possibility of going too far and in this case, jumping in too quick. The Moon–Mars type may jump in and fight your battles, well before you even realised you were at war.

Basically, the feelings of this type are very easily and very quickly aroused. The person is usually used to feeling unsafe and is very quick to smell danger and thus cultivates speedy reactions and responses – the kind of reactions that sometimes save lives. Like Sun–Mars, Moon–Mars may be courageous, enterprising and fearless. To feel is to act for Moon–Mars. The problem may be that they react out of habit, and out of habit they may expect conflict. It can take those with the hard aspects a long time to realise that they and their loved ones are not continually under threat and that there is no reason to believe or behave as if World War III is about to break out at any moment, or that it might do so if one makes the wrong response. Sometimes, *because* the type is so frightened of conflict they can go too far in rushing to the defence, so it may well be a Moon–Mars person who ends up firing the first shot.

The need to protect the self and more especially one's family and others with whom there is an emotional bond is usually keenly developed with all aspects. Not uncommonly, the family were threatened in some way in childhood, if not by anger or violence within the household, then by some threat from outside.

As has been said, frequently those with these contacts came from highly volatile families where the mother-figure especially might be expected to explode at any moment.

One man with the opposition in his chart described to me how threatened he still often feels when confronted with what he sees as very assertive women. He found his own mother to be very explosive, whilst the father was very passive and seemingly unable to express his anger in any direct kind of way. Apparently his mother was the kind of person to make scenes in restaurants and pick fights with his schoolteachers. He describes himself now as '*very sensitive to discord*' and '*reluctant to break any kind of emotional atmosphere'*. A key phrase for this combination might well be 'fiercely protective' and as well as saying something about the individual it will often be describing the mother-figure in an exaggerated and caricatured way. I have known cases where the mother was so pushy and lived so much in expectation of some danger befalling her offspring that she went everywhere with the child. Sometimes she competes with the child and thus on another level unconsciously *wants* something awful to happen to the child (it works both ways of course: Moon–Mars people often fantasise about shooting their mother!).

Returning to this idea of Mum going everywhere, in one case I know of, she even went on the honeymoon. And this is interesting too because there is often a strong sexual tie with the mother-figure and early emotional bonding often has unusually strong sexual overtones.

Often the mother-figure competes with the child (generally or in sexual matters) or with others and sometimes Moon–Mars people have the same kind of conflict with competing that they have with anger, either being over-competitive or frightened of seeming so.

I associate abortion, miscarriage and premature birth with Moon–Mars contacts and sometimes the conjunction, especially if it falls in or rules the 5th house. It's as if the nurturing impulse is too quick, too sharp to go the full term. This quick but truncated nurturing response is usually what the Moon–Mars type is raised on, as if the bottle is always about to be taken away from the baby before it's finished feeding. Little wonder that in extreme cases the Moon–Mars type often behaves like an enraged infant screaming for its food. It is often issues around food and feeding that arouse anger with these aspects.

The hard aspects particularly with these planets can be associated with digestive upsets and stomach ulcers. This can sometimes be traced to the fact that the person eats when they are angry or eats to keep down angry feelings. And early feeding was often itself carried out by an angry and frustrated mother-figure or at least a mother who was always *doing* something. Sometimes she pursued a sexual relationship outside the marriage so that the child feels that they have to compete with this third figure for her attention.

Sometimes the individual with these aspects is born to a very young mother, and again one might think of the Moon–Mars of the woman who gives birth very quickly and also of the image of a very sexual mother.

Inevitably issues of anger and mother go together with these contacts either in that the individual is angry with their mother (almost inevitably) or that the mother was perceived as an angry person (often) or that the Moon–Mars person gets angry on her behalf. Those with the conjunction are usually able to recognise themselves as angry and often as angry with their mother, whilst those with the opposition aspect usually spend some time believing that it is other people who are angry and other people who are responsible for discord.

The anger of the Moon–Mars person, like their sexuality, is often smouldering and broody. Rather like one of these dragons in childhood books, where the dragon is really rather a sympathetic character but breathes steam through his nostrils.

The Moon–Mars type will as often be found fighting on *behalf* of their roots and their past as fighting to get away from those roots. In cases of marital break-up there is often heated debate about property. The individual will often find themselves fighting for their security in different ways in their lives and fighting over the marital home is just one example of how this may become embodied. Fate sometimes seems to ensure that Moon–Mars people are not allowed to feel too physically safe in order that they be forced to discover what really constitutes safety or lack of it on emotional levels.

People with these contacts usually settle down and have a family quite early on in their lives. Often there is a feeling that there will be no time later on to do those things and that there may be no potential partners around to do them with. Basically, the person is often impatient for a home and a family.

Moon–Mars hard aspect types sometimes overeat or over-drink and occasionally may be overweight, if the configuration falls in appropriate signs. Frequently, on many emotional and often physical levels the child was not fed properly and was perhaps weaned too quickly in childhood. Sometimes there was competition for the mother's attention and sometimes actual competing for food. In any event, people with extreme Moon–Mars issues may eat as if they are in a race or as if the meal is going to be snatched away from them at any moment. Being overweight can also often be seen as a way of protecting the self, for the Moon–Mars person often feels unprotected. The vulnerable and fragile individual seeks to protect themselves behind an armour-plating of fat. There is also an impulsiveness about eating with Moon–Mars and indeed an impulsiveness about all forms of nurturance, whether of the self or others. I suspect that those with Moon–Mars hard contacts may often drink and eat out of the need for 'Dutch courage'.

One of the great virtues of Moon–Mars is that the individual with these contacts will usually be honest and direct about expressing their feelings (although some with the hard aspects may be just *too* direct for others' comfort). Usually there is a strong need to make the feelings clear with a corresponding dislike of emotional ambiguity. This combination can be associated with emotional courage.

People with these contacts usually have an instinctual feeling for sexual response and they can also be quite direct about sexual matters.

Men especially, though, sometimes exude a sullen, moody, resentful, smouldering kind of sexuality with these contacts and yet manage to be baby-faced at the same time. An obvious example of this can be found in the chart of Marlon Brando, who has a Sun–Moon–Mars–Pluto T-square which also involves the Moon and Mars signs Cancer and Aries. Sometimes Moon–Mars is not merely baby-faced, but in behaviour seems rather demanding in the way that a baby is, and again I think this can often be traced to issues around the mother putting out sexual feelers to the infant child.

The Moon–Mars combination is a splendid one for active involvement in decorating, carpentry, interior design and all other 'Do-it-Yourself' projects. I often suggest to Moon–Mars people who feel that they have a lot of anger they don't know how to channel, to do something physical around the house – knock down a wall or paint the ceiling or something. This is also an ideal mix for work in the catering trade and for other vocations where the individual is *actively* involved with nurturing others; or where they can legitimately give vent to angry feelings, as might a radical politician or a hellfire preacher.

Moon–Jupiter

Expansive feelings. Exaggerative behaviour. The need for faith. The need to protect. The Mother Church.

Whatever the aspect, the Moon–Jupiter type tends towards a caring, good-natured, emotional expansiveness. This is a sympathetic character who reacts and responds in broad, generous terms. The problem with the hard aspects, especially, is that the individual has a tendency to *over-react* and *over-respond*, to make promises that can't possibly be kept and to agree to wild, extravagant gestures of generosity, because of a feeling that this is how one should behave. In many ways, the behaviour of this type is that of a caring 'Super Mother' but there is the risk of trying so hard to be all things to all people that Moon–Jupiter ends up being not very much to anyone.

As with all Jupiter aspects to the personal planets, there can sometimes be a distinct tendency for this individual to 'play God' in one form or another. At any rate, there is usually a strong need to teach and to preach, either to expound one's belief system or to show off one's knowledge. Indeed, this is a good combination for either the classroom or the pulpit. There is also usually a strong commitment to 'growth' and an awareness that freedom comes with knowledge. Unless other aspects point to the contrary (such as an aspect from Saturn or Uranus), the Moon–Jupiter type usually possesses innate faith in life and can easily discern meaning in life's trials and tribulations. Basically, this type is both optimistic and philosophical about things. There is often a real need for and strong investment in, some sort of belief system, whether this be of a religious, political or philosophical nature. Not only does such a belief system foster feelings of safety and security but it acts as a guide for the individual as to the way to behave and generally conduct oneself in the world. Political or religious feelings are likely to be just that: feelings, as opposed to something more dogmatic, finite or definable. Of itself, this is not a banner-waving aspect: Moon–Jupiter is too casual for that and more concerned with the 'spirit' of a given subject than the finer points of its application. The ideal church for this type would be a kind of all-embracing Mother who would provide refuge and safety for people of all cultures and religious persuasions. Political and other beliefs also tend towards generosity of feeling and freedom of thought.

The Moon–Jupiter person often comes from a background where the maternal figure was rather dramatic and may themselves behave quite instinctively, in a larger than life kind of way. It can be a greedy contact, greedy for nurturance and greedy for sustenance. If we consider greed as an excess of hunger then it becomes, perhaps, a more acceptable human foible. Sometimes the greed comes about because this contact correlates with a mother-figure who herself had not been properly weaned and was still hungry for physical and emotional nurturance – in some cases, so much so, that she was not fully able to meet her child's own emotional needs. Thus a family pattern is set up. So our Moon–Jupiter individual cultivates a warm, caring, sympathetic and protective way of responding in order to receive back the warm feelings so desperately needed since childhood. Since there was a need to cultivate this kind of sensitivity to Mother's needs in childhood, in adulthood it comes as second nature, as does a happy, smiling-face persona. When Moon–Jupiter feels emotionally 'fed' this type has an above-average capacity for sustaining others.

As both planets are concerned with 'protection' there is often an issue of over- or under-protection in childhood, frequently over-protection physically and under-protection emotionally so that maturation comes with difficulty. Be that as it may, this type usually has a very marked protective streak and thus is usually quite easy to hook with a hard-luck story. The desire to protect, to 'shepherd', is usually a very likeable trait but occasionally one sees Moon–Jupiter in the guise of over-protecting. Frequently the mother-figure tried to over-protect the child, often, for example, forcing the infant to eat more food than it needed. Eating issues often loom large in the childhood of the Moon–Jupiter type and sometimes long-term eating problems occur as a result. To over-protect someone can often be a means of keeping them dependent on oneself, thereby inflating one's own self-image and desire to 'play God'. To witness a less pleasant excessive protective streak we might cite Hitler who has a Moon–Jupiter conjunction in Capricorn in his 3rd house; he was of the distorted belief that he was protecting the 'Fatherland' (Capricorn) in his persecution of the Jews. Here, too, we see Jupiter in his arrogant guise of assuming that his is the only right belief system, philosophy, religious conviction, or whatever.

Perhaps this is a rather uncharitable view of this not terribly 'nasty' contact, for on the whole this type is tolerant and charitable, the worst problem in this respect being an inability to recognise one's own intolerances to other people's prejudices. With the opposition especially, Moon–Jupiter may be a lot less humble and a lot more arrogant than it is given credit for.

The Moon–Jupiter person is usually a restless one (especially if mutable signs are involved) and has a strong need to explore, with an accompanying horror of being tied down emotionally, domestically, or indeed in any other way. In all things the behaviour of this type leans towards the casual and the general rather than the specific. Moon–Jupiter might describe it as casual, others might view it as careless, extravagant and slap-happy. At worst, and when reinforced by other chart factors, there can be a tendency to trust too readily to luck, combined with great commitment to avoiding responsibility.

Moon–Jupiter types may well spend at least some of their life living in a country far from their birth, for a multitude of reasons no doubt, including the desire to be free of the restraints of familial obligations. Life overseas also appeals to the emotionally expansive and explorative nature of this combination. Moon–Jupiter is restless and needs to spread its wings mentally if not physically.

Any contacts between these planets tend towards self-indulgence, sentimentality and a certain *laissez-faire* attitude. Moderation is not the greatest virtue and extremist behaviour can occur in all sorts of different areas of life. For example, as has been hinted at, it's common to find people with this contact indulging in quite extreme eating habits, perhaps eating themselves sick one minute and starving to death the next (the latter may be less common but a good example is to be found in the chart of Gandhi, who fasted for his beliefs). Eating issues and the beliefs of the individual will often go together with this combination, which might be expected to be prominent in the charts of not only hunger strikers for example, but also in those of some vegetarians. This may also be the individual who, when cooking for two, produces enough food for twenty. But the Moon–Jupiter type tends to get away quite easily with its overdoing propensity and generally casual attitude of life. People respond well to this contact in an individual and generally overlook their foibles because of their generally good-humoured attitude and easy, warm way of responding to them. Genuinely concerned with the well-being of others, this is a good contact for those occupations that might come under the heading of 'welfare work' as this provides a vehicle for the individual to use their strong protective streak. Though it has to be said that patronising and paternalistic attitudes can crop up as easily with Moon–Jupiter as with Sun–Jupiter contacts.

The soft contacts between these planets also incline the individual to the more self-indulgent, expansive and explorative sides of life but here the person tends to be much less restless and less prone to the self-righteousness that this type can be prey to. Benevolence and kindliness are well marked here but there is less of an urge to go round mothering everyone; in fact the trine sometimes describes someone who expects to be cosseted and pampered themselves.

There is often a strong feeling for the splendour and grandeur of the past (though this really needs to be emphasised in other areas of the chart) with an enjoyment of old buildings (which, by virtue of their age alone are often ecclesiastical), customs and traditions.

MOON–SATURN

Defensive feelings. Controlled responses. Cautious behaviour. The dutiful mother. The need for structure and permanence. Bleak House. Lessons in the home.

> The security of family ties is an illusory one, and it is often very dangerous to assume that one has the right, because of blood ties, to command emotional support from others. Parents can die, partners can leave, and children grow up; and the person with Moon–Saturn is generally courting pain and disappointment if he seeks to bind these external things to himself by emotional need.
> (Liz Greene, *Saturn*)

There is often a feeling of the 'trapped child' in the personality of the Moon–Saturn type. Sometimes this can be observed physically in the woman who wears pigtails or the man who blushes shyly when a woman talks to him. Very often, Moon–Saturn had to grow up rather early and rather like Sun–Saturn missed out on the maturation process, so that there is often a delay in the emotional development of the individual.

Sometimes the child had to take on responsibilities at too young an age, often becoming a surrogate mother, perhaps by being born the eldest child and having to look after younger siblings. Often the mother or other caretaker is overburdened and Moon–Saturn ends up playing mother to its own mother-figure. That lunar aspect of parenting which might be termed 'unconditional love' is often in short supply. The kind of love that says: 'I will love you no matter what, I will be here to support you, to protect you, I will be able to absorb and cushion your anxieties, your fears, your tears, your anger, your rage.' With Moon–Saturn many of these positive features of childhood were rather thin on the ground. And basically, the individual has to learn how to feel and express these qualities from scratch.

The Moon–Saturn child generally gets the message very early on that it has to be emotionally self-sufficient. The child receives early messages that they will be loved only if they behave in a certain kind of way; responsible and unobtrusive, staying in the background, not getting under people's feet. Often there just never seems enough *time* to pander to the child's needs. Often the mother is on her own, perhaps weighted down with responsibilities, often working all day, seldom with any spare time. Usually the child becomes extremely sensitive to her needs and learns how to react accordingly. The ramifications of this are that in adulthood, the individual finds it very difficult to react and respond in a spontaneous kind of way because there is a constant, very often barely conscious, expectation of criticism. People with hard contacts, and the conjunction too, tend to express their feelings with great caution and a certain defensiveness.

The early life may not have been that oppressive, though there is usually what Liz Greene calls a 'business before pleasure' kind of feeling about the home life and the individual's subsequent attitudes. I also think of it as the 'Bleak House' combination as once during a workshop, we discovered that four Moon–Saturn people in the room had either read Dickens' book or had some other association with the name.

The Moon–Saturn combination is common in the charts of people in farming communities where home is also a place of work. As in farming situations, there is often a strong tradition in the family set-up of the Moon–Saturn background. Perhaps for generations, the family may have lived in the same house, or locality, or pursued the same kind of profession. The result of this can mean that it is very difficult for the individual to be able to get away from the duties, responsibilities and history that they were born into.

From the outsider's point of view, the behaviour of the Moon–Saturn type is often very likeable (if a bit wooden and predictable at times) and this can be said of most Saturn contacts, especially to the softer planets, because such contacts tend to be very sensitive. Certainly the Moon–Saturn type is often painfully so. Here we have an individual who tries very hard to please. The classic Moon–Saturn type feels vulnerable and is scared of being hurt and thus will behave in what the individual considers to be as socially acceptable a way as possible. This often involves conforming, in a bid to elicit the approval that they need. Saturn usually inclines to a 'formula' kind of response with regard to the planet it touches; with the Moon, the responses may be overly controlled, under-played and careful or overly eager and gushy.

Perhaps, Moon–Saturn's greatest needs are to feel as safe and secure as possible. Safe in being able to behave as they feel, safe enough to allow themselves to *discover* what they actually *do* feel. The greater the insecurity the more emotional wall-building Moon–Saturn is likely to indulge in. And secure or not, after a while it becomes a habit. Moon–Saturn may have needed a few defences as a child but as an adult the goal must be to feel safe enough to be able to drop at least some of these defences. They must learn to take a few risks with their emotional responses and with emotional life generally. As always, Saturn craves whatever planetary principle it touches and with Moon–Saturn the individual craves nurturance – craves the very deepest emotional bonds, real feelings of security and usually, quite basically, a home and a family, in the hope that they might provide these. Though, as Liz Greene tells us, that kind of security is often illusory. The typical Moon–Saturn person will often seek to own their own home, to have something really solid behind them. Individuals with this contact strong often draw bricks when doodling. Images around stone and brick walls and fences are very appropriate with this combination.

The beauty of the Moon–Saturn person can be that they do take the emotional realm so very seriously. For this is the person who might never let you down, in practical terms anyway. Problems can arise for Moon–Saturn when they take their feelings, and what may have happened in the past, so seriously that they find the whole emotional realm so scary and so emotionally exposing that they won't open up sufficiently in order to receive the emotional feedback that is required.

Because of their need for permanence, Moon–Saturn will always tend to cling to the familiar, tried and tested path and nowhere more so than in relationships. Moon–Saturn often ends up with partners who are even more like their parents than usual, perhaps because there is a vague feeling that any love is good love. There is also a fear of being on one's own and a reluctance to take on board responsibility for a home of one's own. Perhaps basically, Moon–Saturn craves for a mother and sometimes craves to *be* a mother.

I have known several cases of women with anorexia and bulimia whose charts have had strong Moon–Saturn contacts. In such cases, the individual can be seen to be either denying themselves food, controlling (or not) their food intake, or overeating in a bid to nurture themselves, to make up for a time where they have not been 'fed' previously. Some psychologists interpret anorexia as a resistance to mothering, nurturing, adulthood and the feminine generally, coupled perhaps with a strong, unconscious, emotional bonding to the father image, which fits well enough with at least one possible Moon–Saturn manifestation. Moon–Saturn men and women may feel awkward with the feminine, the 'yin' side of themselves and especially that aspect of emotional life which encompasses mothering, nurturing, holding and expressing one's own neediness.

Although I said earlier that there is often an early message of 'be independent' from the parents to the Moon–Saturn child, there is also often a counter-message which says, 'Don't grow up fully because I need you, don't have a family, don't move away'. As adults the Moon–Saturn type will often make themselves available for the parents who maybe get sick or for some other reason are not able to cope on their own. The child remains controlled by the parents and colludes with the situation for many reasons no doubt, not least the fact that the family situation is a familiar one.

Women with these contacts are usually either desperate to have children or cannot bear the thought of doing so. For some, the physical presence of children serves, like a certificate, as proof of the individual's maternal and nurturing ability. Not infrequently also, Moon–Saturn parents look to their child for the nurturance they never had. And a good way of contacting what you want can be to give those things to others. Be being a parent, it is possible to heal some of the wounds of childhood, especially if the individual is aware and conscious that such is the opportunity. The urge for a family can also be part of the individual's hankering for emotional and domestic security. Whilst the permanence of family situations may indeed be illusory, they provide an arena whereupon the individual may learn about those illusions and learn and gain confidence about their ability to care and be cared for, by others. Arguably, it is only through facing their fears about their neediness that Moon–Saturn can emotionally develop into adulthood.

MOON–URANUS

Emotional independence. Sudden moves. The need for space. Rebellious feelings. Inconsistent behaviour. Changing moods. Culture shock.

As an indicator of what we need, the Moon, when coupled with Uranus, suggests that the individual, above all else, needs a great deal of space and freedom on a day-to-day level, especially emotionally and domestically. This person must feel free to feel what they choose and be able to change those feelings at whim. This person hates to feel fenced in, either emotionally or in their domestic life. There is a strong need to feel vibrant, to feel alive and to feel that life could change at any minute and in the most exciting way. Little wonder that Moon–Uranus is usually very restless and often feels 'itchy' for change. This is not a person who feels comfortable with routine or domesticity. Inevitably people with these contacts pursue, and feel much more at home leading, what to others might be considered an unconventional life-style.

Frequently, especially with the hard aspects, there was a childhood experience of shock or trauma; some very sudden happening. Often the child will have witnessed or experienced at first hand some kind of emotional 'cut-out'. This could be sudden loss of the mother or some other trauma in the family that takes the mother-figure away from the Moon–Uranus child, so that the youngster feels abandoned, rejected or cut out. A friend of mine who has a square between these two planets, with the Moon falling in the 3rd house of siblings, had an experience involving her younger brother. Whilst very young, he witnessed the window cleaner fall to his death off a ladder. The shock to the boy was so great and he was so young he was unable to process the experience fully. He didn't cry, he didn't scream but shortly after developed diabetes. He cut out on his feelings and the family did too. His illness, which was quite serious, shocked, shook and radically changed the feeling of the family.

Whatever the actual circumstance, the Moon–Uranus child usually has too early an experience of emotional independence. There are often happenings in the childhood where the child might need comforting, soothing, support and encouragement but for some reason got, or was only able to receive, the cold shoulder instead. The Moon–Uranus experience of giving and receiving mothering, security and emotional holding is nearly always an inconsistent one. The repercussions of this can be that the individual, feeling rejected and cut off in the past perhaps, continually expects to be rebuffed. The type is very sensitive and prone to taking things the wrong way. If there is any ambivalence in the feeling response that the Moon–Uranus person is receiving, they pick it up like lightning and often pick it up when it isn't there. The Moon–Uranus type is usually very intuitive, but the problem with intuition is that it is not always accurate. When feeling rejected, the person will often behave in a brusque, detached and offhand manner as a way to cover up for their hurt. Classically, the other person in the dialogue will just not know what is going on and will themselves feel rebuffed. Another repercussion is that the person often finds it difficult to ask for support and nurturance. Where others may be willing or desirous of helping the Moon–Uranus individual, they hold back, perceiving the person as being too independent to need assistance, too cool and detached to be able to be approached. The Moon–Uranus person, as has been said, is very sensitive but often can only allow themselves to feel in short, sharp shocks. When there is a likelihood of emotional trauma, the individual will often themselves cut out in some way, cut off from their feelings or by doing something drastic such as moving house. I have known several examples where the person faints as a method of protecting themselves. Rather like an electrical appliance that cuts out when the system is overloaded.

The Moon is also, I think, a significator of the inner baby that is within us all. Hard contacts between these planets usually show some sort of urgent need to integrate the needs of being a baby with those of being an independent adult. Sometimes this means that far from behaving in a very independent fashion, as is usually the case, the Moon–Uranus person will go overboard in wanting to be looked after, and not only because of feeling cut off in the past. For some, behaving independently implies that mother will go off and do her own thing, mother will abandon. In such circumstances the individual has been reinforced for not being independent and can find standing on their own two feet quite difficult.

Occasionally the lack of security in early life comes about because of frequent moves, especially if the 4th house is also involved. One woman I know with a Moon–Uranus conjunction on the IC had a father who was a notorious jewel thief; the family moved about forty times in her childhood in order to avoid the police. Looking back, she says she found it quite exciting but it left her with classic Moon–Uranus restlessness and difficulty in putting down roots.

Actually Moon–Uranus often has little time for roots; they don't, for example, usually believe that blood is thicker than water, and classically have no patience for people who are overly tied to the family network. On the other hand, Moon–Uranus can often accept the notion of the whole world being their family.

The Moon–Uranus person often spends a good deal of their life trying to break away from the past. And often rebelling from it too, and more especially rebelling from the mother or other caretaker and all those things that that person stood for. Shocking mother can be a life-time goal. This can happen in a wide variety of different ways. For example, I know of several Jewish people with this configuration who were raised in a fairly orthodox environment but when they were of an age to leave, just did so and pursued what to their family might be considered a very radical and probably shocking life-style. They eschewed the festivals, the ties of the family, the food, the life-style as a whole; they mixed mostly with Gentiles, and so on.

The notion of breaking free from the past does not just apply to the early home-life and background; that too, but the past, as in yesterday or last week. The need for change and to change the self is usually much more obvious on a day-to-day level with Moon–Uranus aspects than with Sun–Uranus ones. This is the person who moves into a new home, is fairly happy with it for a while and then feels this inner compunction to get up and go somewhere else. Or circumstances seemingly force them to do so. People with the hard aspects usually have tremendous problems putting down roots. There is a difficulty because one level of them feels that they do want roots, do want security, and a fixed home. Those with the easy aspects don't usually have this conflict.

The Moon–Uranus person sometimes comes from a background which is radically different from the average mother, father and 2.4 children, and this is increasingly the case, but when the family background is a traditional one, as in past generations, the Moon–Uranus child can often be seen to be 'carrying' much of the inner restlessness in the family. Commonly, the mother may have had ambivalent feelings about motherhood, seeing it as an unwelcome infringement upon her previous freedom and independence, and it falls to the Moon–Uranus child to do all the wild and exciting things that Mother wanted to but couldn't or didn't dare. And of course this can happen quite unconsciously.

Sometimes the Moon–Uranus child experiences their mother or their family set-up as being very eccentric and finds this differentness embarrassing. Those with the soft aspects, however, are more likely to experience the mother-figure as mildly unconventional or eccentric in some way. Perhaps exciting. The individual usually appreciates this quality about her or the family and has no felt need to rebel against what she stands for.

The individual's experience of mothering (both giving and receiving) can embody Uranus in a variety of different ways. Sometimes, the mother is a very progressive kind of person, which the individual may or may not feel comfortable with, depending on the nature of the given aspect and the chart overall.

Often people with these contacts, valuing their independence very highly, choose not to have children themselves. For others, parenthood represents an opportunity for the awakening of all sorts of feelings that the individual didn't know existed. And usually pregnancy, if it comes, does so like a bolt from the blue. In any event, the Moon–Uranus person often finds the traditional family set-up, especially the extended family, quite suffocating, hates all the undercurrents that exist between family members and does not want to replicate this kind of situation. The Moon–Uranus parent usually gives their children plenty of space to do what they want with their lives, which the children will either appreciate or feel abandoned by, depending on *their* lunar contacts. Classically, the Moon–Uranus person finds the family an artificial and hypocritical unit. But in shunning the family, the individual also loses their benefits and in particular, the inner feelings of security which are borne out of the familiarity and therefore safety of something to fall back on. The 'shadow' side of Moon–Uranus is usually dependency. Often the individual deals with this by setting up an unusual family network with friends. The friends may live apart but there is some feeling that they are 'family'.

Often people with hard contacts between the Moon and Uranus feel like an alien in their own family and quite often in their own culture. Frequently the individual will choose to live in an environment very different from the one in which they were raised. They often feel at home in a locality that others from the same background would consider very alien. Classically, they settle in a completely different country or culture from the one in which they were raised. Those with prominent hard contacts between these planets usually rebel against the mother image within themselves and, by extension, in society, even if there is no actual conscious rebellion against the personal mother. Apart from shunning the idea of parenthood there is sometimes a dislike of those parts of the body that might be associated with 'mother': the breasts, the stomach, the more rounded contours of the body. In return for abandoning the more traditional mother archetype, the Moon–Uranus individual often gains true emotional independence and an awakening perhaps to their *own* personal feeling nature.

Whilst the Moon–Uranus individual can have a tendency to cut out on their feelings, usually to protect themselves in some way, when awakened to those feelings, Moon–Uranus is usually very honest about them. Admitting things that might shock others because they would not have the courage to reveal them. Such revelations can create instant closeness and rapport. The Moon–Uranus person may be a very good friend, for, with lightning immediacy, they have the capacity to understand how another person feels. Their own moods may change rapidly and this can also give them tolerance and great insight into the shifts in others' behaviour. The Moon–Uranus person has the capacity to show they care in a multitude of different ways; they do not feel confined by the mores of society and are thus free to react and respond as seems appropriate to them in any given situation. And intuitively, the Moon–Uranus type will often know the appropriate way to respond. But it cannot be relied upon; those with the hard aspects especially can behave very inconsistently. In extreme cases, the Moon–Uranus person can be the type with whom you never know where you are: one minute brusquely independent, the next begging for help; one minute giving a warm welcome, the next seeming to forget you exist.

Nevertheless, being generally humanitarian, egalitarian and desirous of plenty of change, stimulation and excitement, ensures that the Moon–Uranus type will enjoy a whole host of friends of varying ages, backgrounds, cultures and ideas. People find Moon–Uranus types exciting.

Like Sun–Uranus, this is an excellent combination for anyone involved in reform and especially reform which deals with issues and attitudes concerning family life, housing, or social issues. A good example of Moon–Uranus can be found in Germaine Greer, who has a conjunction between these planets squaring the Ascendant and Sun.

MOON–NEPTUNE

Sensitivity to suffering. Elusive feelings. Emotional drowning. Idealised mother. Mother as victim. Saviours in need. The Ideal Home.

> Mother was a tall, thin almost ethereal creature with a romantic nature, who found even the most insignificant unpleasantness difficult to accept. In fact, it didn't exist – nothing unpleasant existed; it was a mistake or a misinterpretation.
> … this talk was necessary, and I would have to stumble in the dark a bit, hoping that I could find part of her that I wouldn't hurt.
> (Shirley Maclaine, from her autobiography: *Don't Fall Off the Mountain*)

It would be difficult to find a better description of a strong contact between these planets than this, coming as it does from one who has a Moon–Neptune conjunction in Virgo and in her 12th house.

Elsewhere Shirley Maclaine speaks of how she couldn't 'find' her mother, couldn't get 'hold' of her and this is a feeling common to many with Moon–Neptune contacts when talking about their mothers and, more to the point, a common feeling to those when talking about their Moon–Neptune friends too!

This is an extremely sensitive and impressionable combination, so much so that the individual with it strong in their charts can have great difficulty in maintaining their own separateness. Their boundaries are weak and, like Sun–Neptune but rather more so, it's often difficult for them to work out just where other people start and they leave off. The type tends to be sensitive to everything and quite capable of taking everyone's emotions and feelings on board. At the same time, it is often difficult for people with this combination to get hold of their own feelings, or indeed to have a very clear idea of just what other people's feelings are. The Moon–Neptune type is often very good at feeling feelings but not necessarily so gifted at defining and understanding them. The presence of air or a strong Mercury can do much to offset this.

Like Venus–Neptune, Moon–Neptune often reminds me of a mermaid: elusive, slippery, enchanting, a little bit of magic that's impossible to catch. The behaviour of the Moon–Neptune person is often like this – elusive in the extreme and reluctant to commit themselves to anything. 'Do we have to talk about that now?' asks the Moon–Neptune person, afraid not only of committing themselves to anything but anxious to avoid dealing with something that might be unpleasant. Moon–Neptune typically would always choose to avoid difficult subjects and having to commit themselves as to what they actually feel about something. Absorbing everybody else's feelings and emotions and soaking up every little happening in the environment renders a typical Moon–Neptune person something of a psychic sponge, getting themselves too waterlogged to be able to differentiate between what is theirs and what isn't.

There is usually a marked sensitivity to suffering of any kind. People starving throughout the world or the old woman across the road that seems lonely, the orphan child or the stray dog. The challenge for people with these aspects is to *do* something about this suffering. Those with the hard aspects, especially, often find such suffering too much to bear and thus look to others to be rescued from having to face all this harshness. The individual with these aspects identifies with the victim and in so doing feels sorry for themselves. Feeling sorry for oneself is often a marked behavioural trait with this combination. This is a very passive combination and the individual needs to direct their energies to other parts of their chart (Mars for example) for a way to make active use of the need to save, care and protect.

Saviour or not, there is usually tremendous compassion and empathy with this combination and the individual often has a marked capacity for putting themselves inside another's shoes.

The mother-figure, or (as Carter and Arroyo both point out) sometimes the father-figure, may embody Neptune in a variety of ways. They may literally be 'lost' to the child, available in some way, or come fleetingly into the child's life like a will-o-the-wisp. Sometimes there is mental instability or sometimes the parent may have been something of a mystic or an artist. Not seemingly fettered by ordinary, practical and earthly considerations. More commonly though, the experience of mother is that she, for whatever reason, was something of a victim and the individual with this combination may have shaky mother–self boundaries. Classically the Moon–Neptune person feels sorry for the mother-figure and identifies with that person's suffering. The mother principle and womanhood generally is often idealised with this combination and classically the Moon–Neptune person is very 'open' to the influence of motherly people. Sometimes there is a strong yearning towards actual physical motherhood. Sometimes, too, the

Moon–Neptune person is peculiarly open to being psychically brainwashed by others. Because the type is often very unclear as to the true nature of their own feelings they can be seduced into believing that they feel something that they don't. The Moon–Neptune person's feelings can often be betrayed very easily.

There is a strong need to escape with these contacts; perhaps this is how the person protects themselves. There is often a need for refinement and a corresponding dislike of crassness, harshness or vulgarity. Typically, the individual would rather not know about anything 'not nice' and if threatened with something unpleasant may retreat into their fantasy life or the comfort of the television.

Whilst one might associate many lunar and Neptunian combinations with imagination, these two planets coupled together must surely be very imaginative. Those with the soft aspects, when asked, will often say that they don't day-dream or fantasise that much. Sometimes though, it can be found that the individual fantasises so automatically and so easily that they are scarcely aware of it.

Moon–Neptune, like most other Neptune combinations, is common in charts of all kinds of creative people. It is extremely common in the charts of actors, although on its own this combination may be too retiring for the bright lights.

An actor is not only someone who can portray a whole gamut of human emotions behind the part they are playing but behind that part they can live life vicariously. They don't personally have to get involved in the messy fray of existence but nevertheless can reflect real-life situations and live out other parts of their chart. For example Shirley Maclaine has a Sun–Mars conjunction in her 8th house. She has embodied some of the sexual issues of that placement through playing a prostitute in many films. An actor also reflects the feelings of the collective. Drama embodies the mythology of the day and the given culture.

People with hard Moon–Neptune contact sometimes have a vaguely parasitical quality. Basically the type seems to yearn for comfort and nurturance and can get quite addicted to anyone who might potentially provide this level of care. As Arroyo puts it:

> There is a hunger for emotional nourishment, caring, and comfort that is extremely difficult to satisfy; for no imperfect human being can ever fulfil the totally giving and selfless image that Moon–Neptune people project on others.

As Arroyo goes on to say, the Moon–Neptune person needs someone or something to devote themselves to, rather than relying on others to give them that devotion.

Basically, there is often a yearning to *merge* with this combination, to merge with the cosmos, to merge with Mother, to retreat into the womb from which one was born.

Whatever the childhood (or even the recent past) was like, the Moon–Neptune person tends to idealise it and weave fantasies around it. Thirsting for a better future, whilst idealising the past, it is often difficult for the individual to make the most out of the present.

It is around the issue of home that Moon–Neptune people often get dissatisfied. Like those with Neptune on the IC, Moon–Neptune people often yearn for an 'ideal' home; something that is not only emotionally tranquil but in the physical sense is beautiful, safe and comfortable – a harbour where the individual can anchor. There is often a very shy and retiring side to Moon–Neptune and this, together with this feeling that one might drown in one's feelings, contributes to this yearning for a safe haven to retreat to.

This is a good combination for anyone whose work actively involves the establishment of 'ideal homes', either in the emotional sense as in the case of social workers who try to find ideal homes for children, or in the physical sense, as with designers and decorators.

Moon–Pluto

Buried feelings. An intense emotional life. Transformation of feelings. Domestic crisis. Emotional blackmail. Powerful mother.

Moon–Pluto's emotional life reminds me a seabird, maybe a gannet, a bird who dives headlong into the water for its food and then comes up to digest what it has caught. The Moon–Pluto individual often has a similar attitude to its emotional life, plunging and diving deeply into their feelings and relationships and then needing time on their own to digest what has been absorbed.

Typically, the Moon–Pluto person needs space as much as intensity in their home and emotional life. Those with the conjunction and hard aspects, especially, have a tendency to feel invaded and intruded upon. Indeed, there seems to be an expectation that in family or emotional situations such an invasion will take place, if the individual does not take steps to avoid this happening.

The feeling life is usually very intense with these aspects but how this intensity manifests can vary greatly and often according to how aware the individual is of their feeling nature. The individual may have a powerful investment in getting to the root of their feelings, the investment being in a need to purge oneself of them. To eradicate them at their source.

Others have a powerful investment in not experiencing them at all and here Pluto can be seen to be 'killing' the feelings. But they are not killed so much as buried, until the time is ripe for them to resurface. Inevitably some of the feelings that the Moon–Pluto type wishes either to purge themselves of or to hide altogether are of a poisonous and destructive nature; revenge, jealousy and pain. Often these feelings do not only belong to the individual but have been absorbed from the whole family. Frequently, those with the hard aspects come from a family with a skeleton in the cupboard. Some sort of trauma or violation. Perhaps something that at the time society might have found deeply shocking; illegitimacy or sexual abuse perhaps. Or sometimes the quality may not have been so much shocking as difficult for the family to process fully: disablement, handicap, madness, premature death.

Doubtless all families have such skeletons but where a Moon–Pluto individual is involved, that person will often be the one unconsciously elected to carry and heal the wounds. And often, to bring things to a head. Rather as poison in the body may eventually surface as a boil, the Moon–Pluto person can often act, sometimes in a professional capacity, as the catalyst which enables the boil to surface, burst and heal.

Sometimes the Moon–Pluto person acts as a thorn in the flesh of the rest of the family, for the individual seems to wear a badge, which they themselves may not be able to see, but which acts as a constant reminder to the family of the poisonous past, the past that they would prefer to see kept hidden from view and preferably permanently buried.

Typically, the Moon–Pluto person acts as a sponge for any negative, buried or unexpressed feelings that are floating around in the atmosphere. This happens in childhood but often becomes a habit, and even as an adult, the Moon–Pluto person often gets emotional stuff laid on them in some way.

Wherever there is a crisis, even if it has nothing to do with the Moon–Pluto person, they usually somehow end up getting embroiled in the matter. These people seem to thrive on crisis and like a vulture may feed on the pickings of trauma – and the type is usually able to smell trauma at quite a distance. Sometimes the involvement occurs because of the type's emotional strength and perceptive insight. People in crisis often turn to Moon–Pluto people for they are strong, can be deeply protective and nothing seems to shock them. Typically, the type has seen it all before, *felt* it all before, and is well aware of and often very compassionate towards the darker side of human nature. At best, the Moon–Pluto person instead of burying feelings, exposes them and can create a safe environment where others can also feel safe enough to expose their feelings and their family skeletons.

If the Moon describes how we feel fed and nurtured, perhaps when contacting Pluto it's describing a need for an intense emotional interaction. Some Moon–Pluto people feel at home living with – or possibly playing the part of – Lady Macbeth. Certainly, the domestic and emotional life of Moon–Pluto is rarely tranquil for long. Often the emotional life resembles a scene from a Shakespearean tragedy: dark, foreboding, full of seething undercurrents that are ready to erupt at any minute. Perhaps saying that Moon–Pluto is at home with the undercurrents is unfair, for the situation is often much more that the individual is familiar with the darker sides of human nature and especially family life. But if the emotional and domestic life of Moon–Pluto is rather dramatic and crisis-prone, this will rarely be in evidence to the casual observer. Commonly, the Moon–Pluto person likes to keep their feelings and all details of their private and domestic life, well hidden from public view. Those with the hard aspects especially, often feel that they have no reason to trust others with their feelings or their secrets.

Often the Moon–Pluto person comes from a background where it wasn't safe to expose one's feelings for it was felt that they would be used for purposes of manipulation, control or blackmail.

The Moon–Pluto individual is often obsessed with their mother (and sometimes obsessed with *being* a mother) and the mother, in turn, will often have been quite obsessed with the child. Typically, the mother-figure is over-protective, controlling and quite unable to let the fledging go. Moon–Pluto mother-love may be devouring and manipulative, although often this is subtle and covert. However in extreme cases and if the combination is strong, the devouring quality of the mother can indeed make her something of a wicked witch or a vampire, a mother that sucks the life out of the child. A mother-figure who 'over-mothers', by constantly invading the child's space, allowing no hiding-place, no secrets and no privacy. It may be that the mother-figure fears that something dreadful will happen to the child and thus is obsessively protective. And this seems to be no less common an experience to those with the easy aspects. Sometimes the parental figure is a grandparent, usually a grandmother and where it isn't, this suffocating history still often has its roots in some powerful, matriarchal line.

I think one can associate Moon–Pluto with very primal feelings. It's as if the individual with this combination emphasised in their chart is fated to embody, work with, and transform some of the deeply rooted instinctual feelings that are common to all of us, perhaps in the collective unconscious. Feelings that the civilisation process has attempted to socialise out of us, often by force.

The Moon–Pluto person may tend to 'crash' through and invade other people's feelings or, in some cases, be very frightened of doing so. The 'crashing' propensity reveals itself in the individual seeming to demand that they be allowed into another's personal feelings and personal space. Such invasion may or may not be appropriate, depending on the motive of the Moon–Pluto person. The motives are often concerned with establishing an intense emotional rapport but they may be to do with suspicion. The Moon–Pluto person, themselves fearful of emotional invasion and as distrustful of others' motives as one might be of theirs, often wishes to delve into the psyche of the other, as a way of protecting the self. Perhaps the philosophy of Pluto contacts generally, and Moon–Pluto ones in particular, runs along the following lines: If you know the other person thoroughly, including their weaknesses, then they cannot do the dirty on you, for you hold the power. Moon–Pluto can be very adept at emotional blackmail.

Whatever the motives, such psychic invasion, positively used, can do much to cleanse and purge but it can also leave the invaded person feeling very exposed. The 'crashing' is usually what the Moon–Pluto person has been exposed to and become used to. It may also form part of their skill and habitual way of operating.

The Moon–Pluto person is often sensitive to and aware of the misuse of power. Providing this quality is well developed, this combination is a very useful one for those whose work involves the exposure, acceptance and transformation of feelings and personal histories that have been kept private. The counsellor, the therapist, the biographer.

Perhaps the most difficult thing for a Moon–Pluto person to do is to let go of their feelings. The urge to purge the self of all the destructive emotions of rage, hurt, suspicion and jealousy is strong but with the hard aspects the fear of letting go seems even stronger.

Life may not be peaceful or tranquil for the Moon–Pluto type but the inner world and often the outer life is vivid, multi-coloured and intense. At best the Moon–Pluto person can squeeze a great deal out of the ordinary everyday experience.

CHAPTER EIGHT

MERCURY ASPECTS

MERCURY–VENUS

Beauty of language. Love of Language. Thinking about beauty. Thoughts of love. Thoughts of peace. Beautiful movement.

These planets can never be more than about 75 degrees apart and thus can only form sextile, semi-square and conjunction aspects in the natal chart. This is not a combination that I have much familiarity with but it certainly confers amiability, charm and tact. A beauty or gracefulness of expression that might find outlet in a variety of creative skills. The combination may be found in singers or those with a beautiful speaking voice. Sometimes it is as easy to fall in love with a voice as it is with a face, and perhaps some of those who attract others with their voice in this way might have Mercury–Venus contacts.

I also associate this combination with creative writing although it is not, for some reason, especially common in the natal charts of famous writers. The Mercury–Venus person will incline to thinking (and talking) about love and relationship and thus if the combination cannot really be associated with writers it is often descriptive of people who get pleasure from reading. Much fiction of course involves itself with inquiring into the nature of various forms of relationship and especially love relationship. The writer and the connoisseur of literature must surely also have a feeling for the beauty of language and value it highly.

Other art-forms such as music may also be associated with Mercury–Venus, although perhaps it is more to be associated with artistic skills and techniques than fine art, skills that require the use of the hands. Many dancers have the combination and so one might also link it to beautiful movement. It is probably the tightest aspect in the chart of Leonardo da Vinci, who had an exact semi-square.

Those whose business is to act as agents in artistic fields might have strong Mercury–Venus contacts and it ought to be well represented in the beauty industry, with those people who have to think, talk or act as agents for beauty products. For example, I know of a woman who holds perfume parties who has an exact 45 degree aspect between these planets.

The Mercury–Venus person may think and talk about their values a good deal, and can be quite interested in money issues. The double Taurus, Karl Marx, whose major life-work involved thinking, talking and writing about values and resources, had an important though fairly wide Mercury–Venus conjunction (a 6 degree orb with, rather significantly, Mercury in Gemini with Venus in Taurus).

If other factors in the chart concur, the Mercury–Venus combination is usually a very diplomatic one. The type thinks about peace. Thus it is a useful contact for anyone associated with diplomacy or public relations in any way.

The diplomatic skills also contribute to the likelihood of enduring and happy relationships. These people seek to say things that they know will be well received and they tend to bend over backwards in trying to be reasonable and fair in arriving at their opinions and expressing them. This in turn confers popularity.

Mercury–Mars

Assertive communication. Incisive, quick thinking. The competitive mind. Sibling rivalry. Putting thought into action.

A 'hard' contact between these two planets can be described as the 'cut the crap' combination and this is just the kind of language that an individual with it might use. For Mercury–Mars types tend to want to cut through all red tape and excess verbiage in their communication and also, perhaps, in yours! The type wants things clear, concise, sharp and honest. Don't look to a Mercury–Mars person for tact, gentleness or delicacy of expression. Their skill lies more in their courage and capacity to 'call a brick a brick'.

Mentally, these people are quick, incisive and competitive. They assert themselves through language and protect themselves by cultivating speed of thought. In some ways, Mercury–Mars types can be a joy in the classroom for they 'cotton on' very quickly. But they also get bored easily and are impatient with minds slower than their own. As a child, this is the student who can be found reading a book under the desk on something completely different to what is being taught. Not only is this a way of asserting oneself but it also expresses the child's boredom. For this type, the mind is the chief weapon and there is a need for ample opportunity to sharpen it.

Intellectually, the Mercury–Mars person needs a lot of 'meat' to get their teeth into. And yet, of itself, this is not the aspect of an intellectual – intellectualism implies depth of thought and staying power, neither of which is this type's forté, unless Saturn is also strong. Indeed, this individual tends to be impatient with academia and at the same time perhaps, threatened by it.

The late British astrologer John Addey, himself the owner of a very incisive mind and a Mercury–Mars square, found contacts (along with Mercury–Uranus) between these planets to be common in the charts of polio victims who, he tells us, tend to share one particular character trait: their mental agility. Polio is thankfully a comparatively rare physical manifestation of the combination of these two planets but nervous tension and irritability are very much the norm. In my experience it is rare to find someone with a hard and close aspect between these two planets who has not at some time been a smoker or nail-biter. Physical problems involving the nerves, including the so-called nervous breakdown, are also not that uncommon. Basically, the impatience and anger of the Mercury–Mars type seems to flood the communicative channels and it's important that a vehicle can be found for it, such as writing, satire or helping others fight their own incapacity to communicate. Mars always needs a cause and here the cause, indeed *the purpose* of the aspect, is to somehow live out the axiom that the pen is mightier than the sword.

One can often sense the frustration of the Mercury–Mars type, for the mind is active and agile and goes so much quicker than either the vocal chords or the pen. Often the words just leap out of the mouth quite raw, before the individual has had time to formulate their ideas properly and certainly before there has been a chance to 'dress them up' a little. Not that Mercury–Mars necessarily wants to soften what they are going to say; this type believes firmly in straight talking, with no punches pulled. In writing and in speech the style can be quite satirical and pithy. If this combination occurs in the chart of an otherwise 'soft' person, the individual might not be quite so outspoken but still usually likes things to be expressed simply and concisely.

Often the Mercury–Mars type came from a very argumentative background where, in the background of the dissension, the child had little opportunity to assert their opinions and ideas, little opportunity to make themselves heard. Later in life there is an urgent need to dominate in some way through communication. Hence Mercury–Mars might talk rather forcefully, quickly or sharply, and in rather a threatening manner, as if they expect opposition. Sometimes the childhood is not so much argumentative as competitive. Sibling rivalry is common as is a situation where one child is constantly reminded how much better their older brother/sister is performing at school. The scenario varies, but the essential issue is that anger in later life, and difficulties in expressing it in socially acceptable terms, can often be linked to this early competitiveness, as can problems in childhood itself (such as undue precocity or petty thieving).

Mercury–Mars is not necessarily argumentative, the individual with this contact knows their own mind excellently and isn't interested in co-operating or in coming to agreement (with all things to do with communication, Mercury–Mars just wants to do their own thing). Neither is the type sufficiently interested in your opinions to want to change them. Where the individual is argumentative it's often because they are so used to arguing that it's difficult to imagine communicating in any other way. Opposition people especially, often go through life accusing everyone else or picking fights, tending to forget that it takes two to make an argument. Even if Mercury–Mars is not argumentative it is certainly prone to getting very heated about things, prone too, to thinking in black and white and to jumping to conclusions with insufficient information.

Mercury–Mars people often have the feeling that 'actions speak louder than words', which is one reason why people with this aspect sometimes don't get involved in discussing things (they usually have a horror of meetings) and are thus often seen, with good reason perhaps, as being uncooperative and undemocratic. Not that Mercury–Mars is necessarily a 'Doer' in actuality, indeed the challenger for an individual with this combination strong is to bring ideas and action together, to have the strength to act on convictions without annihilating others for espousing opinions that differ from their own.

This is something of a 'trickster' combination and is common in the charts of criminals, especially petty thieves such as shop-lifters. Perhaps this is not surprising given the particularly amoral cast to Mercury's character and the self-seeking quality of Mars. Theft also requires those qualities that Mercury–Mars has in plenty: speed of thought and action, courage, sheer nerve and impulsiveness; a capacity to act first and think afterwards.

The way for an individual to use this combination is for them to get themselves into situations that require someone who won't be frightened to speak up. Failure to use the mind as the sharp tool that it is can otherwise result in nagging, discontent, irritability and opinionatedness.

Children with Mercury–Mars contacts tend to be curious about sexual matters at quite an early age, often to the embarrassment of their parents. I have also known situations where the child itself is the victim of sexual curiosity in the shape of sibling incest.

At worst, hard aspects between Mercury and Mars can indicate quarrelsomeness and a tendency to view other people's differing opinions as personal affronts. There can also be undue competitiveness with every conversation experienced as either a threat or a battle. Impulsiveness and impatience are also common manifestations, coupled with great nervous tension, irritability, and a general fault-finding propensity. The impatience is with all forms of communication and also transport. There is no one who hates waiting for a bus or getting stuck in a traffic jam like a Mercury–Mars person. On the plus side, there is the capacity to have the courage of one's convictions, to be honest and 'tell it as it is', coupled with a sharp and incisive mind. There is also often wit and both verbal and manual dexterity. People with this combination make good writers (especially investigative or satirical writers), critics, public speakers, debaters and Scrabble players, and are also sometimes adept in fields such as light engineering. Any situation which calls for an ability to speak up on behalf of something or someone positively needs a Mercury–Mars person. After all, someone had to tell the Emperor that he wasn't wearing any clothes; doubtless it fell to the lot of a Mercury–Mars type who, one suspects, might also have had a Mercury–Uranus contact.

Princess Margaret, well known for her skill with the sharp retort, is a good example of the combination as she has a tight, prominent square between these planets. With the soft aspects the individual is less likely to be so caustic in their comments but there can be an enjoyment of strong language and debate and an easy talent for expressing things clearly and concisely. The sextile is a particularly incisive contact where the mental powers are concerned and is often especially talented at putting ideas into practice and making them work.

MERCURY–JUPITER

Making mountains out of molehills. Thinking about the future. Hoping for the best. The philosophical thinker. Big ideas. Confident opinions.

> [Mercury–Jupiter] ... being inclined intellectually towards principles rather than facts, tends to look inward and to be outwardly mild and genial in bearing. The native with these contacts strong, if called to express himself, has to collect his wits and think out what he wants to say (the exception being his readiness for philosophical dispute and his willingness to give tips). Being preoccupied with ideas rather than things he is usually unobservant except in matters which interest him and provide him with food for thought. If his wife asks him at the tea table if he will have jam or honey, he cannot immediately remember what jam or honey are let alone which, if either, he would prefer ('I'm sorry my dear, you were saying ...'). His movements are often free and careless and he forgets things which you would have no difficulty in remembering. Those who are not the outraged victims of his absent-mindedness are prepared to make allowance and will put a benevolent arm around his shoulders in times of need.
> (John Addey, *Selected Writings*)

In the same section, John Addey comments on how Mercury–Jupiter people may not be especially talkative because of this tendency to looking inwards and the general mildness of expression. Whilst I have found that this is often the case, it is by no means invariable. Sometimes Mercury–Jupiter contacts can incline to what can only be called verbal diarrhoea although this is more usually an extreme expression of this combination when Gemini is involved or Pluto (the compulsive desire to communicate).

Whatever the communicative tendencies of the Mercury–Jupiter type, they may well be the kind of person who will embark on studying fifty major subjects at the same time. Well, maybe not fifty, but quite a few. That statement illustrates a Mercury–Jupiter failing, the tendency to exaggerate! Certainly, the combination may be found in people who are curious about a wide range of subjects. If the contact is a very significant one in the chart, the breadth of interest can be quite staggering and especially around subjects of a philosophical nature, perhaps religion, education, law, travel or politics.

Jupiter seeks to broaden whatever it touches and when contacting Mercury, it broadens the mind. Individuals with these contacts are often able to look at a given subject from the widest possible angle. And they will usually be especially curious to explore what it all might actually *mean*. However, hard contacts between these planets don't always work out that way.

We might associate the easy aspects with balanced judgement and the ability to see the overview of a situation but sometimes this is the challenge posed to those with the hard aspects rather than necessarily the outcome. Jupiter lends a touch of arrogance as well as confidence to whatever planet it links with in the chart, so that with all aspects but especially with the hard ones, the Mercury–Jupiter individual may tend to exaggerate one piece of information at the expense of achieving this overview. At worst the Mercury–Jupiter person may be arrogant about their opinions, always believing that they are right, too confident about what they say and sometimes their ability to say it. This combination may contribute to what I believe is described in the States as the 'grand-stander' teacher, the lecturer who has a wide knowledge of their subject, is charismatic perhaps, but who doesn't really prepare what they're going to say and when it comes to actually talking, merely delivers amiability, massive generalisations and plenty of hot air.

On the other hand, Mercury–Jupiter speakers may be inspirational and uplifting. The type can talk about their pet subjects with great enthusiasm and this can sometimes arouse tremendous interest in others. In this and most other contexts, the Mercury–Jupiter person is most likely to come unstuck because of a tendency to *overstate* their case and to gloss over opinions, ideas or information which are contrary to their own.

The type can also be careless about what they say and sometimes who they say it to. But as with all Jupiter contacts, the person will tend to get away with the careless statement, the glib remark, the error in calculations. This contrasts sharply in my experience with the very careful Mercury–Saturn person who only has to make one erroneous statement for things to go terribly wrong.

Mercury–Jupiter people are less likely to be academics than, say, Mercury–Saturn types. Whereas the latter needs the proof of certificates, degrees or diplomas to vouch for their intellectual accomplishments or articulacy, the average Mercury–Jupiter person is not particularly impressed by those things and has not felt need to prove anything about their brain-power.

Whereas Mercury–Saturn people will often choose to specialise, the Mercury–Jupiter person tends to know a little bit about a great many things. Unless Saturn is also involved, the type may spread themselves too widely and thinly in their knowledge. And often those with the conjunction and hard aspects especially, will sound much more informed than they really are.

Being so intent on knowing everything, and on gaining the overall picture, the student or researcher with this combination can end up with a mass of information but no clarity. In mutable signs especially, the individual often has difficulty in knowing what to emphasise. This is the student with hundreds of pages of notes but no essay. A strong Mars can do much to offset this tendency. The challenge for the individual with these aspects is to set themselves a goal, and indeed cover as much as is possible up to arriving at that goal, but to somehow digest that information before venturing further. Mercury–Jupiter, like other Jupiter contacts, does not want to be bound by limits; this is both the good news and the bad news about this combination. It can give rise to the truly eclectic mind or merely the dabbler.

Typically, the Mercury–Jupiter person will be philosophically rather than scientifically inclined. Unlike Mercury–Saturn there is less felt need for facts or for having things defined. Too much definition is felt to be limiting, confining and narrow to the Mercury–Jupiter person.

As John Addey implies, Mercury–Jupiter is the kind of combination that one might associate with the absent-minded professor, the person who thinks about things of enormous import but excludes the practical details of life from their mental agenda. Mercury in an earth sign or an earthy chart in general, will do much to increase the likelihood of practical thinking though.

Jupiter lends a very *intuitive* cast to the Mercurial mind so that individuals with this combination are usually very good at getting the *gist* of something, good at catching the spirit of a given subject. The type hates anything that might smack of precision or pedantry, and thus there can be difficulties over detailed work or thinking. I have noticed over the years how poorly students tend to fare when taking exams under Jupiter–Mercury transits. They just feel too confident, make silly mistakes and perhaps don't go deeply enough into the given subject.

Hard Mercury–Jupiter contacts can also be associated with misunderstanding. Sometimes these are caused by over-enthusiasm; the individual's mind just races off into the future and thus they just guess what is going to be said or guess the content of what actually has been written. In listening as well as in communicating there can be a tendency to exaggeration, with the Mercury–Jupiter person hearing wrongly, exaggerating certain factors and missing what is the main point to the person who is telling the story.

Unless there are strong indications to the contrary, people with Mercury–Jupiter contacts of all kinds usually enjoy school and, indeed, enjoy and feel drawn to all subsequent learning situations. The type likes to feel that their mind is growing and really the only problem with this can be that the individual's mind grows too fast for them to be able to assimilate everything.

When things go wrong and life seems harsh, as it inevitably does at times, those with Mercury–Jupiter contacts can usually stand back and view the situation philosophically. At best, those with this combination can find meaning and purpose where others only see grim reality. At worst though, those with this contact, especially where hard aspects are concerned, can imbue events with significance when it is arguable, to the individual suffering at any rate, whether there is anything other than the mere grim reality of the situation. Whilst Mercury–Jupiter is busy philosophising and waxing lyrical about the true/inner/real meaning of their neighbour's house having burnt down, more pragmatic friends may be rolling up their sleeves and giving practical assistance. On the other hand, when the Mercury–Jupiter person describes the incident sometime later, the tragedy of it, the awfulness of it will probably be vastly exaggerated.

Since Mercury and Jupiter can be associated with short- and long-distance travel physically as well as mentally, prominent (especially hard) contacts between these planets can be associated with a life filled with plenty of travel. And physical travel as well as educational travel is a very good way to use these contacts. Surely such exploration is the purpose of this combination. Mercury–Jupiter is a good mix for the writer and can often be found in those whose work is read well into the future. Whilst the Mercury–Jupiter communicator will tend to exaggerate what they write or talk about in order to make a social, philosophical or religious point, this exaggeration will lend drama to the narrative and thus will make both the content and the narrator very popular. Thus this is a useful combination for teachers, preachers, politicians and philosophers. Anyone with Big Ideas and anyone who might talk or think about the *future* and, in particular, about an improved future. The concern with the future can point to an interest in youth or work with youth. The combination may also be found in people who enjoy or write science fiction – a genre that usually involves itself with future worlds far from their own. The interest in faraway places sometimes gives rise to an interest in astronomy and in travel. This is a good combination for both the astronomer and travel writer.

MERCURY–SATURN

The voice of authority. Language barriers. Negative thinking. The disciplined mind. Learning the hard way. Defining one's ideas.

Like most Saturn combinations, hard aspects between Mercury and Saturn give rise to two distinct types of background and behaviour and a whole gamut of possibilities in between.

Mercury–Saturn contacts can be associated with people who are serious-minded, thorough and conscientious on the one hand, and those who are frightened to think on the other.

Classically, the Mercury–Saturn person will think before they speak and not commit themselves in any form of communication until they have thought out precisely what they mean to say. This caution in expressing the self sometimes follows a history at school or at home, where the individual felt that what they said wasn't good enough in some way; perhaps not expressed correctly, or not sufficiently interesting. Often the individual will have picked up early cues that what they said was not worth listening to, not valuable enough or more simply and perhaps through no one's 'fault' there really wasn't anyone around who had the time to listen. Often the Mercury–Saturn person comes from a large family where there are just too many people talking at once for one little voice to feel heard. Sometimes it is in the school situation that the listening did not take place. Sometimes the person was made to feel stupid at school and now still fears that their intellectual equipment may not be up to scratch, which makes them cautious about expressing themselves and reluctant to risk making a fool of themselves. Sometimes early learning situations involve learning by rote and the implementation of harsh discipline so that the joy of learning is lost to the individual. The child's own ideas, opinions and perhaps the tendency just to chat, to gabble on, might have been crushed. Often too, the Mercury–Saturn person will come up against language barriers at some stage in their lives so that they find themselves in situations where they are not able to make themselves understood, usually for reasons of language or dialect. Sometimes not a real barrier as in the case of a different language but, in Britain at any rate, a class barrier where voice and accent may be taken, albeit unconsciously, as an indication of the individual's education, upbringing and place in society. This is a classic situation for the Mercury–Saturn child who moves from one region to another where the children speak differently. The child feels ostracised, not so much by what they say as by the way they say it.

The fear that others might be more intelligent or more articulate than oneself may not be a conscious one and may be dealt with in a variety of ways. Typically, when it comes to expressing their opinion, either verbally or in an exam situation, the Mercury–Saturn individual will think they are being 'tested'. Sometimes those with the square aspects especially deal with their fear by putting themselves into testing situations. Mercury–Saturn people may well be academics, gathering certificates as they go along. I suspect that the 'Mensa' organisation may have many a Mercury–Saturn individual in its membership. And I wonder about the contestants on the TV programme *Mastermind*; might they not tend towards Mercury–Saturn contacts as well? Though, given that competition and quick thinking are also required, one might also suspect a strong Mercury–Mars presence. Basically, the Mercury–Saturn person wants a piece of paper from an authoritative body that will testify to their intelligence, knowledge and ability to express themselves. Similarly, Mercury–Saturn contacts are quite consistent with the person who doesn't think you are knowledgeable unless you have a string of letters after your name. Again, this reflects a distrust of knowledge which is not recognised by authority.

Some Mercury–Saturn types shy away from examination situations; they don't allow themselves to be tested, for the fear of failure is too great. As always, where we find Saturn, we take ourselves and the given situation far too *seriously*.

Whether the individual develops into a certificate gatherer or one who shies away from such testing situations will depend, to a large extent, on the background of the individual, the overall tenor of the chart, and the importance that the combination in general and the placement of Mercury in particular, holds in the horoscope.

Sometimes the Mercury–Saturn individual comes from a background where there were no books and no conversation and perhaps little opportunity for education. This can translate into fear around any learning and communicative situations. A fear which the individual may conquer or choose to avoid altogether. Avoidance usually means that the person will then over-trust the voice of those in authority and undervalue their own inner voice and opinions. Rather like the old idea, of believing, for example, that what your doctor told you was infallible and that any ideas or feelings that you might have about your own body or treatment must be nonsense. On the other hand, the Mercury–Saturn person is quite consistent with the person who will accept no voice of authority, who will be sceptical about whatever they are told. Seen positively, this allows the person to become their own best authority on a given issue.

Mercury–Saturn is often associated with, on the one hand, those who seem slow and dull, and with exceptional intellectual gifts on the other. Einstein, who has a conjunction between these planets, would surely fall into the latter category. Certainly some individuals may seem slow and narrow in their thinking with this combination, but closer examination usually reveals great fear of expressing oneself and fear of thinking, more than any actual impairment of the intellectual function. Working at its best, however, Saturn contacting Mercury seems to dry out the mind of all extraneous matter so that the thinking becomes at once much less cluttered, clearer, more measured, considered and thorough.

The mind is often exact and precise with these contacts, and given to defining things carefully. Indeed Mercury–Saturn always wants things very carefully defined and explained. Not content with the gist of the matter, the typical Mercury–Saturn individual wants the 't's crossed and the 'i's dotted. In teaching Mercury–Saturn students over the years I have often found that these are the people who get the most anxious if they feel they don't understand something fully. They don't easily trust the possibility that everything will fall into place in the end, and they are often more troubled than other students by the differing opinions and approaches that various teachers and textbooks might hold.

Mercury–Saturn might feel safest if there were just one authoritative text, one volume, that could be treated as gospel and about which all authorities on a given subject would agree. The same students are often very gifted at calculation work, and in following formulas and feel confident in these areas. Classically, Mercury–Saturn people are good at maths and science, for here there is a 'right' answer. But in interpretation work, where there are less clear-cut rules, where taking a risk is required, where the use of the non-rational mind is needed, Mercury–Saturn often flounders. Usually it's not that the individual doesn't have a perfectly reasonable or 'correct' answer or observation but that they are nervous of risking being 'wrong'. The type feels that they have to know the subject backwards and often, with the tremendous capacity for application and self-discipline that they may have, they do; the individual thoroughly masters a subject – and this is the purpose of the hard contacts between these two planets.

Whatever the academic situation or background, the Mercury–Saturn person often craves to be valued for their knowledge, their quick repartee and spell-binding conversation. But although it sounds like a contradiction in terms, Mercury–Saturn usually has to work at achieving this kind of spontaneity. One person who has achieved this is the writer and poet Maya Angelou, who has an exact square between these planets. She routinely gives one-woman shows and spontaneously talks on the radio in the most humorous way. She is no doubt helped in this respect by a Sun–Jupiter conjunction in Aries. Perhaps another reason for her spontaneity is because she is talking about her own *experience* and it has nothing to do with anything that might be found in books. And perhaps this is a purpose of Mercury–Saturn contacts too – learning the hard way from experience. The playwrite Tom Stoppard also has an exact square between these two planets. Writing, of course, also involves *defining* what one wants to say very carefully. The script is rehearsed.

Teachers and lecturers often have contacts between these planets and it's hardly surprising considering that those with these contacts often yearn, above all else, to be respected for their knowledge and their capacity to express that knowledge. These are the lecturers who prepare very thoroughly, perhaps write down every word they intend to utter and then follow their script very closely when actually talking; the meticulously planned speech that leaves nothing to chance. Such a teacher takes their job very seriously and the effort put in usually shows, for the work will often provide real material, real 'matter' for the students to get their teeth into. At worst though, they can be dry, rigidly traditional academics who squeeze the life out of the subject and lose sight of what it might all actually mean.

Mercury–Saturn types may be people of few words, who 'speak when they are spoken to' and only when they feel it's safe to do so and they are not going to make a fool of themselves. Above all else, typical Mercury–Saturn wants what they say to be taken seriously and their opinions to be respected.

Conversely, some Mercury–Saturn types seem never to stop talking. Perhaps, it is their way of controlling other people and ensuring that they will be heard. Unfortunately other people often do not listen under such circumstances, feeling talked *at*, rather than talked *to*. When the individual learns that they will be heard, will be listened to, they may not need to dominate the conversation so much. I have had several astrological clients with this contact talk incessantly, partly perhaps because they did need to talk and to be listened to, but partly also because by talking they were controlling me and ensuring that I could not say anything, for somewhere along the line perhaps was the assumption that whatever I might say about them, their lives or their chart would surely be negative. The Mercury–Saturn inclines to thinking the worst; inclines to 'negative thinking' and worrying. Little wonder that this combination is associated with hearing problems; at worst the type expects that what they will hear will be negative and so perhaps blanks it out. This over-talking propensity can be useful though, for it can be a way of helping the individual to define what *they* actually do think.

Many a Mercury–Saturn individual finds that easy everyday chatting, and the usual daily interchange of ideas with others, does not come so easily, but the type does have other gifts to compensate. Mercury–Saturn individuals are often extremely good at logical, systematic thinking, with a rare and quite marked capacity for concentration. This is the individual who can think in patterns and who remembers everything you say. And there is often a tremendous capacity for concentration and an ability to plan, to chew things over carefully. This combination is good for any situation which requires planning or organisation of thoughts or data. It is ideal for those who need to think about form or structure, such as architects and sculptors.

MERCURY–URANUS

Free speech. Radical thought. Original ideas. Sudden understanding. Contrary opinions. Progressive education. Rebellion at school. Unique communication. Speaking the truth.

The combination of these planets can be associated with radical ideas and with individuals whose thinking may be far ahead of their times and usually at variance with their peers. With the hard aspects especially, the views and opinions held may seem very extreme indeed to those with a more cautious or traditional outlook. In some cases, the Mercury–Uranus person may just *say* things that are likely to shock others, just for the sake of having fun or making mischief. For the Mercury–Uranus person, communication can be an act of rebellion and a way of asserting one's uniqueness and independence from the rest of the herd.

On the other hand, this individual is rarely *only* being rebellious. At best, one might say of the Mercury–Uranus individual that they are not circumscribed by the opinions of others or traditionally held views. This is the individual who can arrive at their own opinions and views quite independently. Their regard for 'truth' supersedes any other form of loyalty, even to themselves. At best, the Mercury–Uranus person just cuts through all the hypocrisy, undercurrents and unspoken thoughts in a given situation and just 'tells it as it is', both liberating and shocking others with the exposure. This is the person who can shed new light on a situation by looking at it in a totally new way, the individual who can cut through ambivalence, tradition and fear and suggest a completely different alternative. Thus individuals with these contacts can set people free through what they say and the forthrightness with which they say it. This type really doesn't care if their opinions are popular or not; their only yardstick concerns itself with truth, as they see it.

Some might argue that there is no such thing as 'truth', that truth is always relative, that nothing is what it seems and that the most that any individual may arrive at is, in fact, a *portion* of the truth. In any event, what is truth to one person may not be truth to another. The Mercury–Uranus person, especially with the hard aspects, can be quick to forget these things and have too little regard for the implications of what they say. People with this combination are often good at promoting advanced and liberal thinking but tend to have scant respect for the practicalities or emotional issues of the given situation. Also, it has to be said that whilst the Mercury–Uranus individual sometimes thinks their motives are about revealing a truth that needs to be exposed, the truer, more unconscious motive may simply be that the individual has a strong need to rebel and generally to put a 'spoke in the wheel'. In more extreme cases, the Mercury–Uranus person will say that black is white just to be contrary, or so it will seem to their opponents.

With tight hard aspects in the chart, the individual can often be found stoutly adhering to an opinion or belief, when it is clearly inappropriate and no longer resembles the truth of a situation. Thus it could be said that those with the hard aspects just *have* to test the notion of truth and principle for themselves. The type just seems impelled to prove that they have minds of their own.

This is the person who, if necessary, will ostracise themselves from society for the sake of adhering to a principle. It usually depends which side you are on as to whether the principle might be considered worth it or not. Those with the hard aspects, especially, just will not soften what they say for the sake of ease or popularity. Thus this is an ideal combination for any situation which requires the ability to stick to one's guns in pursuit of shifting outmoded beliefs or ideas. Whilst the type may be extreme and partisan in their views, such an extreme viewpoint might be precisely what is required, from the point of view of changing the consciousness of society.

Those with the hard aspects can have difficulty in communicating, not only because of the extremeness of their views, but because of their outspokenness and brusqueness in expressing them. In communication, the individual often shows a marked inability to co-operative or bend, with respect to what they believe is right. The type is just not good at negotiation and it is to be hoped that Venus might also be strong in the chart to offset this. Thus this is a good combination for any kind of situation that requires a talent for *boycotting*. It might be ideal for trade union leaders and shop stewards for example, those that must not be too eager to reach a compromise situation. And I was amused to discover that

that outspoken cricketer, Geoffrey *Boycott*, has an opposition between these planets.

Charles Carter comments that the hard contacts between these planets are not the most discreet. Perhaps this is because people with these contacts communicate so fast it's difficult for them not just to blurt things out or perhaps it is because the Mercury–Uranus person would prefer to expose a 'truth' than keep a secret or protect someone's feelings. Little wonder that Carter also sees this as potentially a rather unpopular combination; unpopular, too, I think because in holding views that are at odds with the rest of society, the Mercury–Uranus person can find they have no one left to communicate with.

Mercury–Uranus individuals are not usually doomed to being unpopular with everyone though, for the type can exhilarate and excite with what they say and the wit with which they say it. This person will be valued by anyone who has a pretty strong ego and a respect for honesty. For the Mercury–Uranus person is not the type to 'talk behind someone's back' or to express views in order to make them popular. Rather, they just have to make what they think crystal clear (often forgetting that other people might not be interested to learn what their views are). The type seems to find it extremely difficult to live with any kind of ambiguity or intellectual dishonesty.

This combination is often linked with a good memory; indeed Arroyo suggests it might be associated with a photographic memory. Certainly, Mercury–Uranus people are often good at remembering and learning about things that they are interested in, though I suspect that the type may have little facility for those subjects they find boring.

Many intellectual and communicative gifts may be associated with this combination which, with some people, can at times think and process information with lightning speed. The mind is very inventive and intuitive with this combination but just as Jung might remind us, intuition, that lightning flash of realisation, is not always accurate and certainly not consistent. The Mercury–Uranus person with hard aspects may get flashes of inspiration but unless Saturn is also strong, such flashes cannot be relied upon to come to order. The combination is useful for work which involves the use, invention or repair of technological or electronic machinery, such as computers or electrical gadgetry.

On occasion the Mercury–Uranus individual can 'cut out' when thinking or talking. Whilst there can be genius with these contacts, with the hard aspects the insightfulness tends to be erratic. For some, breaks in communication manifest literally as in the individual whose voice breaks whilst talking or the person whose phone disconnects at (seemingly) the most inopportune moment. There may be many reasons for this, but sometimes it can be linked to times when the person, had communication continued, might have had to say something they would rather not have done. Sometimes it is as if the communicative channels have become overloaded and have had to cut out as some kind of safety measure. The combination is prone to great nervous tension so the idea of a safety switch may not be such a bad one, especially since 'disconnection' sometimes occurs seemingly because the person gets so excited that they lose their words or get cut off in mid-sentence. There is often something unusual about the way Mercury–Uranus people communicate and this can be part of their gift.

One of the things that the Mercury–Uranus person usually considers to be very important is freedom of thought and speech. Most positively, these individuals do not just pay lip-service to this notion but genuinely advocate it for everyone, whatever their ideas and beliefs. More negatively though, the only kind of truth to a Mercury–Uranus person is their own and the only opinions worth upholding are their own. Thus freedom of thought and communication is often an issue that gets tested with the hard contacts between these planets. The combination can often be found in people who go to prison for exercising their rights.

As Arroyo says, people with this combination are often 'impatient with the traditional system of formal education'. In fact, Mercury–Uranus types will often be found favouring all forms of progressive teaching methods and usually those that are anti-disciplinarian. Usually there are also strong ideas about the curriculum that should be taught. Rather than upholding the status quo, the average Mercury–Uranus person believes that educative methods should cultivate free thinking and liberal attitudes. These are the individuals who are educated at home or who decide to teach their children themselves. Those, too, whose behaviour can be traced to their rebelling against an early school environment. However, whilst the modern Mercury–Uranus person may be found rebelling against current educational practice, it was probably people with these contacts who were responsible for the availability of free education in the first place. And in parts of the world where free education for all does not exist, it might be Mercury–Uranus types who will fight to have it implemented.

Basically, the purpose of the Mercury–Uranus combination seems to be concerned with changing attitudes in society. How comfortable or useful this may be to others will largely depend on their vantage point and whether they believe that the attitudes that Mercury–Uranus are trying to change actually need changing.

Whilst Mercury–Uranus may be associated with extremist views, such views may be necessary for the implementation of any kind of change of outlook. Those who are more moderate are never likely to revolutionise the way the world thinks.

Bertrand Russell, who was a staunch pacifist and held radical views on religion, morals and education, had a square from Mercury to a Jupiter–Uranus conjunction in the 9th house. In 1950 he won the Nobel Prize for Literature for his writing as 'a defender of humanity and freedom of thought'. He was also at one time imprisoned for insisting on his principles. Other examples include Bette Midler (opposition), well known for shocking her audiences; Freud (conjunction), who revolutionised the world's thinking with his ideas; and Douglas Adams, who wrote *The Hitch-Hiker's Guide to the Galaxy*.

MERCURY–NEPTUNE

Inspiring words. The non-rational mind. Creative composition. Undermining opinions. Distortion of information. Idealisation of facts. Infiltrating the mind of the collective.

The typical Mercury–Neptune person (and by this I especially mean the individual with a conjunction or hard aspect between these planets) has a gift for distorting reality. A distortion which can be highly creative or dangerously misleading. It's a common combination for those who work in the media and, more especially, in the advertising industry. As Martin Freeman so beautifully puts it, for Mercury–Neptune 'the truth is adjustable', and this type has a talent for putting things in the best possible light in the given circumstances. And by the best possible light, I mean the portrayal of something in whatever light is required to effect a subtle change in someone else's way of thinking or feeling, perhaps to undermine their opinions or inspire them in a new direction. This combination may surely be linked with journalism and newspaper reporting. For newspapers not only inspire and inform, they also glamorise information, and often raise gossip and scandal to something of an art-form. Even the most scrupulous reporter who may well aspire to factual information, who may indeed idealise facts, will never be in possession of all the facts, for this would be impossible and not, I suspect, what the public would want anyway. So in presenting the material that they do, there is always going to be an element of distortion. Part of the reason for this distortion may also be because facts are seen as a God at the expense of the inner reality, feelings and meaning of the given situation or personalities. A newspaper story or indeed any fictional story refines a given scenario so that the rough edges are erased and the story can be presented in a more seductive, enchanting but possibly more synthetic way. This is the gift and sometimes the curse of Mercury–Neptune contacts.

Neptune commonly undermines the rational, objective function of Mercury but in return enhances the individual's non-rational perception and ability to communicate, especially non-verbally. Thus the individual often has a gift for images or music. This may be the person who can convey images through words or one who bypasses words altogether and communicates through some other art-form.

Those with the hard aspects often feel easily discouraged about their capacity to express themselves in the written word. Certainly the hard contacts are common in the charts of dyslexic people or in others who have so-called 'learning difficulties'. Commonly things like spelling, map-reading, maths and following formulas don't come easily to the Mercury–Neptune person.

Children with these contacts, especially, do best when they are taught imaginatively and when things are presented in an out-of-the-ordinary kind of way. They need to be inspired. Mercury–Neptune is blessed with a highly imaginative and fertile mind. To attempt to put this into a strait-jacket is sacrilege, for the type needs to be enchanted, needs to have its imagination captured before it can learn. Learning by rote would be anathema and probably not possible anyway. All other things being equal the Mercury–Neptune person is unlikely to appreciate purely factual information in any case, and their whimsical imagination can turn something that started out quite factual into something fast approaching fiction anyway. There really is no strong dividing line between fact and fiction for those with this combination.

The Mercury–Neptune child would prefer the world to be peopled by fairy godmothers and wicked witches and in a way this idea is continued into adult life where there is often a marked tendency for Mercury–Neptune individuals to see others, the Government, their neighbours, whoever, as wholly 'good' or wholly 'bad', distorting the facts to make their particular point. Thus this is a good combination for those involved in any form of *propaganda*.

The Mercury–Neptune individual is not usually the vague, woolly or absent-minded person that might be expected from a combination between these planets, although if Jupiter is also involved in the configuration this can be the case. An example may be found in the chart of the astronomer Patrick Moore, who has a tight T-square between all three of these planets. He is obviously an exceptionally learned man but can seem vague and absent-minded. He is interesting too because he seems to idealise scientific fact, which is another way Mercury–Neptune can manifest, especially with the opposition. His attitude to astrology is well known; he seems to ascribe to the view that it is all fairy-tale nonsense and possibly a way of deluding the masses. Thus it could be said that he projects his Neptune (opposition aspect) onto the astrological fraternity. His strong feelings on the subject though, owe much to the presence of Jupiter in the configuration.

The typical Mercury–Neptune person is exceptionally sensitive to external influences. They can often seemingly *infiltrate* other people's minds. The boundary between their thinking and everyone else's seems very weak. This gives an innate talent not only for psychology but also for a form of what can only be called brainwashing. In the process of infiltrating someone else's mind the Mercury–Neptune person seems capable not only of perceiving what is there and absorbing it for themselves but also of subtly changing it. Hence the linking of these planets to advertising and propaganda.

Part of the learning difficulties of those with this combination arise because these people are so impressionable. The mind is so open to everything that retaining or structuring thoughts or ideas is often felt to be difficult. For holding onto facts for example, usually requires ensuring the mind will not pick up extraneous information. It seems to be the case that for the Mercury–Neptune person everything floods in and it's just not possible to sort out and structure it all. It's rather like a very sensitive radio receiver: it picks up everything but takes subtlety to tune it. It could be said that the Mercury–Neptune person has a talent for fine tuning. Classically this person feels that if they don't write something down or make a list they will lose an idea in a sea of other thoughts. Mercury–Neptune people are always making lists.

Like the radio receiver, in my experience the Mercury–Neptune person misses very little. This is the child who picks up unspoken secrets in the family and lets them out at, from everyone else's point of view, the most inopportune moment.

Those with Mercury–Neptune hard contacts are also often inveterate liars, in childhood anyway. This is the youngster who wreaks havoc by telling a shocking story that sends waves reverberating for miles. Even at a young age, the Mercury–Neptune person exhibits a real understanding and mischievous interest in scandal and gossip. The 'tall stories' seem to leak out of the child's lips almost without conscious effort. They both glamorise the storyteller and often move everyone's attention from some other area which might indeed prove rather trying for the child. And more than that, the child is talked about and that is often the real purpose of this kind of behaviour. Mercury–Neptune people don't only sometimes indulge in talking about other people in a scandalous way but will often be at the forefront of such gossip themselves.

If the Mercury–Neptune youngster is good at telling 'whoppers', stories that have no bearing on concrete reality, those stories nevertheless do contain psychic truth for they will vividly describe the youngster's *internal* reality, and as such must be taken seriously and treated with respect.

Telling lies on a large scale is not likely to be an issue for many Mercury–Neptune adults but there is still often this capacity for *the distortion of information*. A capacity too to convey information by painting pictures through sound or the use of the hands. This is probably the combination of the composer, the lyricist and the poet. Examples abound everywhere: Mozart had the opposition; it's Bob Dylan's only square (and the Mercury is angular); John Lennon had a semi-square, Liszt a sextile.

Music is perhaps *the* language that Mercury–Neptune people can understand. Even on a basic, ordinary level, these people often have great ability to carry a tune. Whilst those with the soft aspects may appreciate and enjoy music, it is those with the hard aspects that are really musical and are often driven to create music in some tangible form.

I have also seen the contact in the charts of people who work in textiles; and more especially with those who portray a story or an image on fabric.

As always, we may associate Neptune with the feeling and yearnings of the collective, with the visual representation of a society mythology. Those with Mercury–Neptune hard contacts are in a prime position to give form, to embody in verbal or non-verbal language this mythology. Thus this is the combination of the composer, the poet, or the creative writer who speaks to us all and subtly changes our perception of the world. Individuals with these contacts need a vehicle for their imagination, perhaps a niche in society where their inspired thoughts and fantasies may find a legitimate outlet. Without this outlet the individuals may be prey to the more destructive elements of Mercury–Neptune contacts, the dabbling in scandal and gossip, finding the self at the centre of such scandal (and thus still embodying some collective need). This may be a potential combination not only of the tabloid press reporter but of the individual who becomes the victim of the gutter press. On a more day-to-day level, it might just be scandal-mongering amongst the neighbours. And in its most negative form we may associate this combination with self-deception and a generalised distortion of anything approaching 'real' truth.

Not everyone with these contacts is going to be able to be the next Mozart or Byron but it is hoped that some creative medium may be found for the Mercury–Neptune's talent on a smaller scale.

The fairy-tale writer Hans Christian Andersen had a sesquiquadrate aspect between these planets, whilst C. G. Jung, who studied and wrote about personal and collective dreams and myths, had the quintile aspect.

MERCURY–PLUTO

Knowledge is power. Power of language. Words can kill. Secret information. The researcher. The poison pen. Sabotage through communication. Society's dark thoughts.

People with Mercury–Pluto aspects often exhibit a compulsive desire to communicate as well as an obsessive desire to know. The Mercury–Pluto type may seek unflinchingly to get to the root of the matter. These people often have a feeling that there are secrets hidden from them that must be ferreted out, perhaps in the interests of their own survival. Mercury–Pluto people are usually very talented at finding out others' secrets whilst they themselves may reveal very little. The compulsive need to communicate is usually quite marked with the conjunction and sometimes the easy aspects. The square, however, seems more likely to block communication and here the person is most likely to keep their thoughts to themselves. This only seems to apply on a personal level. Those with the hard aspects may well talk publicly but be hesitant in revealing things about themselves in a one-to-one situation.

Typically, the type takes little on face value. What people say, do, how life appears to be, appearances in general, have little interest and less value for Mercury–Pluto's intense dislike of superficiality and the glib answer. Knowing what is really going on is a survival mechanism for this type, to whom knowledge is power. It's as if knowing the 'right' answer is the difference between life and death. And perhaps as a child, it really seemed that way, where getting to the bottom of the happenings in one's surroundings was the only way, it was felt, that one's sanity might be preserved.

Knowing the right answer can also occasionally be a statement of the educational upbringing, for the type, like Mercury–Saturn, often has what might be termed an 'intellectual complex'. If knowledge is power then one must seek out the very best of learning. Thus this combination is common in those who have done exceptionally well academically. This also owes much, of course, to the type's highly perceptive mind and interest in the deeper motives and causes of things.

Mercury–Pluto is surely a combination to be associated with the 'poison pen writer' and the satirist. The type has a talent for getting to the root of a matter especially if that situation has murky or smelly depths. This person can sniff out the sordid quicker than most and is often very 'sussed' when it comes to human motivation. Naturally a suspicious soul, it is not easy to pull the wool over the eyes of the Mercury–Pluto person. The problem with the hard aspects can be that the individuals may just be plain suspicious to the point of having a dirty mind, always smelling rats where none exist.

The type tends to be incredibly single-minded and relentless when pursuing a topic, when they have a bee in their bonnet. And as well as ferreting out secrets and often being privy to classified information, the person may be found creating secret information. One might expect the combination to be found in the charts of spies, nuclear scientists and the like. Richard Nixon had a tight opposition between these planets and one only had to think about Watergate so see the significance of the contact. Here was secret information that could potentially kill him. It did so mostly because the whole matter was hushed up. With Mercury–Pluto, words can sabotage; secrets can kill. As a child, the Mercury–Pluto individual was often a repository of secrets within the family, either told in confidence or picked up by the curious youngster who misses nothing.

The contact can be descriptive of powerful orators on the one hand and those virtually unable to communicate on the other. In the latter case, there are usually other strong significators that point to communicative difficulties. Mercury–Pluto's combination can be strong, however. For a start this type can find it hard to put into words the depth of their under-standing. There can also be a fear and even horror of the poisonous thoughts that the individual is capable of thinking and saying, and of the information that is held. One can image the child who has uncovered the family taboos, the skeleton in the cupboard, the child who is stunned into silence and cannot possibly reveal or perhaps fully understand the discovery. Hence, too, the obsessive desire to dig out what is going on in a relentless attempt to understand and protect oneself.

For those with communicative difficulties it's as if the Mercury–Pluto person unconsciously believes that their words can kill. And in some sense, they possibly can, but perhaps that should not matter. The purpose of this combination is surely to expose those things that have remained hidden and never been discussed.

I have know of several cases where Mercury–Pluto has been a prominent aspect in charts where siblings have died and profoundly affected the child's ability to communicate. It's as if such children believe that their words or thoughts have killed their brothers or sisters. Such tragedies also kill someone with whom the child would usually have enjoyed if not easy, then certainly spontaneous, everyday communication. And I have also known cases, involving the 12th house usually, where a child had died or a baby had been miscarried prior to the birth of the Mercury–Pluto child. The youngster may not be told of this but vaguely picks up the fact that something awful has happened in the past; so awful that no one can talk about it.

In one example, where the siblings died during the Mercury–Pluto's childhood, she did not speak for three years (though she was physically capable of doing so). She felt at various times that her words were ugly and deformed, that the sounds she made were awful and that she should therefore not utter any. On some level she felt her own life would be threatened if she did talk. There were other things going on in the family too which she didn't want to be involved in. She found that she had more control over the situation by keeping quite. The family had to fit in with her; she manipulated them through saying nothing. Silence can of course be as powerful a way of communicating as speaking in very strong terms, and the Mercury–Pluto can hone this technique down to a fine art.

The contact can also often be found in charts of people who work with those whose communication is deformed or impaired, or at least those who communicate in ways that are different from the traditional norm. Thus this is a common and excellent combination for speech therapists, music therapists or those who work with the mentally handicapped.

It is common enough too in the charts of comedians (professional and amateur) whose capacity to get to the nub of a matter in a less than flattering way can, metaphorically speaking, knock an audience dead. We often speak of funny people as being 'a killer'; they make us 'die laughing'. Comedians also talk about the taboo subjects of life. They talk about sex, and death and take a wicked view of those in power. They satirise.

Mercury–Pluto contacts are also ideal for readers and writers of detective fiction. For as well as being aware of murky undercurrents, the type is interested in motives and causes.

There is also often an interest in 'taboo' subjects, things that are hidden or at least not talked about or openly expressed such as the occult, sex, death, the nuclear age. The Mercury–Pluto person may be a powerful orator on these or other subjects. Enoch Powell (see page 40) had a tight conjunction between these planets. He was a very forceful communicator. This can be a Mercury–Pluto signature; the individual can express themselves with great power, and perhaps venom, to the extent that they can either overwhelm people, leaving them speechless and unable to counter-attack, or totally convert them so that they do not want to anyway. Often the Mercury–Pluto speaks with such power because they expect resistance and this is particularly the case with the hard aspects. The type expects annihilation for holding the opinions they do. Opinions that others may hold but dare not reveal.

Enoch Powell is a good example of Mercury–Pluto also, because in some of his speeches on immigration, he was surely acting as a mouthpiece for much of the unacknowledged racism in the UK. Occasionally, the Mercury–Pluto person does get themselves into situations where they reveal and express some of the darker thoughts of society at large. Certainly, the Mercury–Pluto person often senses such thoughts.

An interest in etymology (the study of the roots of words) is also suggested by this combination. And sometimes there is an interest in the 'dead' languages such as Latin and Greek. This is also a splendid combination for any kind of researcher or detective. One might also expect it to be useful for the gossip columnist!

CHAPTER NINE

VENUS ASPECTS

VENUS–MARS

The romantic adventurer. Love and competition. Romantic triangles.
Sexual love. Assertion and compromise. Putting energy into beauty.
Fighting for money.

All aspects between these planets are to be found in individuals renowned
for their charm, warmth and personal magnetism. All other things being
equal, these people radiate 'personality'.

With all contacts, Mars seems to give vigour to Venus whilst Venus
softens the Mars principle.

This is also a highly creative combination with, as always, the hard
aspects being the productive ones and likely to be found in the charts of
those who actually *do* something creative whilst the soft aspects often
describe the enjoyment of playing at some creative talent, or appreciative
ability. Not commonly, Venus–Mars interchanges (and I have found this
repeatedly when there is not even a Venus–Mars contact but an emphasis
on the Venus and Mars signs Taurus and Aries in the chart) yield talent
with textiles, fabrics and colour and they can be useful for those who
design and work with cloth. Or for those who sew. One woman I know,
with a tight square between these planets, designs her own fabric, mostly
batik, and makes various cushions, pictures and garments out of silk.

The combination is also found in singers, musicians and actors and
doubtless in many other occupations, although personally, I do not
associate Venus–Mars with art (as in painting) so much as creative, craft-
type pursuits. Presumably this combination is concerned with *doing*
something with that which is beautiful or aesthetically pleasing. One
might also expect artistic competition with this combination; situations
where the individual might have to fight for their art, or their ability to
make money out of that art.

But if the creative talents of Venus–Mars are interesting, the relationships are likely to be even more so, for this combination belongs to the
person who cannot really be happy unless in a warm and loving sexual

relationship. Whilst depending on the sign and house placements to some extent, those with this combination strong often give out very strong sexual vibes. The typical Venus–Mars person is erotic and sensual without even trying. This combination is usually not only particularly interested in, but usually better able to relate to, the opposite sex – possibly because those with the hard aspects, especially, often tend to be competitive with their own sex. Venus–Mars types are rarely on their own for long and falling in love seems to come particularly easy to those with this combination prominently placed in their charts. The much-used cliché about 'loving in haste and repenting at leisure' is often very applicable with the hard aspects especially. The type often marries young and often a childhood sweetheart. In the days when couples having sexual relations 'had' to get married, Venus–Mars was very much a signature of the so-called 'shotgun wedding'. Arguably, society is kinder to Venus–Mars contacts now than it used to be as these conventions no longer apply for most people.

Frequently, those with the hard aspects have an early history where love involved *competition*. There was usually some sort of early fighting for affection in the household, either the parents with each other or the child feeling that they were in competition with one parent for the affection of the other. Commonly, too, one or both parents had a lover outside the marriage, so that those in the home could be said to have been in competition with the lover. That's how Venus–Mars might view it anyway. Sometimes the issue of romantic and sexual competition comes about because the individual is raised in a family where all the offspring are of the same sex and similar age and they end up in competition with each other for girlfriends or boyfriends.

In any event, those with Venus–Mars hard aspects tend to have a vague notion that if they are not careful they are going to miss out on something and end up living life out in the cold, and without a relationship – and for Venus–Mars it would be difficult to imagine a bleaker prospect. So there is often an impulsiveness in Venus–Mars people about getting romantically involved, a tendency to jump in feet first as if in some sort of competition to hook the best lover in the shortest possible time. There is often a belief on the part of the Venus–Mars person that everyone else is after the object of their affections. Often they are. I know of no combination as likely to get itself involved in extramarital affairs and complicated romantic triangles as this one – though it may be their partner that is romantically involved in two places at once.

Amongst other things, such goings on can add spice to life and those with this combination like a bit of zest in their romantic adventures – and adventure is what the Venus–Mars individual thrives on; there is usually an enormous amount of energy invested in romantic and sexual involvements.

For this type, to live and to be truly alive means not merely having a partner but being very emotionally and sexually involved with that person. Gentle companionship and the comforting knowledge that someone is across the breakfast table is not usually enough for the Venus–Mars type, who wants and needs affection, warmth and the true and honest expression of feelings. If the relationship doesn't have this vibrant quality then the individual may well be tempted to look elsewhere in the hope of finding it. If keeping a relationship alive means arguments and plate-throwing, that's fine for the Venus–Mars person. This combination must surely be the significator of the classic love-story scene which starts off as a furious argument but ends up in bed. Love and anger often go together with this combination and people in whose charts it occurs often seem as if they have a very traditional 'battle of the sexes' fairy-story, alive and well, and functioning as a whole package within their own psyche.

The Venus–Mars combination sometimes has a reputation for coarseness but this depends a great deal on the signs involved and the relative strength of the two planets. Certainly Venus–Mars hard aspects especially can lack the social graces and seem to some to be quite crude but this tends to be much more the case when Mars is the stronger planet. Certainly Venus–Mars people tend to be very honest with themselves and others about sexual matters and there is no felt need to sweep things under the carpet. This combination usually has a healthy appreciation of the body and is not squeamish about the kind of things that more genteel and refined types might be turned off by. Basically, the Venus–Mars type is *direct* about relationship. This combination is not easily 'turned off' sexually in the way that other combinations might be.

The conjunction and easy contacts between Venus and Mars usually describe people who have very good social skills, who know when and how to be assertive, and how to be co-operative and sharing without in any way losing their own position. For those with the hard contacts, this often constitutes a challenge in at least some areas of the life and often in close relationships. Classically, those with the hard aspects find themselves being overly assertive when they might do better by being more co-operative or giving way; or they are too accommodating, too passive, when they ought to be going for what they want. Classically too, those with the hard aspects especially tend to confuse love with lust and friendship with passion.

Examples of the Venus–Mars combination include the chart for France, that most romantic country, which has a tight trine between these planets. Katherine Hepburn, the gifted actress, who for many years was in the middle of a romantic triangle with Spencer Tracy and his wife, has a square. Raquel Welch has Venus in the 8th house semi-square Mars. Liz Taylor has Venus in the 5th house semi-square a Mars–Uranus conjunction in the 7th. Hitler had an exact conjunction in Taurus in the 7th, *but square Saturn*. However difficult it might be for us to believe now, it seems clear that women undoubtedly found Hitler very attractive. As a young man, too, he wanted to train as an artist – a romantic, Venusian occupation. Above all else, however, Hitler was a racist. Racism can be defined as a feeling of hostility towards, and because of, what a people are, or more usually *what they are imagined to be*. Freud would say that racial prejudice is misplaced aggression. Many studies have linked sexual repression with prejudice. Thus victims of racism are nearly always accused of all sorts of sexual powers and inclinations. The Jews certainly were, and to my mind this is exactly described by that important square in Hitler's chart. With that conjunction, sexual issues (and in Taurus, particularly issues of sexual *jealousy*) must have been enormous for him, and yet with the square to Saturn he was unable to deal with them. So he pushed his sexual feelings and frustrations down into his unconscious, from where they got projected onto a whole race. The fact that the Jews were also seen as commercially successful, were supposed to have *money* (Venus), was obviously also another major factor. Fighting over money can often be a Venus–Mars preoccupation.

VENUS–JUPITER

Expansive feelings. The good life. Wealth. Valuing meaning. Pleasure is God.

Whatever the actual aspect, individuals with contact between these planets are usually very friendly, amenable, and charming and can cope in most social situations, for here we have expansion, if not exaggeration, of the Venus principle. The typical Venus–Jupiter person thrives on having a full social life and is usually very into have a 'good time'. Even in a quiet type of person, disinclined to wild parties every night, the individual is unlikely to find themselves bereft of company or at a loose end very often.

The problem with the hard aspects is often for the individual to learn where to stop as far as fun, romance, spending money and having a good time is concerned. Especially if reinforced by other factors, this is the contact of the hedonist and the 'lush', sometimes indicating a life of ease, indulgence and shallowness.

Basically the individual feeds on popularity, wanting to be loved by all and to offend no one. Often it seems as if the easiest way for the person to gain this popularity is be something of a 'Jack the Lad' and a jolly good sport, usually an up and coming member of 'right' circles, with respect to the person's age, culture and upbringing. Classically though, the individual with this contact sooner or later discovers that love and popularity gained in this way lack substance and have the ring of falsehood. Sometimes, then, another side of Venus–Jupiter comes into play, that of a valuing of the religious principle, sometimes a love of God, or a love of philosophy and an appreciation and valuing of all that might provide meaning in life. Religious conversations and experiences are by no means uncommon, if there is a tight contact between these planets. Unless there are indications to the contrary, the image of God is seen as merciful, loving and forgiving.

Whilst Venus–Jupiter is nearly always sentimental and sometimes even gushy and false, the type is invariably big-hearted, with feelings that tend to go overboard and generally ooze everywhere. Like Moon–Venus this contact can describe the feeling of 'my cup runneth over with love'. Thus Venus–Jupiter is invariably charitable, loving and generally openhanded to those in need, genuinely getting pleasure out of giving, and in so doing, gaining the secondary reinforcement of increasing personal popularity into the bargain. Because of its propensity to be generous, on all levels, these contacts can be useful in the caring professions.

Often the individual with this combination strong in their charts was materially spoilt in childhood or raised in an atmosphere that has a *laissez-faire* attitude to money, or at best, was philosophical about any lack in this area. Sometimes there was a plethora of relatives ever ready to dip their hands into their pockets. Certainly, with the hard aspects especially, there is often an attitude in later life of 'if I love you I will spoil you and if you love me you will shower me with gifts'. With their warm-heartedness, their love of pleasure and perhaps love of luxury and corresponding aversion to any kind of harshness, it is not surprising that individuals with these contacts often marry money, even if they don't actually marry *for* money (not to mention position and status) which is by no means uncommon. Frequently having married money, the resources are then frittered away, but even with the hard aspects, money seems to arrive from nowhere and the person is not usually destined to live in abject poverty for long, however much they squander their (or their partner's) resources. Whatever the actual financial situations, the individual will often *feel* well off. One can surely associate this combination with wealth, a wealth of feelings and love, and wealth in the material sense.

Perhaps the Venus–Jupiter type could be described as being greedy not only for pleasure but for love. Certainly it often seems as if the individual can't get enough affection and one of the main lessons of this contact is for the individual to learn that love cannot be bought, and nor can inner serenity and self-esteem. *En route* to this philosophy the individual with this contact often has a tendency to view the grass as greener over the other side of the fence, especially where relationships are concerned. Somehow the bird in the hand doesn't look half so appealing as the two in the bush. It could be said that Venus–Jupiter is looking for God in close personal relationships. And when in love, the worth and beauty of the newly beloved gets inflated out of all proportion. So much so that whoever the beloved is, that person is just bound to disappoint. Like Zeus, the Venus–Jupiter type can romp their way through many relationships, happily absolving themselves of responsibilities and donning the cloak of the Don Juan.

Others project their Jupiter and instead, find themselves married to something of a *puer aeternus* – a spirited young thing (in heart if not in body) who, in true Jupiter style, means well but can't cope with being burdened with responsibilities and seems to have a perpetual hole in their pocket. They are extravagant with the self and generous with everyone else, and especially to everyone outside the immediate family.

Venus–Jupiter tends to overvalue appearances. On a personal level this can lead to conceit and vanity (sometimes masking an unconscious uncertainty about one's beauty), and in the choice of partners, tends to make the type attracted to 'successful' people. Often the person with hard aspects is forced by circumstance to learn that 'all that glitters is not gold'.

Venus–Jupiter often forms relationships with people from different cultures or from vastly different backgrounds or belief systems. Sometimes the liaison might be with a teacher or someone else who potentially might enlarge life's experience. Encountering a different religion or philosophy in this way can provide the means for the individual to take more of the outer world into their own personal life, a way for the individual to learn and broaden their experience of life. Sometimes relationships of this type can create difficulties as the individual encounters the problems of reconciling different backgrounds. Nevertheless, this is often part of the purpose of these contacts.

The soft aspects, whilst not so prone to the potentially more extreme manifestations of this combination, still like to enjoy a good social life. This, together with aspirations to live a life of ease, can be strong motivating factors behind the individual's other life-choices.

VENUS–SATURN

Denial of affection. Controlled love. Love and discipline. Serious relationship. Definitions of beauty. Proof of love. Time and money. Love and time.

Tell a Venus–Saturn person that they are wearing something nice and they'll probably blush and say something like 'Oh this old thing … yes, it is nice, I paid 50p for it in a jumble sale.' Or 'Yes, it's a pity it's got a hole in it though.' As might be expected there are strong issues here about self-valuation, especially with respect to one's beauty and, in the case of women, one's 'femininity'. With women especially, there were often very early messages that it was wrong to be vain, that looks didn't matter, and that the child was too plain to bother about it anyway. Sometimes the Venus–Saturn person genuinely doesn't bother about their appearance and cultivates other gifts; often though, they are just as aware of appearance as other people but would hate to be thought of as vain, would hate others to think that they think they are good-looking or even that they consider being attractive an especially important asset. This is usually much more obvious with women, who are more likely to be brought up to be concerned with their appearance.

Many people with Venus in tight hard aspect with Saturn will place more reliance on their Moon. With the Venus road blocked, they will take the Moon road to relationship, either being attracted to lunar types or tending to attract others less by virtue of their physical appearance than by being protective, caring and supportive.

There is usually a history of a childhood where there was little affection generally, and more to the point, no affection from the father-figure. Very commonly too, the father will have been seen as someone who did not value himself, was not loved, or did not receive affection. When questioned, many Venus–Saturn people will say that they don't remember ever sitting on their father's knee, let alone ever having hugs from him. The mother-figure may have been more loving and affectionate but there would usually have been strings attached, together with control and discipline. Hardly surprising therefore, that people (especially with hard contacts and sometimes the conjunction) feel very awkward at giving and especially receiving, love and affection from others. For all that, hugs, kisses and physical displays of affection are often craved, and popularity may be pursued above all else. Usually the demonstration of affection becomes a 'Big Deal' for people with this combination. Either that, or the issue of relationship is avoided altogether, and the importance of it is denied.

For some reason, it seems that those with Venus–Saturn contacts come into the world feeling unloved. For many, it takes years for the penny to drop that the issue is really *self*-valuation. Before that realisation dawns, Venus–Saturn people tend to believe, though not always consciously, that it is others that don't care, others that don't love them.

Saturn will always delay the development of whatever planetary principle it touches, and for Venus–Saturn types it takes time for the individual to learn about giving and receiving – and especially giving and receiving with no strings attached.

There is a line in *King Lear* which goes: 'I think I have observed a faint neglect of late.' Whether King Lear was supposed to have had a Venus–Saturn contact is not clear, but the sentiment fits this aspect configuration very well because these types almost expect rejection and are very sensitive to, nay listen out for, any clues which might herald the fact that the other person's love has waned. And the constant demand for proof of affection or for the other person to continually define their feelings often does put a considerable strain on the relationship, as does the continual saying of 'I'm sorry' which is often very much a Venus–Saturn phrase. The scenario can work both ways. Because of the mechanism of projection, the Venus–Saturn person may be the beloved or the one doing the loving. Typically, in heterosexual relationships at any rate, Venus–Saturn men often find themselves doing all the loving of seemingly cold women and Venus–Saturn women don't allow themselves to return or receive the warm feelings of the male partners. Or they fall in love with unobtainable men. It can work the other way round though, usually, as always, repeating a pattern of childhood. In any event, it takes the Venus–Saturn type a very long time to realise that they are really safe in a relationship and really have won the other person's affection. These people really do relate to the idea that one person in a partnership does the loving whilst the other is the object of that love, and it is one of the lessons for the individual to learn that it is not as simple as that.

The Venus–Saturn person often attempts to make themselves indispensable to their loved ones and especially ever willing to give of their time or their money; and this is how Venus–Saturn controls the relationship.

The issue of love and time is often a very big one with Venus–Saturn. You can tell that a Venus–Saturn person cares for you if they are prepared to give you their time and similarly they use the time-factor as a yardstick of your affection. Lack of time and subsequent denial of affection was often an issue in childhood. For example, and this is a very classic case, I know of one woman whose mother wanted to ensure that she (the child) and the father had no relationship with each other. For reasons of his own, the father colluded with this situation. Thus the Venus–Saturn child was forced by the mother to stay in bed (love and discipline go together with this combination) until after the father had gone to work and was sent to bed before he came home. She never saw him. As she grew older, the father started working away from home and was only seen at the weekends. Having no siblings and more especially no brothers, men were foreign to her. Well into adulthood, she was unconsciously chained to the fact that her mother might be jealous of her if she pursued men and having had no relationship with her father, nor having been brought up with parents who themselves had a loving and physical relationship, she was frightened and ignorant of both men and sexual relationship. She had to learn about relating, or at least romantic relating, later than is considered 'usual'.

Although both sexes with these contacts may 'dress down' and the women will usually go for the natural, 'scrubbed' look, the type may go to the other extreme in an effort to compensate. For example, this combination is common in women who use a great deal of make-up and have a very studied kind of appearance. They take the whole thing very *seriously*. It is common too in the charts of beauty queens and those who enter for such competitions. Those who seek a piece of paper, some kind of definition and proof of their beauty. I always associate Saturn aspects with what might be called the 'formula' response, a response that is given to cover up something and a response that is controlled, contrived and over-the-top. It could be argued that the beauty queen exhibits a controlled response as to her looks, her femininity, and more subtly her sexuality, and this can be interpreted as a form of overcompensation, a frantic covering up of an inner feeling of inadequacy.

Liz Greene has linked the prostitute to the Venus–Saturn combination (some might say that beauty contests are a form of prostitution). This agrees with my own experience except that prostitutes often have a history of sexual abuse and this combination, on its own at any rate, is not one I would link with sexual abuse, at least not on a *physical* level. With prostitution, we can again see the association of time with love and money, all of which are usually intimately linked for people with this combination strongly emphasised in the chart, especially by hard aspect. The prostitute is defined by society as one who is sexually skilled. Issues of denial of love, control and love, and love and punishment are also pertinent here. I have also known several women with this contact whose fathers frequented prostitutes. In the one case the father established a deep emotional relationship with a woman whom he had first consulted on such a professional basis. It was very positive for him for it brought him in touch with his feelings, which hadn't happened for a long time. There are masses of issues here but I will leave these to the reader's imagination.

Often the Venus–Saturn person is scared of love, doesn't believe it is really there for them and that if it is then there is always the possibility of it waning. For some the prospect of this can urge the individual to deny themselves relationship altogether. At worst the person builds a wall around themselves and wails because nobody loves them. And nobody will, because they are not allowed to get close enough. Others manage to maintain a not very happy relationship over a long period but do so because they are too frightened to risk trying to find something better. There is at least a familiarity in the pain of it all.

At best though, the Venus–Saturn person through their understanding of pain and especially loneliness can do much to give love to others. At best too, the Venus–Saturn person will face their need for, and fear of, relationship. Saturn always gives endurance and thus the Venus–Saturn person can describe the one who holds on through thick and thin and through doing so, really does make a relationship work, really does learn to give and take. It is through working at relationship that the Venus–Saturn person discovers that the whole thing is supposed, amongst other things, to be fun and that they have been taking things and themselves far too seriously.

Another offshoot of Venus–Saturn contacts can be that the individual finds it hard to enjoy themselves. Sometimes these people just won't allow themselves to have pleasure and sometimes won't allow themselves to have money. This is the person who undercharges for their work, or works for little pay and then cannot afford to go out. Not going out inhibits the social life and thus a vicious circle is built up.

Saturn always insists that we learn the hard way and those with Venus–Saturn aspects, given time, often do learn about relationship at the very deepest levels. People with these contacts do better *after* the initial attraction and illusion has worn off, for the type is in touch with reality and the difficulties inherent and work required to cultivate and maintain a relationship over a long period of time. Like Venus–Pluto, Venus–Saturn contacts are useful for those who actively work in the beauty industry (for example, Vidal Sassoon has a tight conjunction) or for those for whom love and work and controlled periods of time might be issues. I have met a fair number of therapists and marriage guidance counsellors with this combination. In such professions there are no limits to the love that a counsellor may give or receive; perhaps not limits in an emotional sense, but limits in terms of time and personal boundaries.

VENUS–URANUS

Unconventional relationship. Free love. The valuing of freedom. Honesty in feelings. Unusual appearance. Magnetic attraction.

> First of all, people with Venus–Uranus squares and oppositions are often quite afraid of rejection, quite afraid of being hurt, and they act a little like Venus in Aquarius people – somewhat detached, somewhat aloof. They're very experimental when it comes to love, emotional things, sexual things, but they tend to be very self-centred:
> (Stephen Arroyo, *Relationships and Life Cycles*)

Usually the major task facing the individual with the Venus–Uranus combination strong in their charts is concerned with integrating the need for love and relationship, on the one hand, with a need for space, liberty and independence on the other. Whatever the actual aspect, people with these contacts often radiate lots of sparkle and personal magnetism. People gravitate to Venus–Uranus like moths to a light, for they often have a very electric quality.

In relationships there is a tremendous need for space and freedom and this type is perhaps more likely than any other to advocate the notion of 'open' relationships. Neither are they likely to offended by same-sex relationships or relationships which are usually seen as unconventional or 'different' for some other reason. Marriage lines or binding contracts are not necessarily for this person, who prefers to be sure that both parties are in a relationship because they want to be there. And anyway, the Venus–Uranus person prefers to keep their options open. Commonly, the Venus–Uranus type will choose relationships with people they don't have to be with on a round-the-clock basis. An airline pilot or steward is ideal. As well as the desire for freedom, there is also a strong need for excitement. To keep a Venus–Uranus person interested in the relatioship and, more specifically, in you, you need to be full of surprises. Not coming home at night, once in a while anyway, would be preferable to being overly predictable. The Venus–Uranus person themselves may also be full of surprises – or shocks. The type will nearly always get themselves involved in scenarios where the major battle revolves around the question of personal space. It should not be assumed that the Venus–Uranus person is the one who always takes on the role of insisting upon that space either. Because of the mechanism of 'projection' it can work either way. Men especially are notorious for projecting their Venus–Uranus contacts onto women, falling for women who are in some way unavailable to them, perhaps because of an emotional entanglement elsewhere or an unwillingness to give up their freedom. I know one man with an exact Moon–Venus–Uranus T-square who has had no less than three wives walk out on him. One of the reasons for their speedy exits was that he stubbornly refused to co-operate with them. The idea of meeting someone half-way was quite alien to him. When he used to ring up for an astrological consultation, if I was unavailable at the time most convenient to him, he took it as a personal rebuff. The problem was compounded by the lack of air in his chart which made co-operation even more difficult for him. Now he is living with a woman who works for an airline and is away much of the time. They have both taken up astrology and he talks about how exciting and exhilarating he finds this new relationship.

As in this case, because of the insistence on freedom, those with hard aspects, especially, may find co-operating with others rather difficult. As always, change creates resistance, and Venus–Uranus people may be very resistant to changing and accommodating themselves and therefore the partner is forced to 'move', sometimes quite drastically. Most people fit in with others for the sake of maintaining a certain mount of popularity and goodwill. Classically, the Venus–Uranus type sees this as phoney and rebels against playing, as they see it, those kind of games. Being popular and well-liked takes second place to being 'honest' and different for Venus–Uranus. For all that, Venus–Uranus is not always honest about discussing their own feelings; as Charles Carter says – and this is very much my own experience – the person will 'often refuse to discuss his reasons or motives'.

As with all Uranus contacts, the Venus–Uranus individual can be, as Stephen Arroyo tells us, rather self-centred and wilful. Sometimes they need to be wilful because of the resistance they might meet from the outside world as to their choice of partner, or their choice of dress or appearance generally, for that matter. Princess Margaret is an example of this; she has a 1st house Uranus opposing Venus in the 7th. Her choice of partners has kept the tabloids going for years.

The choice of partner is often an act of rebellion for the Venus–Uranus type. The individual may well be all the more insistent on their choice of partner if that person is likely to shock others. Venus–Uranus relationships might be stormy and erratic but usually they are also electrically exciting. As soon as things get boring one of the partners usually does an exit in some way. As might be expected, the Venus–Uranus type falls in and out of love very suddenly.

The honesty, exhilaration and unconventionality that this type exudes ensures popularity; indeed Venus–Uranus attracts other people by being different. Their popularity is often in what might be termed the 'Alternative' camp. This doesn't worry Venus–Uranus, who never wanted to follow the herd anyway. Often, it seems as if Venus–Uranus doesn't care when the fact is that they are merely unable or unwilling to negotiate the social niceties. In its most extreme form, I have know Venus–Uranus to be quite devoid of manners or courtesy or apparent consideration for others. Frequently the Venus–Uranus person can be seen to be rebelling against everyday social mores.

Those with tight contacts between these planets will nearly always be involved in relationships which others are likely to find very unconventional and (privately) rather exciting. It must be remembered, however, that what is new and different rapidly becomes old hat. Uranus is always a trailblazer for change, and when coupled with Venus the change is being channelled through ways of relating to others. If it wasn't for Venus–Uranus people we would all probably be back in the 1880s as far as relationships are concerned.

Typically, the Venus–Uranus person values friendship and a wider, more humanitarian approach to the traditional ways of relating. This person may make friends with anyone regardless of who they are and where they come from. In fact the more different they are, the more exhilarating is their company likely to be. The Venus–Uranus person values humanitarianism in the same way they value and appreciate people's differences and the right of the individual to freedom on all levels.

It is common to find Venus–Uranus in relationships where there is so much space and freedom, with both partners following their own interests and goals, that the couple grows further and further apart until the time comes when there really is no relationship at all.

Perhaps, as Stephen Arroyo suggests, Venus–Uranus is very sensitive, huffy even, about the prospect of being rejected. Usually there is an early experience of being cut off from someone they loved. In any event, rather like Moon–Uranus, Venus–Uranus often has a vague expectation that affection is going to be sharply turned off at any minute. Perhaps that the partner is going to get involved with someone else. And it is probably these feelings that contribute to a 'one foot in and one foot out' attitude to relating, which some people with these contacts exhibit.

Not uncommonly Venus–Uranus is so cold and seemingly uncaring about the prospect of the partner leaving, that they drive the partner to this course of action. At best Venus–Uranus will be honest about their feelings and will deal with them. At worst and commonly, the type deal with situations where separation is imminent in a brusque and offhand kind of way and as if they don't care. The message the person gives off is: 'Sure, fine, great, hope you have a great time.' In behaving so independently and in so detached a manner, the beloved feels that there is no reason for them to stick around, for they are not needed anyway.

The need for social, emotional and sexual excitement can contribute to drinking and addiction problems, for invariably, the Venus–Uranus person wants the social scene to have a certain amount of excitement and 'buzz' and if other factors in the chart concur, they may go to amazing extremes in search of such excitement.

Usually the Venus–Uranus individual will have a unique way of dressing. The personal style is likely to be highly original and individualistic, though one sometimes encounters very 'straight-looking' Venus–Uranus people whose partners look quite out of the ordinary. For some reason this configuration seems exceptionally prone to a very obvious form of projection.

In artistic and creative fields originality is also likely to be a marked feature. This is the person who will deviate from the classic styles to be expected of them from their upbringing, training or background.

VENUS–NEPTUNE

Romantic love. Love of dreaming. Beautiful music. Clandestine relationships. Fairy-tale romance. Idealised beauty.

I like the fact that he lives in another city and has a steady relationship there – there's no pressures on me. Yes, I'd love something permanent but my concept of the ideal relationship bears no relation to reality. Even when I was young I wanted to marry a sailor.

This quote from a woman with a Venus–Neptune opposition clearly illustrates some of the common issues of this combination and especially that of commitment. Classically, these people are reluctant to commit themselves to any one partnership for they do not want to give up the dream of a relationship that is wonderful, romantic and surely made in heaven.

People with Venus–Neptune contacts are inspired by beauty and peace. Commonly, they do not want to know about ugliness or discord. This applies to art, to music, and to relationships.

The Venus–Neptune individual is invariably very romantic and idealistic about relationship. They are in love – so much so that there can be great difficulty in maintaining interest in, and commitment to, an ordinary person and the rigours and (let's face it) unromanticism of the everyday domestic and habitual living with someone.

Shakespeare tells us that love is blind, and certainly when madly 'in love' we cannot see things clearly. Eventually though, we discover the real other person, warts and all. But Venus–Neptune does not want to discover the warts. When the Venus–Neptune person finds that they are no longer waking up in a emotionally drunken state, they can suffer enormous disillusionment but this rarely lasts for long, for the individual usually manages to weave fantasies around the situation. The disillusionment may be dealt with in several different ways. Sometimes the Venus–Neptune person will somehow retire from the scene, withdrawing to suffer and lick their wounds. Sometimes they will ensure that the partner does. And many more will keep up some sort of pretence of relationship whilst pursuing romantic liaisons elsewhere. One can certainly associate this combination with clandestine relationships.

People with the easy aspects tend to find it easy to accept people and their relationships as they are. They are no less idealistic or romantic than those with the hard aspects but there is less of a need for discrimination. For these individuals have few illusions about people. Sometimes it seems that they can just walk into another's psyche and see what is there.

Those with the hard aspects are not so realistic. Their expectations are just too high for an ordinary mortal relationship. They want to make beautiful music with another person, but forget that during rehearsal the music can sound anything but beautiful. They want so much that it becomes difficult for them to accept anything or anyone that is less than ideal. Sometimes the Venus–Neptune person decides to do without the commitment of forming one romantic relationship. Sometimes they try relationship after relationship, doing a subtle exit when the initial glamour and romanticism has worn off. And sometimes the Venus–Neptune person will pretend that things are all right really.

The type has a poor reputation when it comes to discrimination in their choice of partners. Financial loss through partnership is very common. The combination is famous for believing what it wants to believe. The truth must surely be that the Venus–Neptune person does not *want* to see clearly. The illusion is pleasanter, more romantic and just so much more inspiring. Venus–Neptune people are looking for a mystical experience in their personal relationships, something that is made in heaven. Hardly surprising therefore that this configuration is sometimes found amongst people who follow the religious life, for here relationships really can be made in heaven.

Sometimes the Venus–Neptune person chooses celibacy or a platonic relationship for reasons other than religion. Sometimes, the Venus–Neptune person can be found 'saving' themselves for the right person, especially if Virgo is involved in the configuration. Neptune refines the Venus principle and can do so to such an extent that the individual shuns physical love, seeing it as crass and sordid. Venus–Neptune yearns for a meeting of souls but not necessarily of bodies.

Sometimes, after repeated disappointments, the Venus–Neptune person opts for relationships in fantasy rather than in reality. To the Venus–Neptune person the fantasy *is* the reality.

When I first started practising as an astrologer I was several times caught out by Venus–Neptune clients requesting chart comparisons between them and their partners. 'Caught out' in that I entered into their fantasies only to discover, after further, usually very directive questioning, that they were not actually having a relationship with the object of their desire. It could be said that they were having a relationship, but only with a fantasy and certainly without the other person physically participating in it! Maybe the fantasy would be built on the exchange of a few friendly words or a warm smile. Obviously the fantasy is very important and the fact that a relationship with X is yearned for is interesting and provides fertile ground for the astrologer to explore with the client. Why has the person 'fallen in love' with this particular person? What kind of fantasy does he or she embody? And so on. Sometimes, the Venus–Neptune person will talk wistfully about some long-lost love of many years before. The reality may have been very different from the idealised memory, but who cares? I have even known people to talk about a partner they 'lost' to another, when they hadn't even had a relationship with that person!

The typical Venus–Neptune individual doesn't usually have much problem getting themselves into relationships even though they sometimes choose not to. Their romanticism, yearning for affection and openness to love, renders them very gullible and easily seduced. Similarly the type has an above-average aptitude for infiltrating the affections of others so that they are also very gifted in the role of seducer.

When actually in a relationship, the Venus–Neptune person will often idealise the object of their affections (no doubt to buffer themselves from the pain of the disillusionment that would follow if the reality of the person were to be discovered), even though that individual may not seem worthy, to others at any rate, of that kind of devotion and adulation.

The main problem for this type is surely to establish a relationship based on *equality*. Very often Venus–Neptune will devote themselves to someone whom they unconsciously regard as being either a great deal 'higher' or 'lower' than they are; a god to be worshipped or a victim to be saved. Perhaps it will be someone they can in some way rescue, or sacrifice themselves for, perhaps a victim of some sort, by virtue of sickness, impoverishment or criminality. The Venus–Neptune person will often see themselves as the only one who can truly empathise, understand and save the person. And that may well be true. Venus–Neptune individuals are undoubtedly capable of the most altruistic and selfless forms of love. Tears and love, love and sacrifice, often go together with Venus–Neptune. And these people often have little or no difficulty in inspiring the love and devotion of others. Sometimes they themselves take on the role of 'victim' in order to keep a relationship going or make it possible in the first place.

Sometimes the type falls in love with an artistic, glamorous or spiritual type of person, and very often with someone who is unobtainable. If they are unobtainable, then that will often be part of the reason why the person has fallen for them. The partner may appear glamorous and seem able to lift the individual into a seemingly 'higher' order of reality. Such relationships still often avoid 'real' relationship at the outset, but by entering into them (assuming that this is possible) the Venus–Neptune person is offered the opportunity of making their dream of what an ideal relationship should be, into some sort of reality.

The problem with having a relationship with a Venus–Neptune person is that you often feel as if your partner loves not so much the individual that you are but some image that you vaguely resemble. There is often the nagging feeling that another model would do just as nicely.

Similarly, the Venus–Neptune person will often seek to attract others by embodying a particular image at the expense of revealing the person they really are. People with these contacts often fall in love with people who embody the image of the prince, princess or mermaid, or themselves may attract others by seeming like these mirages. By being poignant, wistful, elusive and alluring, they subtly entice, seduce and fascinate.

Whilst an ideal personal love may be difficult to achieve, an all-embracing, compassionate and caring love for all humanity usually comes easily to the Venus–Neptune type. That is both the good news and the bad news about Venus–Neptune people. They have the rare gift of being able to love everyone whilst often finding personal love with one individual particularly elusive. As the individual becomes more able to accept and value themselves *as they really are*, they usually become more able to accept the totality of someone else and thus the opportunity for the ideal relationship is born. Instead of seeking the ideal in others, they need to find it in themselves. The feelings of universal love, compassion and understanding for others can be channelled into any occupations that require genuine altruism and personal sacrifice. Sometimes this takes the form of working in some sort of caring profession.

Sometimes the individual sacrifices personal love for the sake of pursuing their art and giving pleasure to many.

This is often an extremely creative combination and can be associated with all forms of artistic activity, especially music. Work in the beauty industry or in the media is also a possibility. Venus–Neptune people are inspired not only by love, but by beauty. Sometimes the type can inspire the love of others through their creativity; musical talent or appreciation is almost invariable with these contacts.

Perhaps everyone to some extent has an idealised notion of beauty and a romantic idea of love. The media seduces us into believing that there is such a thing as an ideal body, face or appearance; and especially with respect to women. In reality, few people look like the media image and doubtless would appear synthetic and artificial if they did. But human beings seem to need to have some ideal of beauty, some sort of yearning for perfection, something they can aspire to. Similarly, works of fiction, television drama, and a whole host of other mediums, reinforce the notion of boy meets girl and both live happily ever after. As we know, it is not like this and in reality a lot of people would not want it to be. If it were, it would probably be boring. Neither would this imaginary relationship contribute to our own personal growth, which relationships certainly do, but through those aspects of relating that are difficult, tiresome and painful. Nevertheless there seems to be a need for the fantasy. Just as a fairy-story helps a child unconsciously to make sense of their life, the fantasy keeps us going back for more, and — let's face it — perpetuating the species.

Perhaps it is the role and purpose of the Venus–Neptune person to embody the notion of romantic love or ideal beauty, or any other Venus–Neptune images for us all. For surely they act as the people we project these images onto in the first place. When the individual is consciously able to embody Venus–Neptune in this way and through some creative medium, it usually takes the pressure off their relationships for a vehicle will have been found in which they can express their romanticism.

Creative examples of Venus–Neptune abound everywhere. We might cite Mozart (opposition) and Jane Austen (semi-square). The latter is interesting from the relationship angle, for though she was obviously tremendously romantic, and indeed wrote almost exclusively about relationship, she chose to remain single herself. Jane Fonda also has the square; for many she embodies the 'ideal look', the image of the perfect woman.

Venus–Pluto

The Power of Love. Compulsive affection. Relationships crisis. Transforming appearance. Beauty and power. Money and power.

In relationships, both close personal ones and more casual social interactions, the typical Venus–Pluto person (especially those with the conjunction and hard aspects) often seems to have a horror of being rejected in any way and the individual may be capable of any amount of manoeuvring and scheming to obtain and keep your affection or attention. As Stephen Arroyo says, the Venus–Pluto person can be *emotionally insatiable*, always requiring masses of attention. And this coupled with tremendous charm and an ability to know *just how to please* the other person can lead to exceptional manipulative skills. This would be an extraordinarily useful combination for a diplomat.

The Venus–Pluto person usually has a talent for dealing with people in such a way as to make each person believe that they are the most important person in the world to them. And it might be some time before it dawns on the partner that everyone else having any sort of relationship with the Venus–Pluto individual is also at the receiving end of this kind of treatment.

Whilst on many levels, the Venus–Pluto person has a very poor self-image when it comes to how they feel others might view them, on another level, the Venus–Pluto person will often not be able to bring themselves to a point where they are able to accept that the other party is just not interested. Classically the type is just not able to let go. It is not always that the Venus–Pluto individual is necessarily that interested in the other person. It seems much more to be an inner compulsion to conquer another's affection – a compulsion to own that person, body and soul, or at least to ensure that nobody else does. Intense feelings of jealousy and possessiveness are commonplace for the Venus–Pluto type, especially if the signs Taurus, Cancer, Leo or Scorpio are involved in the configuration.

The Venus–Pluto person may eagerly become involved in tense, highly charged relationships, in fact seem driven to establishing such liaisons. Or they may be just too frightened and, like Venus–Neptune or Venus–Uranus, avoid the issue altogether.

There is a need to love intensely with this combination. This is the person who might say, 'If we love each other we must be prepared to die for each other.' There is often a strong dramatic element to the romantic life of the type. Only the deepest most profound type of relationship will do for the Venus–Pluto person, and yet with the hard aspects especially, there is often great fear attached to the prospect of such a relationship. It's as if the person feels that the emotional expenditure will in fact kill them. Some deal with this by avoiding the pain of commitment and tightly controlling those with whom they come into contact, ensuring that friends, or family remain interested but keeping them at arm's length at the same time. Typically, the Venus–Pluto person can overwhelm with charm and intensity to such an extent that it is impossible to reject them.

For many with the hard aspects who do take the emotional plunge, their deeper feelings of unloveableness seem to hurtle them into relationships which are tortuous, messy and deeply painful. Often the partner is unavailable for reasons of distance, emotional unavailability, or an entanglement elsewhere. Like Venus–Mars, Venus–Pluto people often get themselves involved in messy romantic triangles. But whereas a Venus–Mars person may do this to add a little spice and excitement to the love-life, the Venus–Pluto person seems to do so because of the pain of commitment. This combination can often be associated with 'unrequited love', with the individual becoming passionately and obsessively in love with another person who, for whatever reason, is unavailable. In these and in triangular situations the Venus–Pluto person can seem to demand the presence of the other person, without having to contemplate what it would be like in reality to be with that individual on a full-time basis. The Venus–Pluto person often seems to need deeply intense but quite short bursts of relating. In truth, that kind of intensity cannot be kept up for long periods.

As has been said, the Venus–Pluto type can be intensely jealous when the object of their affections shows the slightest sign of letting their attention stray elsewhere, sometimes even momentarily. This needn't be obvious, as always Pluto operates in the most covert and underhand way. And it can work both ways with the Venus–Pluto individual driving the partner into a frenzy of desire.

The sexual needs are often very strong with the hard aspects especially, and it is often this that drives the individual into such seemingly ruthless behaviour. Those with the hard aspects seem to need to constantly test their sexual power over others and are often not too concerned about what taboos have to be broken in order to do this. The greater the taboo, the more proof there is of their desirability.

The Venus–Pluto type often quite routinely gives off sexual vibes, even in non-sexual situations. The individual will usually have learnt to do this at quite an early age. Often it was the only power that the child felt they had. Childhood sexual abuse is by no means uncommon and it is from such situations that the child learns about the power of sex and that it may have nothing to do with feelings of love.

At best, the Venus–Pluto type is not frightened of what might be termed 'real' relationship. They can cope more than most with the crises that inevitably occur in relationships. In fact they not only cope but will often precipitate emotional and dramatic outbursts of emotion. This can be a problem, for the Venus–Pluto person can be exhausting in their insistence on getting to the bottom of every Why and Wherefore of the relationship.

At best, Venus–Pluto relationships may be painful simply because the individual does insist on real relationship and refuses to pretend that whatever problems do exist aren't actually there. This unflinching courage and honesty can indeed raise the art of relating to a completely different level. It is surely Venus–Pluto people who really can transform themselves and their partners from frogs into princes and princesses.

Individuals with strong contacts between these planets are often obsessed with appearance and especially their own appearance, as if they believe that their beauty is their only power. This can take many forms; the contact may occur in those who are always beautifully dressed but also often occurs with the person whose clothes would not perhaps generally be considered beautiful or tasteful by the general populous but who nevertheless chooses to dress that way because it makes some sort of strong statement about the person they are. More to the point, it often makes them difficult to ignore.

The Venus–Pluto person is usually brilliant at jumbles sales, for often they have a talent for being able to 'regenerate dead clothes'. The articles of adornment that others have discarded, Venus–Pluto can pick up, possibly transform, and certainly make their own. Some Venus–Pluto often have a phenomenal talent for 'making do', a very useful talent for those forced to live on a shoestring. Even those not driven to making economies will still often wear old clothes and often in the most staggering way.

A contact between these planets is also often found in make-up artists, whose work involves the transformation of a person's appearance. It is common too in hairdressers, cosmetic surgeons and beauticians, those who recognise the power of appearance and can satisfy their own needs for power by making someone else feel more beautiful and valued.

Money is also power to Venus–Pluto; it represents the power to buy beautiful things, and to make oneself beautiful, and if one is beautiful then surely one is also going to be valued and loved.

In various guises, the Venus–Pluto person often attempts, usually successfully, to 'buy affection'. Inevitably Venus–Pluto people are attracted to those with money and power. This can be quite an avaricious combination. Venus–Pluto people who themselves have money will often use that as a source of power. It may be a Venus–Pluto person who steps in to lend you money when you are broke, seemingly a generous gesture but also a good way of maintaining power over you. Conversely Venus–Pluto is rarely extravagant, for if money is power, there is often a feeling that it must be conserved and preserved. There is rarely a *laissez-faire* attitude about possessions. Some Venus–Pluto people hold out on paying money that they owe until the very last minute, and that again seems to be a way of ensuring that a link remains between them and the other person.

As always, especially with the hard aspects, the problem is usually to do with 'letting go'. The Venus–Pluto individual needs to trust that another person will really love them – and *all* of them, not just their beauty, their sex-appeal, their power or their money. The lesson for the type is often to learn to risk giving the other person enough space to find out if they really do care, enough space to discover if they will hang around even if they don't have to.

CHAPTER TEN

MARS ASPECTS

MARS–JUPITER

The Holy Crusader. Fighting for beliefs. Attacking beliefs. Getting into hot water. Sexual romping. Promotion. Free enterprise. Horseplay.

One can associate any combination of these planets as being concerned with fighting *for* one's beliefs, and, inevitably, fighting *against* the beliefs of others. The beliefs can take any form but commonly there will be strong religious and/or political convictions. The individual can often be found in some cause seemingly fighting for or on behalf of God, and I am reminded of the hymn 'Onward Christian Soldiers' and the idea of 'The Holy Crusader' in this regard. This really is the combination of the crusader and the campaigner in some sort of cause. I suspect those with the square especially, may fight too strongly for their beliefs because it would be just too painful to face their doubts. Perhaps the shadow side of Mars–Jupiter is *doubt* – something that few with these contacts strongly placed have the humility to face.

The contact can equally be found in the charts of individuals who may be found battling against religion, faith, God. An example of this is Vera Brittain who amongst other things was a devout atheist and was also a great peace campaigner.

Whilst these contacts can be found in the charts of anti-violence campaigners it is as commonly found in the charts of those who actually engage in warfare. The oppositions tend to be violently (!) against fighting, and the other aspects are more likely to find themselves in potential fighting situations or at least glorifying heroism and patriotism. Mars–Jupiter implies the idea of fighting abroad as well as adventuring overseas. Every woman I have ever met who has joined the forces in peacetime has had strong contacts between these planets. It doesn't necessarily seem to apply to men, who perhaps join up for different reasons. A good example of a Mars–Jupiter person is Spike Milligan who has a tight trine between these planets and who is well known for, amongst other things, his humorous books on his wartime experiences.

Mars–Jupiter can often be found to be espousing a cause which seems to be being fought on behalf of a higher authority, such as having to fight for one's country or one's God, and being involved in such a cause may well be as suitable a vehicle as any for using, in the case of the hard aspects, the excessive enthusiasm and courage to be found with this combination.

There is great enthusiasm with these contacts, an enthusiasm to assert oneself, to grow, and to explore, coupled with great talent for inspiring others, and imbuing them with faith, confidence and enthusiasm.

The major problem with Mars–Jupiter hard aspects, and sometimes the conjunction too, is the tendency to get overly carried away, a tendency to *overpromote* the idea, ideal or product. Clearly this is a very useful contact where an ability to be able to promote something is required, and it is often found in people who work in sales-type occupations. But in situations where being able to sell something is not a requirement the individual can come across far too strong in espousing their beliefs and sometimes run the risk of 'putting other people's backs up'.

In his book on accidents, Charles Carter associates Mars–Jupiter with scalds, and perhaps this physical manifestation is hardly surprising, for this combination can be associated with the notion of *getting oneself into hot water*, on all sorts of different levels. This can be a very adventurous combination in all sorts of different areas of life and in the bedroom as much as anywhere else. I am reminded of the old Brian Rix farces, where there was lots of horseplay, slapstick and half a dozen characters, often half dressed, engaged in complicated rushing between bedrooms to meet and avoid certain partners.

In mythology, Zeus romped his way through many a sexual adventure, leaving behind his jealous wife Hera, who involved herself in the occasional rather half-hearted infidelity in a bid to make Zeus jealous. In his way, Zeus was faithful to her, although he was forever jumping from one sexual adventure to another. Like Zeus, Mars–Jupiter people need lots of space to explore sexuality, as indeed in most other areas of their lives. Monogamy doesn't come easily to the typical Mars–Jupiter type, although the contact is as common with those who play the part of Hera in their relationships as with those who play the part of Zeus. One is again reminded of the mechanism of projection here, and also of the fact that when Zeus was out philandering he was giving Hera quite a bit of time to explore her own interests, which might well have been some compensation for her. The Mars–Jupiter person needs space in order to grow.

In all sorts of areas of life Mars–Jupiter can tend to get carried away, indeed sometimes it seems they believe they can get away with anything (and because they believe it is so they usually do) and they get themselves into hot water simply because they over-extend themselves. Too easily taking more and more on, becoming careless and eventually taking on just too much. One hopes for a strong Saturn in the chart to offset the potential dangers of a hard Mars–Jupiter contact.

This Mars–Jupiter person is usually an adventurous sort, happy to take risks. This individual might be interpreted by some as courageous and by others as foolhardy.

The soft aspects are not potentially so dangerous as the conjunction and the hard aspects, for the soft aspects incline to acting wisely, whilst the hard aspects especially suggest that impatience and impulsiveness can get in the way of the taking of wise action.

The company Townsend Thoresen, owner of the fated *Herald of Free Enterprise* which sank off Zeebrugge, has a tight angular Mars–Jupiter square. This company, established in the 1920s, has a reputation for being very competitive. It has consistently bought out smaller companies, becoming a large fish ever opening its jaws to smaller fish. Various accidents that have befallen the company as well as the sinking of the *Herald of Free Enterprise*, which occurred when this square was triggered, might be interpreted as the result of a more negative manifestation of a Mars–Jupiter square. Even the name *Free Enterprise* is very Mars–Jupiter for if those with this combination believe in anything, it surely is the principle of 'free enterprise'. Margaret Thatcher herself has a square between these planets.

Another example of a Mars–Jupiter contact can be found in the chart for Salman Rushdie, author of *The Satanic Verses*, who has an opposition between these planets.

Despite some of its more dangerous possibilities, the Mars–Jupiter combination is a useful one for anybody who has to embark on large projects, for it yields tremendous energy and zeal, and a real spirit of adventure. It's a good combination for sport, religion or politics.

MARS–SATURN

Fear of fighting. Fighting for or against authority. Fear of competition. Tests of strength and courage. Domination, stamina, endurance. Sexual control. Hard labour. Heavy metal.

As with all aspects, Mars–Saturn contacts can manifest in a wide variety of different ways. However, I think that it is safe to say with all contacts that individuals with this combination strong in their charts will consciously or unconsciously gravitate towards situations where their capacity for strength, endurance and stamina will be tested and stretched – sometimes to near breaking-point. Those situations which require that endurance may be physical, emotional or mental, depending on all other chart factors.

All contacts between Mars and Saturn suggest that the individual has to integrate seemingly alien energies: fear with courage; assertion with control; impulse with discipline.

The conjunction and hard contacts especially, have long been associated with, on the one hand, paralysis of the individual's will and an inability to assert the self with, on the other, the application of extreme self-will, courage, and possibly aggressive domination. Personally, I suspect that the more violent manifestations of Mars–Saturn occur when Venus in the horoscope is difficult for the individual to access.

The Mars–Saturn person will often find themselves fighting on behalf of some authority, as for example in the forces, or waging war against those in authority. Conflicts with authority-figures can inevitably be traced to childhood battles or situations where the child felt that their will was thwarted.

The Mars–Saturn individual may get themselves into situations where they are the scapegoat, the whipping boy, the person who is dominated. Or they may find themselves as the individual who holds the whip-hand. In any event, this combination speaks of life lessons that are concerned with contacting one's own inner authority and thus not needing to dominate and control others or be dominated and controlled by them. Inevitably, individuals with these contacts will find themselves in situations where some sort of control and discipline has to be implemented – the schoolteacher in an unruly class for example.

In authority or not, the Mars–Saturn person often finds it difficult to get angry, difficult to assert themselves, to go for what they want, *without going too far*. Like Mars–Pluto, Mars–Saturn can suffer with great rage that they don't know what to do with. Frequently they will have been told at an early age that it is wrong to lose their temper, or not so much that it is wrong but that it is useless to do so. Nevertheless, once aroused Mars–Saturn can fly into the most terrific rages. It's as if all the unexpressed hurts, angers and irritations get saved up. The person has controlled their temper for so long that when they *do* get mad they really let rip, though usually only when it is safe to do so, perhaps in the presence of, or directed towards, seemingly weaker individuals who are unlikely to retaliate.

Mars–Saturn can be an exceptionally courageous combination. Those with the square especially are usually frightened that they lack courage and have to put themselves to the test. The individual will only discover their courage after they have faced their own fear. It's the same with competition; the Mars–Saturn type is often frightened of competition, and they take competitive situations far too seriously. Presumably therefore, they are also frightened of not winning. This can mean that the individual avoids any situation which might involve their engaging in competition with someone, or even with themselves. Or they will continuously get themselves into competitive situations where their ability to win is constantly being tested, challenged and stretched. Typically, women will take the first option and men the second, but this is not necessarily the case.

One way for Mars–Saturn individuals to use these contacts is to get themselves consciously involved in such situations which require the testing of strength. Through doing so the individual is forced to face their fears of failure and impotence. The tragedy of Mars–Saturn occurs when the fear of challenging and not winning, the fear of not succeeding, is allowed to stifle the impulse to dare, the impulse to initiate, confront and compete.

As best, Mars–Saturn describes cautious daring and the ability to control and direct the will so that the achievement of great things becomes possible. The combination is good for those situations that require discipline, courage, endurance, organisation and control. There is no time-wastage with Mars–Saturn energy. Sometimes individuals with this combination strong can direct each moment towards the accomplishment of whatever project they are engaged in.

Subjecting the self to enormous physical tests of strength is a common manifestation of Mars–Saturn hard contacts and sometimes finds a vehicle in the working life as in the welder, the miner, the blacksmith, the mountaineer, the engineer, the person who works with 'heavy metal'. Or the person who engages in superhuman sporting challenges. This is a very good combination for sport. Saturn touching Mars will often crave to be the first, the strongest or the bravest and, more than that, needs to be seen as such.

The Mars–Saturn combination has long been associated with violence, either given or received, and whilst this is not the usual manifestation, it is by no means uncommon. The reasons for the association are not hard to find. Firstly, the classic Mars–Saturn type is frightened of being a coward, and is usually frightened of violence generally, their own and other people's. Sometimes there is a strong personal history which lies at the foundation of this fear. The trepidation can have several different outcomes. The person may try to ensure that they do not get themselves into vulnerable situations. But not challenging, they hope to avoid being challenged by others. This approach renders the individual quite passive and impotent. Or sometimes the person overcompensates and in attempting to prove to themselves that they are able to defend themselves, they can go totally overboard, flying into the most amazing rage (or more likely feeling like doing so; Mars with Saturn can have tremendous control over the will) whenever their will is thwarted. Also, years and years of frustration can just build up into anger which is so great that it has to find an outlet.

Usually this kind of rage goes right back to childhood and is a response to abuse (physical or sexual) that the individual as a child may have suffered. The child, by virtue of age, limited strength and size, had no resources to resist or fight back. Such a childhood can have several repercussions. One can be that as an adult the individual becomes determined to be stronger than anyone else; the prize-fighter or the war hero, for example, who not only wants their strength and courage defined by the outer world (perhaps in the shape of medals and trophies) but challenges others to test that strength. Sometimes, in the face of an abusive history or merely a childhood where the child felt thwarted, the youngster learns early on that they are powerless and in adulthood remains too frightened to discover whether they actually are.

Women especially are likely to take this passive route, for society reinforces this as the way a woman should be. Women with hard aspects especially between these planets often fear men and fear the masculine principle within themselves. I have known many women with these contacts (I am not convinced that the 'easy' aspects are immune) to become involved with harsh, rough or brutal men who have been violent or at least thoroughly dominated them. Inevitably, this kind of scenario is more common where there has been a history of previous abuse in childhood. The woman has low self-esteem. On some level she believes unconsciously that if she were good/nice/beautiful then she would not have been abused in the way she was, and that therefore she must deserve that abuse. She feels impotent. She learnt early on that she did not have the strength to cope. She perhaps gives out secret messages that she is vulnerable and thus her own unexpressed and unacknowledged rage comes back to her from an eternal source. Ironically, for reasons already stated, the perpetrator of the violence may themselves have difficult Mars–Saturn contacts. Like attracts like, as homoeopaths would say. Not surprisingly, therefore, Mars–Saturn has been isolated by many astrologers as the combination to be associated with masochism and sadism. The Marquis de Sade himself had Venus conjunct Mars tightly squaring Saturn, the same combination as Hitler. But to illustrate the potential usefulness of this combination, perhaps it should also be pointed out that Albert Schweitzer also had a tight square between these planets as part of a grand cross with Uranus and Pluto.

Sometimes, the violent individual can often be seen to have great control over their temper outside those brief moments of blind rage. This is very much a Mars–Saturn hallmark, a blowing hot and cold with respect to one's anger and also one's sexual impulses.

Hitler himself suffered at the hands of a cruel and harsh father and some individuals with the hard aspects especially do suffer a similar fate. The violent father with these contacts also has problems with assertion and classically dare not assert himself with anyone who is his equal in strength. So like all bullies, he unconsciously selects the weakest victims:

his woman partner or his child. Usually he would have been abused himself in childhood.

More often the father-figure embodies the qualities of the two planets by being very hardworking. He may be a harsh, rough, violent kind of man but equally he may work in a trade which is harsh, heavy and rough or be engaged in some other occupation which demands tremendous stamina. Gardening, mountaineering, labouring. Commonly he would have been in the army. He may also have been a gentle man who was unable to express his own anger and frustration but kept tight control over it.

Having looked at some of the unpleasant manifestations of Mars–Saturn contacts, perhaps the fact should be underlined that this combination does not always give rise to violence and many people with these contacts suffer no abuse whatsoever in childhood. As always, the astrologer has to look at the whole chart. There are many more ways than one in which a configuration can manifest. Nevertheless, the conjunction and hard aspects especially may describe a more covert atmosphere in the home that the child plugged into. An atmosphere of suppressed rage perhaps or suppressed sexual energy. People with difficult Mars–Saturn contacts frequently have parents who don't sleep together and the child often picks up vague sexual fears and tensions in the home. The child may inherit the feeling that physical love-making is bad and sometimes comes to associate the sexual act with domination by one partner over the other. Very frequently, there is an early thwarting or denial of sexual curiosity and experience.

For Mars–Saturn the sexual act and control go together and where there is fear that physical love-making involves domination, that domination may be experienced as deeply satisfying or intensely frightening, depending on the individual – sometimes both. For some, feelings of sexual inadequacy propel the individual into being something of a sexual athlete, the lover with amazing staying-power but less talent perhaps with the softer more gentle side of love-making. More positively, where we find Saturn is often where we learn the hard way and where we really do learn through personal experience. Mars–Saturn people may well become an authority on sexual matters and an authority on Martian matters generally. People interested in kundalini yoga, for example, which involves control of sexual energy, often have Mars–Saturn hard contacts. Yoga generally is probably good for Mars–Saturn because yogic practices emphasise controlling but not forcing the body.

The fear of domination looms large for Mars–Saturn people of both sexes, which is why some individuals get themselves into situations where they can dominate others. Commonly individuals with these contacts choose partners who are in some way weaker than they are. Partners who are not going to pose a threat, are not going to compete. The perceived threat will depend on the sign and house of the planets and the person's history but it need not be physical. The perceived threat could, for example, be intellectual, emotional or even related to an individual's earning potential.

Depression is known as the common cold of mental illness and both conditions can be associated with Mars–Saturn contacts. Unexpressed anger and feelings of impotence are invariably at the root of Mars–Saturn depression. Frequently that anger is with early authority-figures.

The cure is often to 'do' consciously whatever the Martian energy in the chart indicates, as well as acknowledging the unexpressed anger. Whatever the possible difficulties, the Mars–Saturn individual has many potential strengths. Commonly, Saturn will caution and control the Martian impulse to fight, assert and win. And Saturn will provide Mars with staying-power. In any situation which requires strength, force or courage, a Mars–Saturn individual is positively required, for this person can keep going long after others have fallen by the wayside.

MARS–URANUS

Originality in action. Decisive action. Precipitate action. Sexual excitement. Sudden violence. Electrical fires. Fireworks. Freedom-fighters. Revolutionaries.

Typically, the person with a prominent Mars–Uranus contact seems hyperactive, and as if they are living off a highly strung nervous system. This can be the person who just never seems to stop. Sometimes the physical energy comes and goes in fits and starts as the individual grows older but mentally the dynamism remains, especially if any of the Mercurial signs or houses are implicated.

People with this contact not only tend to know what they want but also the fastest route towards attaining it. This is the person who can't wait and won't wait, the pedestrian who has little use for level crossings or traffic lights but crosses the road wherever they happen to be.

This is a very decisive combination, and having decided, Mars–Uranus will usually let nothing stand in their way. Those with the hard aspects especially can be very impatient, and not only impatient but sometimes frantically wilful and stubborn too, although these traits are usually 'softened' by other factors in the chart, especially if accommodating and co-operative Venus is also prominent. And the soft aspects are not nearly as wilful and the manifestations are rarely so dramatic.

Whilst often productive of great extremism, this is nevertheless an extremely useful contact to have in any situation which requires decisive and immediate action. And Mars–Uranus is not merely decisive but resourceful too. Those with this combination strong often have great talent for getting themselves out of tight corners and they are often highly original as to the way they go about doing things.

Mars–Uranus has a reputation for being accident-prone especially where accidents are the result of taking precipitous action, or the needless taking of risks, and failure to heed rules and take precautions. As a rule, the Mars–Uranus person is in too much of a hurry to pay any attention to safety and too wilful to listen to anyone else's opinions or warning cries. So accidents can occur and inevitably they will happen very suddenly and often rather dramatically, involving perhaps knives, or other weapons, metals or sharp tools. Perhaps electricity. Fires, especially fires, seem to be signified by Mars–Uranus too. This is a common contact in the charts of those in the fire brigade and is present (a tight conjunction square the Moon, the significator of food) in the chart of the only fire-eater I know of. Mars–Uranus must also surely be a significator of fireworks and of sudden outbursts of violence generally. J.F. Kennedy, who of course died after receiving a sudden gun shot wound, had a Mars–Uranus conjunction in his 8th house.

If either Mars or Uranus are significators of work in the individual's chart, then that work will often involve sharp instruments such as cutting tools. In fact Mars–Uranus people are often quite at home with machinery or gadgets and good at fixing appliances when they go wrong. It's not necessarily that Mars–Uranus knows how the thing works, so much as the fact that they have no reluctance to take a risk (if it occurs to Mars–Uranus that they might make the thing worse, they won't let this thought hinder them) and often these people have a kind of intuitive rapport with machinery. And anyway, taking something to be mended at a proper repair shop takes so long. Some people, however, usually with the hard aspects, seem to have machinery, especially electrical machinery, forever cutting out on them, as if their own electricity is getting in the way of the circuit. I suspect that this might also be attributable to the extreme impatience of the type.

Mars–Uranus is a great contact for getting people going, inspiring others into action and, sometimes, into trouble. 'Come on, come quickly, this is exciting' is the war-cry of Mars–Uranus, who themselves might be the first to respond to such a plea.

'Come quickly' can also be a sexual statement for Mars–Uranus too, for these people seem to need and have a talent for generating great sexual excitement, the only problem being difficulty in staying the course. For Mars–Uranus may get tired of you as soon as they have discovered that you are (to them) as boring as everyone else. Women with this contact are especially prone to living out their Mars–Uranus aspects by getting involved with 'exciting' men, rendered exciting perhaps by their fast-paced life-style, or possibly by their tendency to live on knife-edge dangerous situations. Men who risk doing damage to themselves (or others) on an almost daily basis. Like Venus–Uranus, Mars–Uranus seems especially prone to projection. I have known quite a few women with these contacts who have not exhibited any of the behaviour usually attributable to Mars–Uranus but their partners most certainly have.

Basically Mars–Uranus positively thrives on excitement and danger and this needn't necessarily be as negative or as violent as it sounds. I know one woman whose Mars–Uranus square involves her 8th house and who works as a Sister on a recovery ward in a hospital. She tends patients who have just left the operating theatre after surgery. Her work, unlike any other form of nursing, involves no routine (routine is usually anathema to a strongly Mars–Uranus person) but calls for the immediate making of life-or-death decisions coupled with the ability to carry them out with speed. It could be said that her work involves dicing with death on a daily basis. She was also instrumental in setting up the unit, one of the first in the country and rather a progressive move, which also sounds fairly Mars–Uranus. Interestingly, Ebertin associates this combination with surgery. Given that both Mars and Uranus have a very cutting quality, this may not be surprising. Operations (and accidents) also of course involve the sudden release of blood (of which Mars is the significator).

I heard the astrologer Dennis Elwell in a lecture once associate Mars–Uranus with 'flashers' and this set me thinking. Obviously Mars–Uranus is a fairly common combination and sexual flashers are not, as far as I know, that common. Certainly the typical Mars–Uranus person has the urge, as has been said, to generate and receive a great deal of sexual excitement. Perhaps most Mars–Uranus people flash their sexuality around in ways other than by 'flashing' in the popular sense. The Mars–Uranus individual is very quick to take their clothes off. Perhaps this is a common combination in nudist colonies? Anyway, this must surely be a good combination for the model and the stripper, those who, amongst others things, trade in sexual excitement and in the case of the stripper especially, those who are quite happy to flout convention. For Mars–Uranus classically does like to flout convention in a variety of different ways and is impatient with social mores and well able to point out the inconsistencies and hypocrisy in society's sexual values.

Acting in its purest form, unfettered by other factors in the chart Mars–Uranus will say: 'This is what I am going to do ... damn you if you don't like it.' Classically, the Mars–Uranus person hates and ignores any kind of constraint. Little wonder then that Mars–Uranus is a contact often to be found in the charts of those who pursue an unconventional or alternative sexual life, for at best, the Mars–Uranus individual has the courage to pursue whatever path they choose, sexual or otherwise.

The Mars–Uranus hankering for speed sometimes reveals itself in a love of fast cars or motor bikes, or in any form of racing. To Mars–Uranus, speed is not frightening but exhilarating.

This is also a good combination for fighting on behalf of humanitarian issues. Fighting for progress. A good combination for anything that requires the pushing forward of some sort of reform. One might expect it to be a prominent combination in those active in the Trade Union movement. And perhaps at a more extreme level, freedom-fighters, mercenaries and revolutionaries. Like the typical revolutionary, Mars–Uranus tends to want action and change *now*. It's good too for flag-waving about reforms that might relate to sexual matters. Sometimes drastically so, for one might expect the combination to be the significator of sex-change. Like Venus–Uranus but perhaps even more so, Mars–Uranus is a good significator for the continually changing and – one hopes – progressing sexual mores of society.

MARS–NEPTUNE

Victims of violence. The illusion of strength. Fighting on behalf of the underdog. Passive aggression. Putting ideals into practice. Seduction. Sexual fantasies.

Just as Venus–Neptune may be associated with a glamorised, sometimes rather synthetic media image of the feminine, so may Mars–Neptune aspects be associated with the pin-up male or the fairy-tale prince. An image that, like the Venus–Neptune one of women, is perhaps designed to ensure the continuance of romantic love and the perpetuation of the species.

Thus it is not surprising perhaps that Stephen Arroyo has linked this combination to particularly charismatic actors and sports personalities.

Drama and sporting activities certainly do provide an excellent way of using the hard aspects between these planets. Anyone with a strong Neptune in their chart may have a need to embody, or find themselves propelled into embodying, the dreams, fantasies, feelings and yearnings of all of society. When coupled with Mars, it is often through sporting or other Martian activities or by embodying society's sexual fantasies in some way, that the individual is able to do so. The combination is to be found in all glamorised hero situations and especially those that might involve some kind of fighting for some ideal. On a literal physical level, one imagines fighting at sea; and the contacts can indeed be found in those who join the navy or the marines. Inevitably we all project our aspects onto others and it is surprising how many with these contacts do literally become involved with sailors!

This combination can also be found in all sports situations and especially those that appear glamorous or raise the physical use of the body to something of an art-form. Sport builds up strength, stamina and an ability to compete — useful assets for the Mars–Neptune type. It also allows the individual to let off steam. Those with the hard aspects often idealise and fantasise about the notion of winning and sometimes fighting. This may propel them into having a go, but equally they may let self-doubt get in the way of allowing themselves to try. Those with the hard aspects especially, need to put their dreams of winning, achieving and conquering to the test and this obviously doesn't just apply to sporting activities.

The challenge for those with the hard aspects between these planets is often to act on their dreams, visions and ideals, to put them into some kind of practice.

Sometimes action to do with a Neptunian enterprise is indicated and thus work with film, photography, the fine arts, and the stage are all implied. Such artistic mediums may also provide a vehicle wherein the individual may give form to the myths of all society. Thus in the film industry, one might imagine the actor, director or whoever dramatising violent situations or situations where saviours fight to rescue victims in some way. Television and film also provides a vehicle for the embodiment of the sexual fantasies of the collective as well as the sexual fantasies of those who actually write the script, play the parts, shoot the scene or direct the show.

I have known both men and women with these contacts go in for body-building and the type generally is often quite muscular if the aspect is prominently placed. And I think one of the reasons for this frequent physical show of strength is that people with hard contacts between these planets are often doubtful as to their strength and their courage and therefore have a strong need to give the illusion of courage or strong physique both to themselves and to others. They idealise and perhaps glamorise physical strength. Typically too, the type is frightened of becoming a victim of violence and at the same time may dream of saving and rescuing others from such experiences.

A very good way for people to use Mars–Neptune hard contacts is for them to fight consciously on behalf of the underdog in some way. Thus it's hardly surprising that these contacts are common in the charts of social workers and the like.

The Mars–Neptune person's real strength usually lies in their sensitivity, compassion and imagination.

Both sexes can sometimes be heard to talk about 'Real Men'. Whilst men may sometimes try to embody the image of what they think this means by working out at the gym, women often fall in love with someone who embodies the illusion of strength. In the classic man-woman scenario, when she takes him home he turns out to be more of a victim than a knight in shining armour. The Mars–Neptune contact is in her chart and she rescues him – from his insecurity, his vulnerability, his lack of direction, his drinking or a whole host of other possibilities.

In extreme cases, I associate hard aspects between these planets with the 'gaolbird', and with those that wait on the outside for them to come out. And Mars–Neptune actors may play such characters. Nowadays, a lot of people wind up in prison on drug-related charges, which is also very fitting for this combination.

One of the reasons why, in extreme cases, Mars–Neptune people may sometimes find themselves in gaol is because they often imagine that there will be no restraints imposed upon their actions. This is sometimes because they themselves find it difficult to put restraints on the actions of others. Another reason is that the type is also often easily led. The Mars principle gives direction, the conscious impulse to do something and the drive to do it. When linked with Neptune this sense of direction feels undermined and thus is often unclear and diffuse. The individual wants to do so much that committing the self to just one project, a project which might fail, is felt to be quite difficult. If the individual has not got their own clear sense of direction, then they are frequently particularly open to being seduced into furthering the goals of others, particularly if such projects sound glamorous or hold the possibility of a future glamorous life-style. One can imagine that in a criminal situation, it would be the Mars–Neptune member of the gang who wound up getting caught.

Any hard aspects to Mars create issues around the experience and discharge of anger. For those with Mars–Neptune contacts, the problem can be in getting hold of these feelings in the first place. The hard contacts may occasionally be found in people whose anger seems to know no bounds, and thus like most Mars hard aspects can produce aggressive behaviour. Unlike Mars–Saturn rage, for example though, the Mars–Neptune person often has no one or nothing specific to direct their anger towards and thus it may spill out all over the place. Mars–Neptune rage can be more dangerous than that of Mars–Saturn for there may be no control over its expression.

More usually though, Mars–Neptune anger just dissolves and the individual finds themselves crying when they wanted to be shouting. Classically the Mars–Neptune type is highly emotional whilst at the same time disliking, and impatient with, shows of weakness and even displays of sentimentality, either in themselves or in others. As always, the type idealises strength, often without having a clear idea of just what strength actually is. And as noted before, the type's real strength usually lies in their sensitivity, compassion, empathy and imagination. It often seems that the purpose behind some of the happenings in the individual's life is for them to discover this.

Often the Mars–Neptune person (especially with the opposition aspect) sees themselves and others as 'victims' of other people's aggression. Mars–Neptune individuals are very prone to thinking in terms of 'goodies' and 'baddies'. And those with the square aspect often find it particularly difficult to assert themselves, their ability to do so is often blocked by feelings of self-doubt and idealistic notions of pacifism.

As always the possibilities are endless, but usually Neptune refines the aggressive impulses of Mars and despite outward appearances of strength the Mars–Neptune individual often feels incapable of self-defence. People with all aspects are particularly prone to passive aggression and masochistic behaviour. Unable and sometimes too sensitive to express their own anger, they meet it from an outside source and do indeed become the victims of others' aggression or, at least, angry feelings. In actuality they are really victims of their own unexpressed anger. For example, I have known women with these contacts have extremely unruly children. As toddlers, the youngsters are overly aggressive and completely disruptive, often actually physically hitting their mother and scarcely being restrained from doing so. They were like this because their Mars–Neptune mothers were unable to be tough with them. The mother would sometimes feel too impotent to cope whilst at the same time would really be too enchanted and seduced by the child to be able to say 'no' with any real authority. And in being so soft, they received from the child their own unexpressed anger.

Many sporting activities also have a masochistic side to them. The racing-driver who might get killed, the boxer who is asking to be punched.

The Mars–Neptune individual is often the type of person who on witnessing or experiencing an injustice, sets out to punish the wrongdoer but then finds themselves unable to do so because they end up identifying with that person (who has now of course become the victim).

People with Mars–Neptune hard aspects do often become victims of their own aggression in others ways too. In its most negative manifestation, the type seems peculiarly prone to strange psychosomatic illnesses or the self-inflicted disorders related to drink or drugs. Being ill is occasionally a way of punishing the self, asserting the self and often of hurting others and making them feel guilty and at a loss as to what to do.

Several astrologers have spoken of the Mars principle as being concerned with the ability to shrug off disease. Certainly, people with Mars–Neptune hard contacts, and sometimes the conjunction, often find it difficult to do so. 'Bugs' often seem to infiltrate the body system and the type seems particularly prone to catching colds, flu and mysterious viruses.

Despite the usual Mars issues with anger and aggression, at best, the Mars–Neptune type is able to temper their assertiveness and need to maintain their individuality with compassion and sensitivity for themselves as well as for others. And they often easily enchant others with these qualities.

A whole book might be written about the sex-life of the Mars–Neptune person but I will say little here beyond sign-posting the reader to Stephen Arroyo's excellent material. Basically, in sexual matters as elsewhere, the type may be seduced into almost anything for, at worst, the individual with the hard aspect does not know what they do want for much of the time. They are also often very seductive themselves. The sexual act is often very idealised and the individual inevitably thirsts to lose themselves in the ultimate sexual experience. Although the Mars–Neptune type may get themselves, in extreme cases, into some very messy, unromantic romantic situations, where in fact they are not valued but instead taken for a ride, it may be through a certain amount of experimentation and fantasising that the type is able to find the sexual expression that is right for them. The problem with the hard aspects can be that the individual is so busy looking outside of their relationship for Superman or Wonder Woman that they fail to work on the relationship that they actually have and therefore miss the possibility of ensuring that the earth really does move. For Mars–Neptune, mysticism and oneness with the universe must go together with the sexual act; it is only through practice and experimentation that this may become possible and the individual may be able find out what is right for them, if only by discovering what isn't. Those with the soft aspects often find the attainment of heavenly relationship much easier to obtain. And as always, those with the soft aspects tend to accept what they have and where Neptune is concerned one might say idealise the romantic and sexual relationship that they have.

Not infrequently those with the hard aspects between Mars and Neptune were conceived out of a 'made-in-heaven' kind of sexual relationship and it is as if they come into the world having been totally disorientated by this, and at the same time driven towards repeating it.

Although difficult aspects between these planets in extreme cases may not always have the most pleasant repercussions, these perhaps have been exaggerated here. The presence of a strong Saturn will do much to nullify the more extreme manifestations of this combination, although if that planet is actually plugging into the configuration it may actually increase the tension.

Creative examples of Mars–Neptune contacts abound. Leonard Bernstein, creator of *West Side Story*, a modern-day *Romeo and Juliet*, had

Venus conjunct Neptune in Leo tightly square Mars in Scorpio. Writer Roald Dahl has the same square. His children's books very much concern themselves not only with children's dreams but with the rescuing of victims from their oppressors. Sidney Poitier, the cinematic defender and sometimes embodiment of the underdog, also has a tight square between Mars and Neptune. He is also the personification of the refined macho image. Lauren Bacall, who tended to fall for 'baddies' in her earlier films, has the opposition; she usually comes across as very seductive as well as open to being seduced.

MARS–PLUTO

Fighting to the death. The fight for survival. Compulsive winning. Assertion of power. Sexual power. Buried rage.

> Let me not pray to be sheltered from dangers but to be fearless in facing them.
> Let me not beg for the stilling of my pain but for the heart to conquer it.
> Let me not look for allies in life's battlefield but to my own strength.
> Let me not crave in anxious fear to be saved but hope for the patience to win my freedom.
> Grant me that I may not be a coward, feeling your mercy in my success alone; but let me find the grasp of your hand in my failure.
> (Rabindranath Tagore, *Fruit-Gathering*)

This combination has the reputation for being singularly ruthless and fiercely competitive, but as with most Pluto combinations this may not always be obvious to the casual observer or even to the individual themselves. The ruthlessness is sometimes turned inwards upon the self. Nevertheless, this is the contact of the person who might say to themselves, unconsciously if not consciously: 'I will win, I will fight, I will survive at all costs.' *Survival* is usually a very big issue with this combination. Even in a small way, those with Mars–Pluto contacts can sometimes be found exhibiting a compulsive need to win. This is the person who *must* win the game of tennis, Scrabble or Monopoly or if they can't will choose not to play at all. The feelings of there being a strong need to survive and fight are usually the same whatever the aspect, but behaviour indicative of these feelings is much more obvious with the opposition and square. Often people with these contacts seem anything but able to fight (overtly at any rate) as if Pluto has in some way 'killed' the Mars impulse. Like Mars–Saturn, with most aspects, and certainly with tight conjunctions or hard aspects, there is usually a childhood history of 'might makes right', where the youngster's right to say 'I want this' or 'No, I don't want that' was severely thwarted in some area. This usually makes the individual uncertain of their capacity to assert themselves in later life, with all the feelings of disempowerment that go with that. Individuals may then either over-assert themselves to be sure of getting their own way or not seem to bother at all, preferring instead to err on the side of diplomacy and compromise, believing that it is useless to fight anyway for they have no hope of winning. There is usually a pronounced manipulative quality then, so that the person gets what they want through more covert and subtle means.

Whilst this latter situation is by no means uncommon, the more usual manifestation with the hard aspects is the tendency to be overly forceful.

As always, Pluto tends to bury the planetary principles it touches. When coupled with Mars, the burial is of rage, energy and a kind of bestial sexuality. However, like a boil coming to a head, these qualities will surface when triggered by appropriate transits, and when they do so, it will often be with the most tremendous force.

Mars–Pluto anger is not so much anger as rage, the rage of the screaming infant who, for whatever reason, was too frightened to get angry when young. And the anger that was never discharged settles and becomes congealed. In childhood, there was usually a lot of free-floating rage around, commonly with sexual roots. In any event such feelings were often unconscious or largely unexpressed.

Mars and Pluto together are usually thought of as the significators of rape and one thinks of rape in the sexual sense, which would apply here as Mars–Pluto is a common contact in the charts of both the raped and the rapist, but the real meaning of the word is to 'take by force' and this can be viewed in a variety of contexts. Those with Mars–Pluto contacts know all about 'taking by force'; that's usually a quality of the environment in which they were raised. Succumbing to such behaviour themselves is not the usual manifestation but it can happen and it is what one might expect to happen to any child who has continually felt thwarted and powerless and angry. The idea of 'taking by force' and resisting pressure from outside can be positively or negatively used. As Arroyo says, 'there is a compulsive drive for power with these aspects'. Such power can provide the strength out of which great things are made and out of which great personal transformation occurs but it can also be at the root of great cruelty and violence.

People with tight hard aspects, and not uncommonly the conjunction, will often themselves have had a history of physical violence, cruelty or sexual abuse. Rape is a common manifestation of this combination and I have known cases where the individual was not actually abused themselves but felt as if they were and absorbed a great deal of the underlying sexual rage in the household. I have also met people with these contacts who were conceived out of a rape situation.

Mars–Pluto people of both sexes usually have a deep distrust of men and what might be termed 'masculine energy' within themselves and often projected onto men. These contacts are common in women who pursue a lesbian life-style and in men who relate almost exclusively to women.

People with these contacts often get themselves into life-situations which mean they have to confront sexual taboos of one sort or another. Sexual relationships with their own sex or with people from a very different culture, and usually a different skin colour, might be examples of this. What constitutes a sexual taboo will vary from family to family, from society to society, and will change over the years. For example, an Indian friend of mine, a Hindu, encountered the most enormous taboo from the point of view of her family and culture when she divorced her husband and went to live with an Englishman.

For Mars–Pluto there is an aspect of sexuality which is experienced as dark, savage and bestial, and this can be viewed as deeply exciting or life-threatening. The individual often carries around with them savage images of the sexual act, seeing penetration more as an assault than anything else. Life becomes much easier for the Mars–Pluto person when it can admit to feeling murderous at times and can discover that they are not alone in having these feelings. The real problems for Mars–Pluto when falling in the charts of otherwise 'soft' and humane people, can be of owning their own violent feelings, and this is why the type can often find it difficult to allow themselves to express anger and also can be so ruthless with themselves. Not owning their rage can also result in the person attracting other people or life-situations which are violent or require superhuman courage or endurance. Through encountering such situations the Mars–Pluto person is forced to access their own ruthlessness, anger and strong survival instinct.

Because the Mars–Pluto person usually knows something about violation of one sort or another, the individual can have a deep under-standing of some of the more hidden aspects of our society, and more especially of the sides of life that humanity's civilised persona would rather not admit to having. Not surprisingly therefore, these contacts are often found in the charts of people who work with those that have abused or been abused.

This combination can be associated with 'fighting to the death' and sometimes with fighting off death. Elisabeth Kubler-Ross has a tight square between a Sun–Pluto conjunction and Mars. Through her work she has been one of the first people to examine the taboos surrounding death. She also teaches the philosophy of living until you die. The lines by Rabindranath Tagore which open this section are those chosen by her to open her book *On Death and Dying* and very much reflect a positively used Mars–Pluto interchange.

Perhaps because there is such a strong survival instinct with this combination, people with it often have a tremendous resistance to disease and especially to everyday things like colds, but I have seen charts of Aids and cancer sufferers with tight Mars–Pluto contacts. In such cases the individuals, on learning that they had a life-threatening disease, have exerted themselves not only to survive but to reach the peak of physical fitness. Others have used the experience to penetrate the workings of their psyche and transform their lives. Even Mars–Pluto people whose lives are not threatened will often react to situations as if they were.

People with this combination are usually capable of extraordinary courage and powers of endurance. The courage will often be emotional as opposed to physical, although this combination is useful for those who physically push themselves to and beyond the limit: dancers, athletes, mountaineers and the like. In fixed signs especially, the Mars–Pluto person can put up with the kind of extreme situations that might be expected to crush any human spirit.

The way to use this combination is for the individual to engage legitimately in something that, for them, does require superhuman effort. And whilst the exertion needn't be physical, engaging in such activity, as in work-outs or sport, is often a good way for the person to make conscious use of these contacts. Tennis and squash, for example, provide a legitimate vehicle for giving and receiving a good thrashing. Because anger is so good at fuelling action of all kinds and because Mars–Pluto people can be so frightened of getting angry, their physical energy can also get 'dammed up' and some sort of physical exertion is often required to shift it.

Dance is sometimes a therapeutic activity for the Mars–Pluto person, for as well as requiring a great physical expenditure of energy it can also be quite sexually cathartic. Drumming is also ideal. Mars–Pluto lends itself very well to jungle imagery and drumming and free-flowing dance is one way of accessing and using this energy. Keeping or working with animals is also a way of contacting the bestial within oneself. I think one can also associate Mars–Pluto with interest in magic and the occult and thus with all forms of hidden power and the idea of mind over matter.

The performance or experience of music can also provide a vehicle for a tremendous release of emotion. Perhaps a double dose of Mars-type energy, as might be associated with Mars and Pluto, calls for a double dose of Venus: music, love, acceptance and forgiveness. Expressions of love can do much to heal the scars of this combination.

Examples of people with Mars–Pluto contacts include: Albert Schweitzer (opposition), Aleister Crowley (exact trine), Shirley Bassey (square) and Ringo Starr (conjunction).

JUPITER ASPECTS

JUPITER–SATURN

Tests of faith. The definition of wealth. Philosophy of materialism. Fear of abundance. The large superego.

This can be an easy combination to get hold of if one simply imagines how each planet might affect the other. Saturn will tend to define, restrict, restrain and add an element of fear to all those things we associate with Jupiter; namely faith, meaning, joy and enthusiasm. Whilst one of the other major issues of this combination seems to revolve around the fact that, similarly, Jupiter expands, enlarges and increases the Saturnian principles of order, responsibility, discipline and caution.

Our image of Saturn as being the internalised schoolteacher, the inner figure that uses words like 'should' and 'ought', and for whom nothing is ever good enough, is inflated with these contacts. What a Freudian might describe as a large superego, an unconscious exaggerated morality and, not infrequently, great depression because of the individual's inability to live up to their own inflated sense of right and wrong.

On the plus side, Jupiter and Saturn together usually yields great persistence, patience and perseverance, coupled with far-sightedness and at best cautious optimism. Certainly these qualities are to be expected with the soft aspects and often the conjunction. At worst, and this is especially a feature of the hard contacts, the individual swings between optimism and pessimism, believing at one moment that anything is possible and that they are capable of earth-shattering achievements and the next, that life is meaningless and they themselves are less than worthless and capable of only the most menial tasks. In material terms, it's the hallmark of the youngster who one minute fantasises about chairing the Board and the next considers applying for the job of assistant, apprentice dogsbody. And the life in reality, may take either form. Nevertheless, this is perhaps *the* combination associated with solid material success, and the easy aspects especially seem buffeted in this area of their lives. On the whole, individuals with the soft aspects and sometimes the conjunction between these planets are judicious, which according to the dictionary means 'wisely critical. Prudent, careful and capable. Wise in adapting means to ends.' Those with the hard aspects may have to work to arrive at this judicious position, depending on the overall feel of the chart. Often there are problems with timing, with the individual being overly cautious when taking a risk might pay off, and taking a gamble, a wild leap of faith, when it might be unwise to do so. Nevertheless, strong contacts between these planets can do much to offset an earthy lack in a chart and being a worldly combination will also increase the feeling of earthiness in a chart already strong in that element. This is a common contact in the charts of economists, who could be said to be concerned with the philosophy of materialism. It is common, too, in the charts of others who define wealth and take on duties and responsibilities for it.

The major problems with this combination usually revolve around the area of faith. Commonly, the individual was educated in a strict moralistic, if not religious code. The kind of religious background that is of the 'fire and brimstone' variety. The religious experience conveyed not as a joyful one but as the ultimate method of controlling an individual's behaviour; conveyed as a threat, the threat being that if you do wrong you will incur the wrath of a vengeful God. The internalised image of the Creator is not of a person who is kindly and compassionate but of one who is a source of punishment, a stern arbiter of a strict justice. This is obviously a Judaeo-Christian image, and the exact image carried by the individual will obviously vary according to the belief system that they were raised in, but the feelings will often be similar and there will often be a very patriarchal feel about it. Sometimes the upbringing is not a religious one; indeed faith of that kind might be strictly denied, but then instead there are commonly strong philosophical or political beliefs which are themselves pursued with religious zeal, or strong ideas about 'right' and 'wrong'. Whatever the belief system, the source is usually the school or the father. Father looms very large with these contacts and the image of God sometimes becomes identical with the image of the personal father. Commonly, the individual internalises this figure, both becoming and fearing it. This combination relates very well to the Jungian archetype of the 'senex' (which in Latin literally means 'old man') and I have know several young people with this combination whose behaviour has been quite out of keeping with their generation. This is the signature of the 18-year-old who, for example, always wears a suit and leather shoes, is never dressed in jeans or sneakers or caught behaving in the silly or outrageous way that might be expected of this age-group.

As always, Saturn craves what it touches and with this combination the individual craves real meaning in life both in the personal and religious sense. And with the hard contacts and sometimes the conjunctions, finding this meaning can be a major life-quest. I have known many individuals with hard contacts between these planets who have eschewed the religion in which they were raised but then either returned to it many Saturn transits later or replaced it with another fairly structured belief system. Whatever the faith, for individuals with this contact it must have a distinct form. A clearly defined dogma and distinct rites and rituals. One reason why true meaning and purpose in life can seem so elusive to the Jupiter–Saturn type is their insistence that faith, meaning 'God' (whatever one means by that word), should be definable. The nature of existence can perhaps never be known as fact, can never be defined in the laboratory or the court of law. As Liz Greene says writing on Jupiter–Saturn: 'Genuine faith is about knowing in an intuitive and non-rational way, that there is meaning and purpose to one's experience and that it will unfold according to a pattern which contains intrinsic wisdom and purpose.'

Classically, the Jupiter–Saturn person wants to believe that things are either true or are not and finds doubt particularly difficult to live with. And because doubt is so difficult for the Jupiter–Saturn type they may either present a face of excessive jollity, exuberance and confidence or, at the other end of the spectrum, appear never to believe anything that anybody ever says. And perhaps the Jupiter–Saturn type should not believe what they are told. Their journey is surely about finding out what they believe for themselves.

Jupiter–Saturn people do not always reject the belief system in which they were raised, and this is a common enough combination in the clergy and in those who regularly attend church. Often then the challenge is for the person to face their fears and doubts as to what life might be like without the structure of the Church, if its rituals and dogma were stripped away. Often though, this life-style is not a cover-up for a genuine faith, not a Saturnian over-compensation, although it might have started out as such, but a formal expression of it. I suspect that for many a Jupiter–Saturn person, the way for the person to contact genuine faith is by going through the route of an orthodox church, complete with its ritual, dogma and, inevitably, attendant doubts.

The Jupiter–Saturn individual often craves, and frequently reaches, an influential and executive position in the world. The type is often concerned with law on all levels and is frequently found in the legal profession, the clergy and in education.

Material success comes easily to those with the soft aspects but is not usually denied those with the hard aspects either, though they will probably have to work harder for it. Having a secure position in the world and money in the bank whilst frequent, is not always the outcome of Jupiter–Saturn hard contacts. Sometimes people choose to discern meaning in their lives through self-denial and deprivation. The type is rarely self-indulgent unless other factors in the chart point this way. Typically, the materially successful Jupiter–Saturn person with hard contacts will have all the trappings of material solidity: the nice car, the beautiful home, the excellent dinner parties but on their own, live very simple and even frugally. There can be a fear of having abundance, as well as a fear of poverty, both material and spiritual.

The Jupiter–Saturn person is usually frightened of taking risks with their lives and with their money but it's surprising how often those with the hard aspects are literal gamblers. As always with the hard aspects, the individual when afraid of doing something, can go too far in over-compensating. The combination is consistent both with the person who never takes any risks and the individual who often does so. The hard aspects may be no less productive of material advantage than the soft ones in my experience but with the latter, if the individual has not earned this advantage themselves, there is often some sort of nagging guilt. With these people and with those who have not managed to achieve in a worldly sense there is often a feeling that one needs to do something very big before one is too old. And betting (and losing) on the horses or the Stock Exchange is a quite common manifestation of this urge, especially in the individual who has not found personal meaning in their life and perhaps believes that they can avoid facing the pain of this realisation by achieving material wealth.

Sometimes the hard aspects between Jupiter and Saturn operate in the area of education. These contacts are consistent with individuals who are highly educated but also with those who missed out on higher education when young and evermore feel threatened by what they see as the better educational qualifications of others. In such cases, what Jupiter–Saturn misses out on in terms of pieces of paper is usually more than compensated for by a certain streetwise quality, a knowledgeability and dexterity with the real world. Nevertheless, it is often useful for this person to go back into higher education in later life, if only to heal this wound and renew faith in the self.

The late Dag Hammarskjöld, the famous diplomat and economist, is a good example of the Jupiter–Saturn type, in terms of his upbringing, beliefs, career and, at times, suicidal tendencies. Throughout his life, he jotted down his thoughts and feelings and after his death they were published, as he had requested, under the title *Markings*. A wonderful and profound book, *Markings* provides a rich study in the Jupiter–Saturn life-process. Hammarskjöld had Jupiter in Gemini exactly squaring Saturn in Pisces. Surely his words exactly describe this:

The language of religion is a set of formulas which register a basic spiritual experience. It must not be regarded as describing in terms to be defined in philosophy, the reality which is accessible to our senses and which we can analyse with the tools of logic. I was late in understanding what this meant. When I finally reached that point, the beliefs in which I was once brought up and which, in fact, had given my life direction even while my intellect still challenged their validity, were recognised by me as mine in their own right and by my free choice.

Perhaps this defines the purpose and challenge of Jupiter–Saturn: to arrive at one's beliefs the hard but thorough way through personal experience. It is through facing their doubts and fears as to the meaning of life, and in particular the meaning and purpose of their own life, that the Jupiter–Saturn person can find true faith in the self and in the life-process.

JUPITER AND THE OUTER PLANETS

When an aspect occurs between Jupiter and either Uranus, Neptune or Pluto, it will do so for all horoscopes over a period of days or even weeks. This is not to say that the contact will not have personal significance for the individual in whose chart it falls. Indeed it most certainly will, but the relative importance of the configuration will need to be *very carefully weighed up*. If the combination picks up an angle or a personal planet, or important midpoint, it will be of much greater importance.

JUPITER–URANUS

Big radical ideas. Integrating faith with truth. Changing beliefs. Belief in freedom. Sudden journeys. Sudden strokes of luck.

Both Jupiter and Uranus symbolise aspects of the psyche that want space and freedom. When combined together, these requirements are usually a very marked feature. And this applies on physical, emotional and intellectual levels. This is a highly independent combination, given to free and often radical thinking, ideas and beliefs. Concentrating on the hard aspects and the conjunction, there is usually a strong streak of originality and contrariness to the personality. Whatever the actual aspect, Jupiter will expand the individual's Uranian issues and traits. So there is likely to be a very large need to rebel in at least one small corner of the person's life. Uranus is descriptive of behaviour that is stubborn and non-conformist and when picked up by Jupiter can be doubly so and quite fanatical.

The purpose and major usefulness of these contacts is often concerned with shaking the rest of society out of their outmoded beliefs (whether political, religious or otherwise) and exposing the double standards frequently prevalent in the upholding of them.

Above all else, this combination is concerned with integrating the concept of truth with that of faith and meaning. Jupiter–Uranus individuals often find their meaning in life through more seemingly unusual or unorthodox channels – astrology for example. What the Jupiter–Uranus person can sometimes forget is that what is truth to them may not be truth to everyone else.

Basically, those with these contacts have to find their own personal truth for themselves. The typical Jupiter–Uranus individual is unlikely to feel comfortable with whatever belief system or moral code they were raised in. Sometimes this might have been a traditional religious faith such as Judaism or the Catholic Church, and if so the individual will normally exhibit a strong urge to break free from it. This is the classic contact of the 'lapsed' Catholic. Sometimes there may just have been some sort of moral code pervading the household or the school environment. Whatever the situation, there is usually a strongly felt need to rebel against it. If focusing on religion the individual is often concerned with what they see as the hypocrisy of the Church, for example in the wealth within that institution and the poverty in the world at large. Or they may turn their attention to what they see as the narrowness of the Church's moral stance.

It is hardly surprising that the combination is common amongst atheists and agnostics; people who want to be free of religion. It is also to be found in the charts of people who join up with more unorthodox, unconventional and radical beliefs, whether these be religious or political.

Sometimes in pursuing their new beliefs, the individual winds up being as fanatical about them as the more extreme exponents of the ones they broke free from in the first place.

Some Jupiter–Uranus individuals do stay within the fold of their political or religious background but become radicals within the system. The rebels who call for change.

Hardly surprising given the nature of the planets involved, whatever the belief system, the Jupiter–Uranus person will often espouse strong views around issues of freedom and personal liberty. These people might also be staunch supporters of progressive educational reform.

There is often a great deal of activity devoted to that other Jupiterian pastime: travel. The Jupiter–Uranus person may thrive on excitement and sudden embarkations for unusual places. Mentally and physically there is a liking for the wide open spaces.

Commonly, people with these contacts are interested in different peoples and their cultures. This would be a good combination for an anthropologist. Sometimes Jupiter–Uranus individuals feel more at home with the beliefs and customs of cultures other than those they were born into. This is likely to be especially the case if the Moon, or the 4th house or its ruler is involved.

Jupiter–Uranus is sometimes associated with sudden strokes of luck. Ebertin speaks of the combination as being concerned with the 'sudden release of tension or strain' and has named it 'the Thank the Lord' configuration.

Examples of this combination include: the explorer and anthropologist Thor Heyerdahl, who has the conjunction; trade union leader Arthur Scargill (square); Ken Livingstone (square); and Nelson Mandela (opposition).

JUPITER–NEPTUNE

Big dreams, grandiose fantasies. The mystical experience. The Great Escape. Spiritual pride. Explorers at sea.

This is often a very altruistic, philanthropic combination. Jupiter–Neptune individuals sometimes have a strong urge to sacrifice themselves in some way for the greater good of the whole. There is usually a tremendous sensitivity to the world's suffering and sometimes a desire to 'save the world' in some way. Contacts between these planets can undoubtedly yield tremendous compassion and humanitarian impulses, but occasionally may also be at the root of great spiritual pride, arrogance and a misplaced belief in one's own sainthood.

There can be a very strong religious and mystical yearning; the individual with these planets strong and aspecting each other yearns to merge with God or at least with something that transcends the ordinary crass reality of living in the mundane, workaday world. This yearning may be satisfied by spending three weeks in the Bahamas or by taking up Buddhism or a course of study on the cabbala, depending on the individual.

The Jupiter–Neptune person often has a great understanding of intangibles, and both seeks and feels at home with all that is boundless in life. To Jupiter–Neptune, God is infinite, and permeates and infiltrates everything and everyone. At best the Jupiter–Neptune person really can see the world in a grain of sand,

At best, the individual yearns for, and genuinely wishes to work towards, a higher order of reality; at worst, there is an ever-present urge to look for the Big Escape Route. Mysticism may be a way of escaping from the true reality of one's life and the person one is, and this is the most obvious danger to those who have these contacts. The mystical experience can be used, not as a way to touching a higher plane of consciousness but as the route to avoiding the rigours of one's life.

Contacts between these planets are common in nuns and monks, those whose life could be described as escaping from the world or transcending it, depending on one's viewpoint. For Jupiter–Neptune, freedom lies in escape or transcendence.

People with hard aspects between these planets can be prone to big disappointments in their lives. Every dream, for individuals with these contacts, can become an enormous bubble that is simply asking to be deflated.

I know of a young man who was for quite a long time an apprentice mechanic for Rolls Royce cars. When qualified, he could expect to earn an amazing salary. He has a Jupiter–Neptune opposition falling across a Taurus–Scorpio Ascendant–Descendant axis. He dreamt of a time when he would be able to escape to idyllic tropical islands with sun-drenched beaches, sipping pina coladas and generally living the life of the lush. That was his big beautiful dream and the car he was working on, the Rolls Royce, could also be described as a big beautiful dream, for it is surely a car (aptly named 'Silver Cloud') quite unrealistic for most people's purse and life-style and certainly his. Sadly, his bubble burst when he was made redundant. This is very typical of Jupiter–Neptune hard aspects.

The mystical experience, the relationship with God, can also be built up into something very unrealistic, giving rise to almost inevitable disappointment and disillusionment. A strong Saturn can do much to offset such problems.

Mike Harding tells me that Jupiter–Neptune contacts are also common in the charts of stockbrokers, who apparently have a very intuitive feel for which way the market might be going. Seemingly they have an almost mystical approach to their work. One imagines too, a proneness to grandiose fantasies about how many millions might be made playing the market.

Thus hard contacts between these planets are equally common in the charts of those who want to escape from the material world and those who find spirituality within it. For some, the religious experience is ecstasy; for others, ecstasy might be putting £500 on a horse at Doncaster.

In all ways, shapes and forms, Jupiter–Neptune is prone to what can only be called Big Illusions and it's difficult to know sometimes whether someone with this combination is generally inspired and hearing celestial music and seeing visions that only they have the sensitivity to hear, or whether they have deceived themselves to the extent that, from an earthy Saturnian perspective anyway, they are completely deluded. Certainly this combination can be very gullible, woolly and vague. Individuals with this combination strong may want everything to be beautiful to the extent that they want to avoid anything that is not. They run the risk of failing to face up to any kind of reality. The challenge offered to those with the hard aspects is to actually make the dream a reality.

Travel can be important too to the Jupiter–Neptune individual. Dreams of wonderful summer holidays or three-month treks across India can keep many a person going through a boring working day. And a fairly harmless way of dealing with this aspect is to escape abroad every now and again.

It is through long-distance travel of the mind or of the body, that the Jupiter–Neptune individual can quite literally lose themselves and transcend ordinary life. Examples of the Jupiter–Neptune combination can be found in the chart of Mother Teresa (square) and Pope John Paul II (conjunction).

With Neptune's association with the sea, this also sounds like a good combination for marine explorers and long-distance sailors.

JUPITER–PLUTO

Hidden wealth. Wealth in buried matter. Enormous power. Exploring the underworld. Mining and recycling.

For individuals with this combination prominently placed in their charts, there is usually a life-theme around what might be described as 'the wealth of buried matter'. This wealth can take different forms: sometimes a very physical form, as in the charts of those whose work involves mining of various types of ore, coal, oil or other minerals; or sometimes a more psychological form – the wealth that is buried in the unconscious.

We are used to thinking of the unconscious aspects of ourselves, the 'Shadow', as housing the more ugly elements of our psyches but many psychologists, including Jung, would be quick to point out that those ugly and socially unacceptable parts of us are fertile, potent and useful, and house a great deal of buried treasure. It's rather like the compost heap at the bottom of the garden: it is composed of decaying, dead and rotting matter, stuff we have discarded; but it miraculously transforms itself into mineral-rich nutrients that can be ploughed back into the soil.

Perhaps those with this combination may be exceptionally aware of the potential wealth that exists in discarded material on a physical level and so one might associate this combination with various aspects of recycling. Both the therapist and the recycling advocate are concerned with regenerating discarded matter so that it can be used again. They are both concerned with the avoidance of waste.

I think Jupiter–Pluto can also be associated with 'hidden wealth' in the financial sense. The enormous sums of money which are exchanged through the banks, the finance houses, the insurance companies; money that is hidden from public view but exerts the most tremendous power.

Not uncommonly, enormous sums of money often do go through the hands of Jupiter–Pluto people. This aspect can refer to the inherited wealth of the upper classes but can just as easily be found in the charts of those who themselves are poor but work in banks, stockbroking and insurance companies. Again, it can be associated with various mining industries, for there is wealth in fuel and especially, at the current time, in oil. Neither Jupiter nor Pluto symbolise money but together they form the significator for Big Power and that kind of power usually does involve large sums of money, in covert if not overt terms. It also involves a great deal of secrets and we might associate Jupiter–Pluto with big secrets.

When picking up the angles in the chart or the personal planets, the individual with this combination is likely to be very ambitious. Typically, Jupiter–Pluto wants to do something very big. Just what, will be shown by the planets or points the combination picks up, but this can be a very relentless and ruthless combination.

There is usually a very strong urge to reform with this combination, whether the reform be political, legal or religious. It can be psychological too, concerned with the reforming of the self, continually bettering and improving one's life and one's being.

Jupiter–Pluto has what Sakoian and Acker (*The Astrologer's Handbook*) describe as 'the faith that will move mountains'. This can be interpreted in a religious sense but may also be a statement about the individual's faith on a wider level. The Jupiter–Pluto person will often believe that anything is possible, that whatever is wanted in life is obtainable if only one can set one's mind to it. It is not surprising therefore that the combination sometimes yields an interest in magic, for magic is simply concerned with the power of the mind over matter and it can be used for good or ill.

The ruthlessness of Jupiter–Pluto's philosophy can be seen where death or punishment is viewed as acceptable if it is for the greater good of the whole. The most obvious example of Jupiter–Pluto can be found in the chart of Margaret Thatcher, who has a tight opposition between these two planets in the 2nd and 8th houses – so appropriate for one who had such power over the economy (see page 69).

CHAPTER TWELVE

SATURN ASPECTS

SATURN–URANUS

Cautious reform. Fear of change. Breaking with tradition. Breaks with authority. Unexpected brakes. Rebels in control.

Saturn and Uranus represent such opposing principles that when they are contacting each other, especially by conjunction or hard aspect, a very taut kind of tension is created. The conflict is perhaps obvious: Saturn concerns itself with tradition, authority, discipline, duty and responsibility whilst the Uranian impulse is individualistic, anti-establishment and highly rebellious.

The most recent example of the Saturn–Uranus combination occurred with the 1987 conjunction. In Russia, as in other places, it heralded a period of major reform, the breaking away from tradition and the drastic cutting of defences, all under the helmsmanship of Mikhail Gorbachev, who himself, rather appropriately, has a Saturn–Uranus–Pluto T-square.

Uranus was the first of the outer planets to be discovered and as any text book will advise, its discovery ushered in a period of revolution: the French Revolution, the Industrial Revolution, the American War of Independence. It marked a period where there was a revolution in the thinking of ordinary people, a time when individuals started challenging the rights of those in authority to rule and the right to shape the rest of society's ideas. Perhaps whenever Saturn meets up with Uranus in the heavens, then this original challenging of authority or tradition is again invoked.

People born during times of Saturn–Uranus contacts are raised against a backdrop of accelerated reform or a major change of ideas in the collective. And usually the right of individuals to exercise free choice gets into conflict with the constraints imposed by the state or other segments of the community. Many traditions and institutions are forced to change or go under; for example a lot of factories may close. The Old Order or established ways of doing things may be drastically and suddenly swept away. Not surprisingly, such changes meet with a good deal of resistance. The resistance comes from the Saturnian perspective and constitutes an attempt to preserve and conserve tradition, as well as a fear that the oncoming changes will be too fast and too drastic.

Uranus is concerned with the progressive and changing ideas of the collective. The Saturn–Uranus combination suggests the giving of form to new ideas popping up in society. Such ideas may literally be embodied in form, as in the case of advances in technology or there may be a revolution in the opinions of the people, or more particularly a change of direction by those in authority. Ideas that only a few years before might have been considered extremely radical and too shocking to contemplate take form and become both institutionalised and acceptable.

The introduction of the car, the telephone, flight, electricity, votes for women, computers, to name but a few examples, would all have been new, progressive and a novelty at one time. The introduction of each would have met with some resistance but would soon have become part of everyday life. Time turns what is new into what is old. New ideas, inventions or attitudes heralded by Uranus actually take root and *materialise* when that planet meets up with Saturn. People born during periods of Saturn–Uranus contacts are perhaps born during such times, and if the combination is of central importance in their charts, they may be the people who will give form to changing ideas in the years to come.

Saturn–Uranus contacts also often mark a time when old things resurface in a new way or with a new and exciting impact. For example, both these planets can be associated with astrology. In 1987, astrology was front-page news when there was speculation as to the extent to which Ronald Reagan consulted the stars. The oldest of subjects created great shocks by being in the news for weeks.

In personal terms, people with these contacts often have a gift of looking at an old subject in an entirely new way. In various aspects of their lives, they will also often experience internal conflict as to whether to take a firm anti-establishment, progressive and radical line or whether to respect authority, tradition and that which has stood the test of time. Somehow the individual has to integrate both ends of the spectrum, and people with these contacts often exhibit a curious mixture of radicalism and fear of change.

How the interchange is likely to manifest in an individual will largely depend on which, if either, of the two planets is stronger in the horoscope. If Saturn is stronger, an aspect (especially a hard aspect) may give rise to an individual who is frightened of change, suspicious of anything new and unable to let anyone or anything that is the slightest bit 'different' or unconventional into the life. The individual attempts to castrate progress. And of course sometimes the onset of 'progress' and the advance of technology needs to be checked, and in particular the feelings of people need to be taken into account. Where Uranus is stronger, the individual continually kicks against authority and rebels against the established way of doing things. This again may be entirely appropriate for both the individual and society.

Not uncommonly, the Saturn–Uranus person is conservative and conformist whilst young but increasingly stands out as a rebel as the years advance or at least until after the Uranus opposition cycle. Sometimes people with these contacts cling to a fashion that everyone followed when young, but as they get older they become conspicuous or are viewed as eccentric by still adhering to the former way of being. Thus these contacts may be found both in people who fight for change and in those who firmly resist it. Usually both attitudes co-exist.

Charles Carter describes Saturn–Uranus as being 'democratic in spirit and autocratic in method' and this combination has long been associated with inflexibility and a tyrannical and dictatorial attitude. It might well be someone with a Saturn–Uranus contact in their chart who, as they shake their fists, will say we *are* going to be democratic or we are going to introduce computers into the company. In introducing a new regime or a new order, the Saturn–Uranus type may be as tyrannical and controlling as whatever or whoever they are trying to overthrow. In some cases people with these contacts can just go too far (from other people's point of view anyway) in insisting on their viewpoints so that they meet with some kind of unexpected brake on their action. Transits between these planets often precipitate broken bones, or else people with these contacts find some other kind of enforced 'break' imposed upon them. The Saturn–Uranus capacity for strength is very useful but it can also render the individual quite unable to bend or shift to changing circumstances; hence fate seems to ensure the implementation of the most dramatic kind of breaks or brakes.

I have certainly known people with Saturn–Uranus contacts who have experienced an authority-figure, and often the father, as having demonstrated this kind of bullying behaviour. In later life, the individual finds themselves rebelling against that person for evermore and, by extension, kicking against all others in society who are in positions of control. And in extreme cases, becoming more and more like their father (or whoever the early authority-figure or regime was) in their own behaviour. For those with Saturn–Uranus less prominently placed, the bullying quality of these planets may be more descriptive of the experience of the political figures of the time. Occasionally, those with these contacts experience their father as unconventional or 'different' in some way.

This combination is productive of great determination, perseverance, extraordinary will-power and strength.

It is common enough in politicians and others who have to resist mutiny in the ranks or hold fast to a particular course of action. It is a useful combination for anyone who has to push through major reforms or conversely for those who need to resist the introduction of unwelcome changes.

SATURN–NEPTUNE

Transcending boundaries. Escaping responsibility. Fearing lost of control. Idealisation of authority. Undermining of authority. Lessons of purification and refinement. Guilt and reparation.

When I wrote this book (Spring 1989) Saturn and Neptune were exactly conjunct in the sky, picking up the Sun and Midheaven in the 1801 UK chart. The conjunction heralded news of salmonella in eggs, listeria in soft cheeses and numerous stories of poisoned water and contaminated food. In all cases, there was confusion as to the real extent of the dangers and uncertainty as to who, if anyone, could be held responsible. Other Saturn–Neptune stories abounded the undermining of various institutions, stories about rain or lack of it. (One is reminded of Poseidon who, out of spite, flooded the lands or caused extreme drought as befitted him.) Ecological issues were to the fore, with society becoming more aware of the continual erosion being made to the earth and the dangers of pollution. There were calls for lead-free petrol and less polluting of the seas. Society was feeling guilty. That new awareness of the loss of and undermining of our planet can be attributed to and interpreted as a positive manifestation of the Saturn–Neptune conjunction.

We can see that children born over that year period were born against the backdrop of those issues. And one can start to get a good feel for how these major but non-personal configurations operate.

Ebertin, Charles Harvey and others have long isolated the Saturn–Neptune midpoint as being a point to be associated with *sickness*, so the tales of dangers to food are hardly surprising. More specifically, Saturn–Neptune seems to describe poisoning and, more generally, lessons around purification and refinement.

Saturn–Neptune contacts in the heavens can last for appreciable periods of time and by themselves cannot usually be taken as indicators of illness. However, when coupled with appropriate houses and certainly when used in a midpoint connotation, this correlation has certainly agreed with my own experience. Sometimes, the issue is paralysis or a psychological feeling of 'caving in' and not being able to cope. Typically, Saturn–Neptune people are frightened of loss of control and occasionally fate seems to ensure that they literally have to relinquish some form of control in order to learn lessons of some sort of non-attachment.

I have known several instances where Saturn–Neptune has fallen across the MC–IC axis and it has been descriptive of a sick father. In one case where a woman had a tight opposition across that axis, the father had some strange neurological disorder which not only confined him to bed but apparently made him especially sensitive to noise and disturbance. Through his sickness, he managed to control the whole family, who moved around him as if he were a precious piece of porcelain that might crack at any minute. At the same time of course he escaped from having to take any real responsibility, financial or otherwise, for the family. I also know of two other cases, with Saturn–Neptune conjunctions in the 4th, where the father was disabled and rendered more of a burden, a victim, an object of compassion, than a head of the household. With these contacts the father is not attached to the real world in some way.

More commonly, where Saturn–Neptune is taken as a significator of the father, it is descriptive of a man who is usually quite ordinary, a mild, agreeable, retiring type but not able or willing to take on responsibility, and sometimes extremely anxious to avoid it. By seeming incapable of doing things, he ensures that others will do them for him. Agatha Christie, who had a tight square between these planets, had a father of this type. A man of independent means, he never needed to work and spent his days at his Club. He obviously had a very agreeable personality and was in no way a disciplinarian. When he died, it became clear that in financial terms, at any rate, he had failed his family. He had failed to safeguard his resources, and make adequate provision for them. He died when Agatha was about 12 and this fits a classic Saturn–Neptune pattern too. The pattern of a missing or weak father figure, the father who gets it 'wrong' not because of what he does but of what he fails to do. A father who is not and doesn't set himself up to be, the voice of authority. Often the individual longs for that authority in their lives, looking for it in all sorts of places and in all sorts of people and ultimately from within themselves.

There will be other, possibly stronger signatures of father in the chart, like aspects to the Sun and angles for example, so too much weight should not be placed on Saturn–Neptune contacts as being entirely descriptive of the experience of father unless there are other strong supporting factors. Though in most cases it will describe an *aspect* of father-figure. And an aspect of what society was feeling about authority at the time the individual was born.

Agatha Christie worked as a chemist during both wars and there obtained her knowledge of poisons which was to become her favourite weapon in her detective stories. Another Saturn–Neptune signature, as was her own 'disappearance'. It seems clear that she disappeared because she wanted to escape from, and felt unable to cope with, all the responsibilities she found herself saddled with after the death of her mother and exit of her husband.

The role of father can be difficult too for both sexes. It's not easy for people with this combination to mete out discipline or to impose boundaries.

On the whole, Saturn–Neptune finds it difficult to be overtly controlling, though passive controlling through sickness or inability to cope sometimes occurs, if the aspect is prominently placed for some reason. Frequently the person seems to lack, or fear they lack, authority, in the same way perhaps that father did or the government did at the time they were born.

Sometimes Saturn–Neptune people idealise and inflate the idea of taking responsibility and imagine it to be far more onerous than it need be, or sometimes more glamorous than it actually is. Often it is difficult for the individual to get a true perspective on responsibility. Certainly there is an awareness that the more one is involved with the reality of living in the real world then the less one has time for pursing one's dreams and visions, which can be another fear of those with strong hard contacts between these planets. The challenger for Saturn–Neptune is to make the vision, the dream, a reality in the real world and to find enchantment there too. Sometimes though, the notion of being in a responsible position is too much for Saturn–Neptune and they yearn to escape from all the ties and duties that their life might involve. At other times the scenario is more that in being a responsible citizen, dutiful member of the family, Saturn–Neptune feels they have sacrificed their own dreams.

Guilt is very much a feeling that one might attribute to this combination, but the guilt is often caused not by the real failure of those with the contact to cope with the material world and all its obligations but by the fact that the whole issue has been so exaggerated, frequently because it loomed so large as an issue in childhood. According to the Oxford English Dictionary, the word guilt may come from the word geld meaning 'to pay', and that's often the key to Saturn–Neptune behaviour, for the individual on some level often feels as if they are in debt for something and must continually be making reparation, paying a penance, often paying the father's (or society's) debts or avenging those that are indebted to him. This can be interpreted, of course, in the religious sense of the father as well as in the case of the personal father.

Neptune is a significator of the imagination and when touched by Saturn can give rise to an imagination that tends to think the worst, especially with regard to the areas of life it has rulership over, as shown by the houses, which is often what gives rise to the feelings of inadequacy. Day-dreaming will often revolve around the imminent possibility of suffering and sacrifice and it's not uncommon to find those with these contacts adopting the role of martyr in various guises. Saturn–Neptune can be associated with *renunciation*.

Perhaps the most famous act of renunciation of the twentieth century was that of King Edward VII, who had a trine between these planets. He was inspired by the idea of renunciation. In more ordinary life-stories, it can be that consciously deciding to use this contact usually does involve surrendering something as well as the exercising of considerable self-discipline in order to pursue whatever the dream, vision or ideal may be. Little wonder that this is a common combination in the charts of those who pursue the religious life, for it is surely the combination of the ascetic. Indeed, the image in one's mind is of a monk or a hermit (the true meaning of the word ascetic).

I do know of a nun with this combination strong, who had come from a very wealthy family. The 'idle rich' she called them, she felt guilty about their life-style and spent much of her life seeking to make amends for them. And in devoting her life in this way, she too was escaping from or transcending (depending on how you look at it) the rigours of the everyday world. The combination, too, is common in the charts of people in the West who follow the Buddhist faith which, amongst other things, teaches non-attachment and considers the reasons for the suffering of humankind.

Obviously not all people with these contacts strong will follow a life of abstinence, meditation and prayer but the theme of sacrificing certain areas of one's life, cutting out what is superfluous, and disciplining oneself in order to make some vision a concrete reality, is a common one. It can be seen as a purpose of this combination and can find outlet in a variety of ways. One can also associate Saturn–Neptune with the giving of selfless and disciplined service to others – a kind of practical compassion. The challenge of the hard aspects (and often the conjunction) between these planets is concerned with the need to integrate on the one hand the side of the person that is worldly, a materialist constrained by living in the mundane world, with a side that is more compassionate, idealistic and otherworldly. At best this is the combination of the practical idealist, the person who has an awareness of their own limitations and the limitations of the given situation but nevertheless works to make some ideal a reality in the concrete world.

The preferred life-style of Saturn–Neptune can be seen as being the opposite of that desired by Jupiter–Neptune. The latter would dream of a life of splendour, luxury and profusion, whilst Saturn–Neptune would seek a simple and uncluttered life free of any kind of opulence or excess.

This combination is often also commonly found in the charts of artists and musicians and those involved in film or video. And here the artist can be seen as giving form (Saturn) to the dreams, fantasies and feelings of the collective (Neptune), as well as providing a medium and a structure wherein the individual can express their own fears and fantasies.

SATURN–PLUTO

Controlled use of power. Sabotaging of authority. Fears of annihilation. Lessons of survival. Obsession with order.

As Liz Greene comments when discussing people with Saturn–Pluto contacts, 'the moment you attempt to impose any ideology upon them, or assert any kind of control, you get a very perverse and very violent reaction'. Saturn–Pluto aspects often manifest, in personal terms, as a fear of power. Either fear of owning and expressing one's own power or a fear of the havoc that collective power can wreak. People with these contacts not only often exhibit a deep distrust of those in authority but usually have a strong reluctance to being 'in charge' themselves, although accepting positions of authority is sometimes precisely what is required of those with these aspects.

Paradoxically, people with this combination emphasised in their charts (and it must be remembered that its effects can be largely generational unless it is also plugging into personal planets or the angles) often carry authority rather well and they are also usually exceptionally responsible people. And yet despite this, or possibly because of it, they sometimes express no desire to be in control.

Saturn–Pluto people often feel persecuted. Even if there is no obvious reason for such feelings, one manifestation of this combination is of the individual who identifies with people who have been ostracised from society for some reason, or who have suffered a cruel fate. Perhaps persecuted because of their race, their colour, their sexual orientations, their religion or some 'taboo' in their life which society shuns. Whether or not the Saturn–Pluto person actually belongs to the group, or has the necessary qualifications to join it, there is often an *identification* with what the individual sees as the group's suffering. Some Saturn–Pluto people work, campaign or become involved with what they see as the victims of society, although such manifestations are more likely if Neptune is also very active in the chart.

The Saturn–Pluto person may be able to identify with and take responsibility for those who are persecuted but will often find it very difficult to accept any collective responsibility for the role of persecutor. It is as if unconsciously the individual takes responsibility for all the oppression and torment in the world and thus on a conscious level seeks to distance the self as far away as possible from those segments of society which may be seen as the oppressors.

Perhaps Saturn–Neptune people are born during or just after periods of exceptional persecution, as just after World War II, as Liz Greene suggests. Some people born in the 1940s and 1950s with these contacts will have had fathers who witnessed and perhaps had to commit atrocities. The scars of which would have been taken home. Certainly it often seems that individuals with these contacts carry the memory of an earlier threat of some kind, buried deeply within them. What would it be like to be born during the time that the full horrors of Auschwitz became known, or the day Chernobyl blew up or the week that Wall Street crashed, or in the wake of such happenings, for example? Surely such experiences would be somehow imprinted in the unconscious. In actuality, Saturn and Pluto are not usually the main significators (although they may be highly active in the midpoint structures in the chart of the country concerned) for such happenings and are often not making any kind of contact at all, but Saturn–Pluto aspects do equate with the *aftermath* of dreadful events when the collective is reeling at the horror of what has occurred and beginning to get some sense of what the repercussions might be. Saturn–Pluto seems to correlate with the *delayed reactions* of a previous atrocity occurring in the collective. I have occasionally urged people with these contacts to find out what was happening at the time they were born, in the hope that they will be able to share consciously in the *collective* responsibility for such happenings in the future, without taking unconscious *personal* responsibility for what happened in the past. Saturn links up with Pluto fairly frequently and thus these periods cannot always mark periods of such obvious horror but there may have been plane-crashes or earthquakes in the news, some kind of mass annihilation that, on some level, the individual continues to feel persecuted by. Saturn–Pluto may also mark the beginning of a recovery stage, when society realises how dreadful the situation is or was, but that it has survived.

Perhaps Saturn–Pluto might be linked with the lessons of survival. Sometimes the threat might be of a disease (polio, tuberculosis, Aids) which causes restrictive behaviour and scare-mongering, and sometimes the fear of massive financial loss. Certainly, Saturn–Pluto generally seems to mark periods of economic depression and hard or brutal times. For example the two planets were in opposition in 1930 and more precisely in 1931 when the horror of the 1929 crash would be really starting to make an impact and the way forward for survival would also be starting to surface. Saturn–Pluto times may also mark periods of accelerated fear concerning the dangers of nuclear power or the possible threat of nuclear war.

All this needs further research but assuming that such thinking is along the right lines, perhaps it is not surprising that people with these contacts prominently placed in their charts, often seem to build extremely strong defences. People with tight contacts between these planets often have a suspicion of psychology as well as a fear of their own unconscious processes. Sometimes there is an above-average fear of the nuclear threat, a fear of collective and personal annihilation. Whilst such a fear may be a very fitting and appropriate one for our times, the fear is often of the bomb within the self, a fear of the darker side of one's own unconscious, and a fear of the collective unconscious and the pain, brutality and havoc it can wreak.

Liz Greene associates Saturn–Pluto with the urge to sabotage those in authority and repeatedly this seems to be so. Whilst Saturn–Pluto can be associated with, on the one hand, very strong personal defences it can also, conversely, be associated with the demolition of defences, authority-figures, walls, barriers and boundaries. The dark face of authority sometimes has to be demolished in order for something new to be born. An example can be found in the chart of Mikhail Gorbachev, who has a Saturn–Pluto–Uranus T-square.

This is a good combination for demolition workers of all kinds although in psychic terms perhaps the walls have to be brought down slowly, brick by brick. It's ideal too for anyone who can take responsibility for collective power, whether this power be physical (as in fuel for example) or confined to paper or the exploration of the psyche. At best, Saturn–Pluto is concerned with the responsible and controlled use of power and this can manifest in a wide range of activities, whether these be physical, emotional or intellectual.

CHAPTER THIRTEEN

ASPECTS BETWEEN
THE OUTER PLANETS

Due to the slow-moving nature of the outer planets, aspects forming between them occur for very long periods of time and are descriptive of the major physical, political and psychological changes that occur on a world-wide basis. The cycles of these planets contribute to the history of the planet, the discussion of which is beyond the scope of this book.

However I will say that almost any 'disaster' which involves unexpected crisis, sudden violent death, some sort of shock that jolts and horrifies the collective, invariably has tight contacts involving both Uranus and Pluto in the horoscope. Commonly, the Sun (or another important factor) will fall exactly at the midpoint of these two planets.

The reader is signposted to Liz Greene's *The Outer Planets and Their Cycles*, Reinhold Ebertin's *Combination of Stellar Influences*, and *Mundane Astrology* by Baigent, Campion and Harvey, for further information on the cycles of the outer planets.

PART THREE

THE ANGLES

CHAPTER FOURTEEN

THE ASCENDANT–MIDHEAVEN COMPLEX

THE ASCENDANT–DESCENDANT AXIS

> Any planet's position on the horizon (i.e. near the Ascendant) can be
> considered to *indicate an unusual prominence* of that planet's qualities
> and energies in the life of a person at that moment. Imagine a full
> harvest Moon, glowing orange and gold just above the horizon. It
> looks *huge*, easily twice its normal diameter [italics mine].
> (Stephen Arroyo, *Astrology, Karma and Transformation*)

When considering any aspects to the Ascendant, it's important to realise
that we are actually dealing with an axis, that the Ascendant does not come
on its own but is paired with the Descendant. Any planet aspecting the
one will also be making aspect to the other.

The Ascendant/Descendant axis is the most personal point in the chart
as it is based on the actual moment and place of birth. We are born on the
same day as millions of other people and whilst we may share many characteristics and life-patterns with our birthday twins we will at the same
time be very unlike them. It is our birth-time that makes the difference.
The birth-time determines the angles and houses and basically the
structure of the whole chart. This alone gives us a clue to how important
the angles are.

Clearly though, in trying to interpret the Ascendant and Descendant we
have to grapple with much more than simply the signs on the axis. As
Stephen Arroyo points out, we are really dealing with a *complex*; a complex
described by the signs on the angles, any planets conjunct them, any planets
making aspect to the axis, together with the Ascendant ruler by sign, house
and aspect. Any aspects to the Ascendant, and all the details surrounding
its ruler, will greatly modify whatever the message of the Ascendant sign
actually is. All aspects to the angles will be significant and noticeable but,
as Arroyo says, the importance of a planet when it is conjunct the
Ascendant is vastly magnified. The labyrinthine nature of the Ascendant
complex makes it particularly difficult to categorise individual meanings in
a cookbook style as in the pages that follow. Thus the reader is urged to

use these with caution and in the light of all other factors in the horoscope.

The Ascendant (and by this I do mean the whole 'complex' from now on) will often very graphically describe the birth moment. This is not easy to prove since we cannot remember our birth and unless we resort to rebirth techniques, have to rely on the memory of those who might describe it to us. One example of this that I really like is of a woman who has Aquarius rising but Jupiter conjunct the Ascendant in Pisces. It was very cold (Aquarius) just before she was born. So much so that the pipes froze in the house and there was a flood (Pisces). The mother brought on the birth prematurely by overstraining herself in trying to mop up all the water. More curious still is the fact that this same person has the long-term goal of living on a boat and travelling round the world in it.

Planets contacting and ruling the axis seem to describe not only the birth experience but other very early situations and feelings that the young child is exposed to. These very early experiences permanently affect our attitude to meeting the outer world. We automatically expect things to be that way. Clearly our relationship with the immediate environment is not a passive one. It's a two-way process. On some level we somehow 'choose' what experiences to extract from our environment. As always, things don't just happen to us, we hook them.

In any event, the Ascendant clearly does describe, amongst other things, how we greet the world. How we approach life and those within our immediate environment. And as has been said, this will depend to a marked extent on how we expect that environment to be, based on how we experienced it in early life and, I believe, more specifically, with how we experienced it the moment we came in.

I have heard Lindsay Radermacher liken the Ascendant to being at Wembley Stadium or any other large arena. Whilst everyone will be looking at the same performance, the view of that performance may be different according to where one is actually sitting. Our Ascendant describes our particular vantage point, the seat we happen to be sitting in, the perspective from which we view the action and perhaps participate in it. The place in which the performers, were they able to do so, would also be able to see us. The Ascendant describes our *outlook*.

The Ascendant is often described as a lens, our own personal lens through which we view the world and through which the world views us. When having our sight tested, the optician puts different lenses in front of our eyes and whilst with each different piece of glass we are looking at the same view, with each lens it will *appear* differently to us. The image works better if we imagine the lenses as having colour. Dark glasses, rose-coloured spectacles, clear glasses and so on. Pluto rising or Scorpio on the Ascendant clearly would most closely fit dark glasses! Keeping with the metaphor, if the eyes are the mirror of the soul then clearly glasses can either allow or stop the outsider looking in. They also change the wearer's view of the world. If the world is a dark place, as with dark lenses, anything might be lurking anywhere. It might not feel safe, then of course the individual takes steps to shield themselves.

The Ascendant is also commonly described as the persona, the particular mask that we wear. The Ascendant is that part of ourselves that we choose to mediate between our whole person and the immediate environment. This persona may reveal and harmonise with the whole individual or present a very false image. Our Ascendant says much about our *advertising*, the *badge* we wear about ourselves.

At the risk of continually mixing metaphors and coming up with too many images, the Ascendant might also be described as the front door to our house. Everything and everyone goes in and out that way. In order for other people to reach us and explore who we are, they have to enter by the front door. And in order for us to get at ourselves, to look through all our different rooms, it is as if we also have to go the way of the Ascendant. The Sun may describe the task, the purpose, the hero, the way we have to go, the room we have to get to, but the Ascendant surely shows the way we have to go. Our Ascendant describes the journey and the *vehicle*.

Some definitions of vehicle I think are helpful and these are taken from the *Oxford English Dictionary*:

1. Substance, liquid or something which serves as a means for the readier application or use of another substance mixed with it or dissolved in it. 2. That which serves as a means of transmission, or as a material embodiment or manifestation of something. 3. A means or medium by which ideas or impressions are communicated or made known. 4. The form in which something is embodied or manifested.

Our birth-time is the time we *manifest* as individual beings. The time of an event is also when the energy of that event manifests. When something 'out there' takes form, a riot might take place. The energy that created that riot would have been around for some time, but the time for riot is when it actually happens, when the fighting actually breaks out, and that is the moment for which we would set up the chart for the event – the time it manifests.

One more definition:

5. A Material means, channel, or instrument by which something can be transmitted or conveyed from one point to another.

The Ascendant has always been associated with the physical body. As well as being a mode through which things are carried, and transported, a vehicle also has an outer covering. A covering that protects (or doesn't) what is inside as well as either revealing or concealing it.

We may find a physical analogy here. Human beings have brains, livers, kidneys and all manner of things going on inside their bodies. But what we each see of each other is the outer covering. Our skin, our clothes, the impression we make, conceals a multitude. On the other hand, it doesn't lie. If we are enormously fat, our skin has to stretch. If we are ill it shows in our face and in our eyes. If we look at a potato, we can usually get a rough idea of what it's like inside by looking at the skin.

The skin is our outer surface fabric; it acts as a waterproof covering and as a first line of defence against injury or invasion by bacteria. Tough, supple and self-renewing, it also covers a vast area in proportion to other body organs. Our Ascendant should also be like this; supple and yet tough, able to move and able to grow. If the Ascendant is too strong, too inflexible, as with Saturn or Pluto rising for example, it can be rather like wearing too tight a body mask. The individual may become trapped behind their image. Incarcerated in a vehicle that is so strongly fortified that nothing can penetrate it or leave.

Staying with the analogy of the skin, it also registers sensations; it registers touch, pressure, pain, warmth and cold, and having picked up these sensations can modify the temperature of the body through perspiration or goose pimples. In the same way our Ascendant says something about how we *register* the outer world and adjust to it.

Research has shown that people do not necessarily look like their Ascending signs and planets but rather like an amalgam of the Sun, Moon, Ascendant and Ascendant ruler, or, in individual cases, just one or two of these. Nevertheless, aspects to our Ascendant, particularly conjunctions, usually have great bearing on how we come across, the impression we make. Arroyo describes it as the *image* of the person that is seen by others.

The *Descendant* is also often seen very quickly by others. Sometimes it is difficult to tell the difference between the two halves of the axis but, put simplistically, at the Ascendant we act, we initiate and at the Descendant we *react*, we respond to initiatives from others.

If the Ascendant is how we approach others and the environment in general, the Descendant describes how we react when approached. With Aries rising for example, one might greet the world, eager to launch into action, to be first. Keen to start things. Decisive and competitive. In early life, the individual may have experienced the world as a competitive place and one in which the individual feels their attitude must be 'I'm gonna do it, I'm going to get out there and show them.' Libra is on the Descendant though. Other people might say: 'I cannot make my mind up. OK, you want to lead, that's fine by me' – an attitude which would reinforce Aries rising. But equally the other person, the world at large, the not-self might say: 'Hang on a minute have you ever considered X, Y, Z, or what about me? Is that course of action really fair?' The response to that might be, 'Yes, maybe you're right.'

Through relationship, Aries rising realises how much it needs another person, for how can Aries be first unless there is another person, another situation to compete with? Through relationship Aries learns co-operation.

For the sake of completeness perhaps we had better try it the other way round. With Libra rising, the individual might go out into the world being concerned with balancing various factors in the life. Libra rising might approach everyone wanting to keep everything nice, peaceful and har-monious. Libra rising goes out into the world being concerned with co-operation and fairness. Libra might say. 'I go out into the world wanting what you want, whatever I do in life is coloured by the fact that I want to make a pleasing, harmonious and co-operative kind of impact.'

But with Aries on the Descendant other people, especially the partner, might respond thus: 'That's a bit wet isn't it? That means I have to make all the decisions. OK, I will. I want this. This is my decision.' Libra might return with: 'That's not fair … I'll fight you for it.' Through interaction with another person, Libra rising finds out about being direct, assertive, taking the initiative, and possibly getting involved in all-out battle!

The Ascendant–Descendant axis works very much as a duo; sometimes it's difficult to see which side of the dialogue one is actually on, because we tend to oscillate between one side and the other. The sign on the Descendant and planets in or on the Descendant are often just as obvious as those on the Ascendant. This is hardly surprising if we consider that the Descendant describes how we deal with the not-self.

THE MC–IC AXIS

As with the Ascendant–Descendant axis the MC and IC again need to be viewed as a complex. Conjunctions on the angles will be very important but other aspects to the axis need also to be noted, together with the ruling planets by sign, house and aspect.

A common image for the MC and IC is of a tree and I think this is a very good one, for a tree cannot have masses of branches and foliage unless it also has strong and mature roots.

The MC is the highest point in the chart. We look up to it, just as we look up to the top of a tree. We *aspire* to whatever is described by our MC complex. But it takes a long time to get there. The planet nearest to the Midheaven is known as the most 'elevated' planet and greater importance is traditionally conferred upon it because of its elevation.

When we first walk into a room of people that we don't know, at a party for instance, we are likely to come across as our Ascendant. That's what we feel safe with. With people we know, we may behave more like our Moon or other factors in the chart. Later on, perhaps we will get chatting to people at the party whom we have not met before. Someone is bound to ask 'And what do you do?' It's a common enough question in that kind of situation and it's a question that reflects not so much an interest in one's work as a curiosity about one's social position. The answer to the question can be taken as an indication of prestige, status and role in society. In a way, it is also saying what is your upbringing? Your class. And as such has Saturnian overtones, but basically it is an MC-type question. The MC of the individual asking the question might describe whatever answer you could give that would impress them, whilst your MC might describe the answer that would impress you.

The MC complex may be taken as an indication of the different ways we seek to *impress* the world at large. The first person we ever sought to impress would probably have been a parent figure and it would have been that same person or persons who would have socialised us as to how we should behave in society. It can already be seen why a complex is at work with this axis, for there can be all sorts of complicated messages coming from parental figures wanting us to succeed or fail in different careers and be viewed in society in different ways and for various reasons. And having different ideas about how we should get to wherever we are going. And then there is our own sense of 'calling', which may be quite at odds with all these other messages. The different aspects and significators will describe all the various internal dialogues.

Basically, the sign on the MC will usually show the *way* we go about getting ourselves to where we want to be. That sign, and more especially any planets on the axis, may describe the nature of the vocation but this may also be shown by the ruler of the MC. And where there are planets in the 10th house in a different sign, that also has relevance. I suspect that the 10th house has much more to do with the actual vocation whereas the MC has much more of a bearing on the image (which may not have that much to do with work) one wants to cultivate and the image one has of oneself in later life; the kind of life that one would want to live. In many ways, the MC describes our dreams and goals for the future. The whole complex, including the 10th house, seems to have bearing on what we would like to be held in esteem for, remembered for, what might be the summit of our contribution to the world at large. So it says a lot about our aims. Above all else the MC describes the *direction* we are going in.

Where the Equal House system is used, the MC and IC can fall in a variety of houses and the MC may not fall in the 10th. Although this complicates matters, I do not consider it a reason not to use the Equal

House system. Rather, it may be used to give additional information. The house the MC falls in may describe another aspect of one's career or where one sees one's public. For example, MC falling in the 9th might suggest vocational activities to do with education, publishing, law, travel, other cultures and all else we associate with this house. It might also be saying that for a person with this placement, it is people in these vocations that they would most like to impress or that impress them, who constitute their personal public, rather than say the business world, or a parent (10th) and so on.

The IC is the lowest point in the chart; we have to dig to get to it and like the tree can probably never get at all the roots. The IC represents our own personal history and that is never-ending, for it would take us back to dinosaurs and beyond, if we could go that far. Thus the IC probably links us with the collective unconscious.

The IC describes where we are coming from, as opposed to the MC which describes where we are aspiring to go. It is the past in the sense of describing family atmosphere from where we have come and thus both parents and the whole family is implied. It often describes the emotional quality of our childhood. It represents our heritage, our family history, our roots, our racial origin, our home, our source. It is our platform, our base, our foundation. It is the place that we retreat to; the place that we go to for privacy; the part of us that is hidden from public view. Because the IC forms an axis with the MC, any planet aspecting the IC will also aspect the MC and vice versa, thus a planet on the MC may also describe the family roots and all the other IC issues.

Traditionally, the IC is associated with the end of the matter (in horary astrology) and the end of life. I am never quite sure whether this means where you are buried or cremated in a literal sense, but this area of the chart, including the 4th house, does often say something about the end of one's physical life. This also fits well with the tree analogy. The fruits of the tree fall to the ground and the seeds take root. In the 10th house we do our bit in the outer world, in the 4th we retire, we go back to our roots and hopefully enjoy the fruits of our labours.

The IC represents the family in the personal sense whereas the MC is all of society, which in turn is composed of millions of families.

Parents and the MC–IC Axis

There is tremendous controversy as to which parent should be ascribed to the MC and 10th house and which should be considered to be concerned with the IC and 4th house. Liz Greene and, apparently, Lilly and Manilius[1] before her, have suggested that the MC is more likely to indicate the mother and the 4th to describe the father, despite the fact that Cancer is traditionally associated with the 4th and Capricorn with the 10th. Much learned material has been presented on the subject in the astrological press.

I do not really wish to get into the debate here. My own experience confirms the mother – 10th/father – 4th associations but suggests that hard and fast rules just cannot be made. One can usually see *both* points as being descriptive of *both* parents. What is consciously lived out by one parent is often pretty strong in the unconscious of the other. And surely our whole chart reflects our childhood, with obviously some planets and parts of the chart maybe doing so more than others. We might also view the birth-chart as a horoscope for a first meeting, the first meeting with our mother. It is not necessarily the chart for the first meeting with our father, whom we don't necessarily meet. It might equally be viewed not only as a chart that potentially describes the individual's relationship with the mother but also as a relationship chart for whoever else was in the room at the time. The midwife or obstetrician for example!

I think it has to be remembered, too, that some people are not raised by a mother and a father, and what do we mean by these terms anyway? We know what we mean in a *biological* sense, but parents in the biological sense seem to me to be as clearly described by the Sun and Moon, as do the internal images of 'mother' and 'father'. Some people are raised in institutions, some by one person, others by two people of the same sex, still others in a community. It can be very complicated and whilst the reality of the whole situation will be reflected in the chart overall, I feel that we need to be much more flexible in dealing with parental issues generally and ascribing parental roles to the MC–IC axis in particular, especially since such roles are changing and vary greatly from culture to culture. In my view, the most that we can say about the MC–IC axis is that it describes our roots in both the widest possible and narrowest senses.

To illustrate the idea that, in my view, both ends of the axis describe both parents, but in different ways, I would like to look at the charts of June and Jennifer Gibbons, the so-called 'Silent Twins', taking into account not only the angles but the Sun and Moon. If the reader is unfamiliar with their story it does not matter, for I only wish to look at a few basic descriptions of their parents and the grandparents and show the complexity of a family myth. As with all such complex stories, out of which we are all born, the myth cannot be thoroughly explored by the astrologer alone. The individual whose chart is being examined has to be consciously engaged in the process too, and over a period of time.

Briefly, June and Jennifer, as children, hardly ever spoke to anyone except each other. And when conversing with each other, they did so in private or too fast for anyone to follow and in a special language that no one else could understand. They were bonded to each other totally and it seems were unable to live with each other and yet were unable to live apart; bonded by love but also by intense rivalry. After a few attempts at theft and arson as teenagers, they were sentenced to Broadmoor top-security special hospital, from which they were released many years later. Unfortunately Jennifer died in 1993, an event that whilst tragic at so young an age, may have released June from the stress and confusion of a shared identity and so tight a psychic bond.

Though born only ten minutes apart the twins were different. Jennifer had a Gemini Ascendant whilst June has Taurus rising. In harmonic astrology, the differences in the charts become much more apparent, and the reader is directed to an excellent article by David Hamilton[2] on this subject.

All material and quotes are taken from *The Silent Twins* by Marjorie Wallace.

The mother's name is Gloria: *Leo on the IC.* Above all else, Gloria seems to have been a friend to the twins; *ruler of the 4th house in the 11th*; or *Aquarius on MC square Moon!*

The twins' father, Aubrey, really enjoyed his friends, with whom he liked a drink and a chat: *Sun in 11th house, Aquarius on MC.*

Aubrey 'wanted, needed, to be liked and accepted. But already his yearning for social acceptability was having an effect on the family which saw less and less of him.' *Saturn on the MC in Aquarius square Moon–Neptune.*

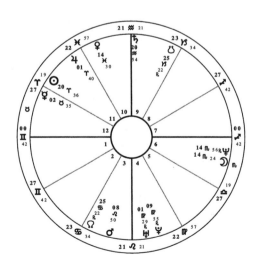

Fig. 17

June Gibbons 11 April 1963, 8.10am local time (5.10am GMT), Aden, Yemen, 12N47 45E02

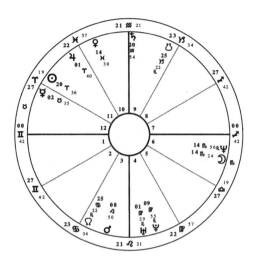

Fig. 18

Jennifer Gibbons 11 April 1963, 8.20am. local time (5.20am GMT), Aden, Yemen, 12N47 45E02

Gloria comes across as a very loving mother who refuses to see anything is wrong with the twins. When reading about her in the book she seems difficult to get hold of: *Moon conjunct Neptune in the 6th house trine Venus in the 10th*. She is described as very hard-working and she seems to take most of the responsibility for the children: *Moon–Neptune is in the 6th house and squares Saturn and the MC*. Aubrey apparently felt that 'his contribution to family life began and ended with providing shelter': *Moon square Saturn*.

Gloria's father was 'a strict Barbadian, who was ambitious for his eldest daughter whom he wanted to become a teacher'. Gloria took a job as an infant teacher for a while 'but hated it': *Saturn on MC, ruler of the 9th house of education*. The MC conjunction can be interpreted as her own unlived ambitions. Gloria mostly worked as a telephonist before she met Aubrey: *the Moon rules the twins' 3rd house*. Gloria's mother played the organ in the local church: *Moon conjunct Neptune trine Venus in Pisces*.

Aubrey was in the forces — the RAF: *Sun in Aries; Sun is ruler of the 4th house*. Aubrey was very bright as a child, but his home life was dreadful with his parents arguing violently all the time. His mother left his father half a dozen times but always went back. Aubrey couldn't cope; he rebelled against his father and the family wishes for his future: *Saturn in Aquarius on the MC and Uranus in the 4th*. Aubrey rebelled against his father. The twins rebelled against *him*. He wanted to be a respectable member of society. The managed to get themselves put in Broadmoor! Because of his (probably quite appropriate) rebellion, Aubrey was unable to fulfil 'the family's dream to become a lawyer or doctor'. He says, 'I feel I failed, I was a disappointment to my family. I'm not what they wanted me to be': *Saturn on the MC.*

Because of service life, the family had to move a great deal in the twins' early life. And of course their first move was to England, for their roots were really in Barbados and they were actually born in the Yemen: *Uranus–Pluto in the 4th house.* This is surely descriptive of feelings of rootlessness and a feeling that you can never put down roots for they are sure to be pulled up at any moment – not that this might not be exciting as well as unsettling.

Looking at the charts more from the twins' point of view, we might interpret Saturn on the MC as fear of not receiving public recognition. With that placement there can be enormous investment in achieving, and a tremendous parental investment in their going so and in their being respectable. Judging from the biography, this certainly would have been Aubrey's wish. In Aquarius, there could be a need to make some sort of unique contribution towards humanity. With Saturn on the MC achievement may be such an issue that the individual might not manage it at all. Certainly one would expect individuals with this placement to be 'late developers'. This Saturn is saying, 'I must achieve something and be known for something that will stand the test of time.' It might be some sort of innovation or invention or I might get to where I am going through some sort of unorthodox route. One might expect seemingly eccentric aims and ambitions, and with the Saturn in Aquarius and Uranus in the 4th house there is, as has been mentioned, a strong need to *rebel* against family pressures. On another level, the twins may have been doing Aubrey's rebellion for him. Unconsciously, this may have been what he or Gloria wanted. But that is very much conjecture.

In any event, the twins have become very well known. They have become famous for their silence: *Saturn is exactly quintile Mercury.* They are well known through becoming the black sheep of their family. Saturn even exactly sextiles the Sun in the sign of the sheep, Aries. One can also consider the rootlessness of Uranus–Pluto in the 4th and the need for security described by Saturn opposition IC and as described by their incarceration behind bars for so many years.

NOTES

1 *Astrology*, Vol. 59, No. 4, Winter 1985/86.
2 *The Astrological Journal*, June/July 1987.

CHAPTER FIFTEEN

PLANETS AND ANGLES

THE SUN AND THE ANGLES

Those with Sun conjunction Ascendant often find it impossible to be inconspicuous. In their immediate environment they tend to be always noticed, wherever they go, whatever they do.

Those with the Sun rising in their charts were born at dawn, at the beginning of a bright new day. Characteristically, Sun rising people like to be in at the beginning of projects and usually have very marked leadership potential. These people tend to be self-motivated and keen to pull the strings in their life, to be master of their destiny. This person is usually in no way a fatalist.

The birth moment is often marked out in some way. Perhaps there is an especial sense of occasion as if the arrival of the child has actually created the beginning of the new day. The emergence of the new arrival is properly recognised or humoured. It might just be the dawn chorus. Just imagine all the birds starting to sing at the moment you are born.

There is often an early childhood history where the child felt constantly 'watched' and noticed. Aspects to the Sun will describe the reasons for this and whether it was a pleasant experience or not. Often the child was expected to shine, or sometimes to 'perform' to others. The parents, especially the father, were usually proud of the child, who perhaps was the first born. With luck this should make for a self-reliant and confident individual but aspects to the Sun need to be carefully studied for confirmation of this.

In any event, those with the Sun on the Ascendant or into the 1st house tend to watch themselves a good deal; they are 'self-conscious', seeming often to have an ability to step outside of themselves and look at themselves, and watch other people looking at them. The person with Ascendant and Sun in the same sign not only usually embodies very strongly the characteristics of that sign but also often comes across with great presence. And authenticity. There is no persona for the individual to hide behind. Or one could say that the person *identifies* with their persona.

The father was often a strong influence in the child's life and was frequently present at the birth, even when this was a less common occurrence than it is now. The person will tend to identify with the father, his outlook, attitudes and sometimes how he is physically. This person can literally 'follow in Father's footsteps'.

Where the Sun is in the 12th house and especially when it is actually out of orb of conjuncting the Ascendant, the individual often feels overlooked as a child, not recognised as an individual in their own right, in the background or behind the scenes. People with Sun in the 12th house often work 'behind the scenes' in some way but as Gauquelin's research seems to suggest, this placement is also often to be found in the charts of world leaders. (Margaret Thatcher is an example of this, although in the Equal House System, which I favour as much as the quadrant systems, her Sun actually falls in her 11th house.) Personally, I think one of the reasons for this is that if a person has had a history of feeling overlooked then quite often the individual will make very sure that they are not overlooked in the future. Also of course, in leading a public life, an individual has to sacrifice much of their personal life, which is fitting for the Sun in this Pisces house.

Those with Sun on the Descendant can sometimes seem to 'give' their Sun to others, in as much as they give power to other people. I have particularly noticed this with Sun–Descendant clients, for they seem to take more than usual notice of what might be said during a consultation, tending as they do to ascribe far too much importance to the view and opinions of others at the expense of their own and frequently looking to other people to make their decisions for them. The astrologer–client relationship like any other counselling situation is based on equality and sharing; if one person could be said to be more 'important' than the other then that person is clearly the client. At its most extreme, Sun in the 7th, when in the role of client is often reluctant to accept this. They give away their importance, they fight shy of the limelight and try to manipulate the situation so that the counsellor is centre-stage and the one pulling the strings in the client's life. Where this does happen it is usually repeating a situation that has been created in their other partnerships, whether personal relationships or working partnerships. All too easily, Sun–Descendant can believe that their life is fated and that they are merely pawns in the hands of the heavens or others' superior power.

This is not always the case of course, but certainly Sun–Descendant, rather like a Sun Libran, does like to share the decision-making process and does like someone to do things with. Relationship and partnership are very important to this type. It's a good placement for people who work in a partnership and indeed for anyone who works in a one-to-one situation. In some cases, the Sun–Descendant might say, 'I am nothing without a partner; life has no meaning without another person.' More positively, Sun–Descendant people might say, 'I find myself through close interaction with another person.'

Significantly, analysts Freud, Jung and Laing all have their Suns on the Descendant or in their 7th house. They found their identity through close interaction with another person and similarly in a one-to-one situation they have enabled others to shed light on themselves. It could be said that they 'fathered' their clients. So it is a very good placement for analysts, therapists and the like. In the case of these famous analysts, they also of course achieved personal distinction and recognition through relationship. It's common in the charts of lawyers too; they often work in partnerships and on each case they work in partnership with their clients, and usually lawyers are involved with litigation with 'open enemies', working, ideally, for justice and fairness.

The father of the person with Sun on the Descendant was usually viewed by the individual more as a husband to the mother than a father to the child. Sometimes this is literally true, where the father-figure in the home during the formative years is not actually the biological father, but usually this is more the psychological experience than the actual one. Father was concerned with being a partner (in the marital or business sense) above all else. It is hardly surprising, therefore, that Sun in the 7th places such a high premium on marriage (and I mean the contract of marriage, not living together) for it is through marriage that the individual (of both sexes) seeks a relationship with the father archetype either by playing that role themselves or by expecting the 'other' to do it for them. Where the individual considers working partnerships to be especially important the Sun is usually to be found on the 6th house side of the Descendant or the ruler of the 6th is in the 7th or vice versa. In any event the individual is still usually 'fathering' others in the sense that they are providing some sort of identity for others.

Descendant–Sun people are proud of their partnerships. This is the type who, aged 70 or 80 can be found linking arms with their spouse and stating proudly that they have been married fifty years or so. Not that relationships are more likely to last with Sun on the 7th or that it is necessarily a 'good' thing too if they do, or that the relationship is necessarily 'better' than anyone else's; it's just that with this placement, relationship tends to be the most important thing, and something to be proud of.

Traditionally, Sun conjunct the MC is supposed to mark out an individual for great success and honours. There are many different types of success of course and many a yardstick for measuring it. Success or not, the goal of many with this placement is to be important, noticed, recognised and respected in the world at large. Famous in fact. It's hardly surprising therefore that fame often does knock at the door of those with this contact, or at least success in their field.

Classically, it is found in the charts of those who find themselves in charge of something, a leader in some way, the one who heads the company, the school, the hospital and so forth. Whereas Sun conjunct Ascendant finds it difficult to be inconspicuous in their immediate environment, the noticeability of the person with Sun conjunct MC is usually much more public, or at least that is often the goal.

All other things being equal, this is the person who winds up being a pillar of the community, renowned for their integrity, respected for the position they hold and the responsibility it carries. Executive positions, or public positions, but of course aspects to the conjunction have to be very carefully weighed.

I associate this conjunction with prizes – *honours* I suppose would be more accurate. I have even noticed that a progression from or to the MC by the Sun often coincides with the individual receiving some sort of prize. If a child, this might be some sort of school or sports prize but as an adult it may take the form of some other type of publicly recognised honour. An example of this can be found in the chart of Pearl Buck, who has Sun conjunct Mercury conjunct MC and has been awarded both the Nobel and Pulitzer prizes for literature. As a child, the person with Sun conjunct MC would have been encouraged to gain public recognition in this way. The father is often well known and acts as a model for some kind of 'stardom'. And sometimes it is the fact that he wasn't well known that makes the child so anxious to become so for him.

Those with Sun conjunct IC usually would not wish for public recognition or the star treatment, although it is important to emphasise that individuals with this placement are no less likely to be successful. But the home life is likely to be even more important, as is the need to tap one's roots, either literally or emotionally.

Individuals with this configuration sometimes retire from the world, even occasionally to live as a recluse. At any rate they invariably want some privacy. They might be hidden from society in a variety of different ways, and in extreme cases by being sent to goal or hospital. The father was also often a hidden kind of figure.

Square aspects from the Sun to the MC–IC axis suggest a long hard climb to the top, but a determination to get there. It sometimes suggests that the individual's ultimate goals are actually out of keeping with the character that they are, and integrating the two takes time. The person may also feel pulled between personal and professional life.

Soft aspects to the MC–IC axis suggest no such conflict. The individual achieves success, whatever is meant by this term, comparatively easily and is motivated by doing so. But the achievements are not likely to be so record-breaking. Other configurations in the chart may say differently of course.

THE MOON AND THE ANGLES

Moon conjunct Ascendant suggests that the individual will approach the world and those within it wanting to care for and protect. If other chart factors concur, they will appear as being very responsive, adaptable, impressionable and either keen to satisfy the needs of others or to have their own needs satisfied.

There is often a strong identification with the mother-figure and often the mother role itself. There is usually a very strong female presence in the early years. One man I know with this placement was brought up living with his mother, grandmother and aunt. They were all responsive to his needs and he was to theirs. People with this placement will sometimes have been (or had to be) exceptionally sensitive to the maternal figure's needs and perhaps had to protect that person. In some cases, they act as mother to their own mother and thereafter go out into the world wanting either to feed others emotionally or be fed by them.

The individual with the Moon rising, rather like Neptune rising, can be so receptive and sensitive to everything and everyone they meet that they find it difficult to work out where they leave off and others begin. They absorb whatever they encounter. I have known several instances where the mother had psychiatric problems and the child had to take on the role of mother to the mother from a very early age. To keep her behaviour relatively sane, the child develops what Howard Sasportas describes as 'a radar-like ability' to pick up and read her signals and quite soon the ability to read signals from everyone they come into contact with. The ill mother also sometimes copes better with the child whilst it is still a baby or infant and still dependent on her. Thus as an adult, the Moon rising person often still exudes a powerful neediness and often a childlike dependency. The Moon seems to describe the child in relation to early mother-figures and thus Moon rising people sometimes approach the world revealing the part of themselves which is a needy child, wanting to be protected and cared for.

Moon conjunct Descendant suggests that there is a very strong need for relationship and all the emotional, familial and domestic security it might provide. A need for relationships which will provide some measure of nurture, containment, protection and dependency. Whatever the real nature of a particular relationship – child–parent, employer–employee, or that between two lovers – those with the Moon Descendant somehow or other find themselves in a parent–child relationship, with them to be found at either end of the spectrum.

People with this placement often find, maybe several years into a relationship, that they have 'married' someone who closely resembles their mother or are re-enacting the relationship they had with her or would have liked to have had.

Sometimes the early mother-figure was experienced more as a wife, either to the child or to the other parent and it is from this situation that a mother–spouse linkage is formed. In any event, mother issues and relationship seem even more intermingled than usually with this combination.

People with Moon conjunct Descendant are often very nurturant in relationship and indeed, in all one-to-one encounters, though as Howard Sasportas says of Moon in the 7th, it may be 'over-sensitive or over-adaptive' to the needs of the partner. This placement is indicative of the formation of very strong bonds with women. People with this placement who are in therapy, for example, usually feel more comfortable with women therapists.

The placement can also be found in those who meet others through providing some sort of lunar skills; such skills might range from cooking and catering to working in security or even such things as furniture restoration: those who provide some kind of service which involves caring or providing some kind of protection.

The Moon on either end of the MC–IC axis is suggestive of exceptionally strong parent–child ties. Those with Moon on the Midheaven sometimes take on the role of some kind of public mother, perhaps the person in the company who 'holds' everything together and provides some kind of containment. Sometimes the vocation chosen is concerned with looking after one's own home and family, but sometimes the vocation is concerned with protecting, caring and nurturing in a much more public sense. Obviously the sign is of great importance. Moon in Gemini for instance could suggest that the individual is concerned with protecting language or nurturing through language; Moon in Taurus or Cancer would suggest a career in agriculture, horticulture or catering.

Like Sun conjunct MC, there is a need for personal recognition with this placement, coupled with a sensitivity to what the public thinks and feels. Thus this is a good combination for anyone who has to be very responsive to the needs of the public.

The Moon on the IC is naturally at home. This placement suggests a rich familial history and also that the past will exert an especially strong pull on the individual. This might be the past in terms of the family in which the individual was raised, the past in terms of the family's history or much further back still. This is an ideal placement for historians or those who seek to trace their family tree.

The need to feel emotionally and domestically secure is likely to be very strong in an individual with this placement. There is usually a need for privacy, a place of retreat and safety and even seclusion. A need, too, to keep one's feelings private. Often the individual has a strong awareness and sensitivity to the notion of protecting or nurturing planet earth; this can manifest in a variety of ways from gardening to involvement in ecological issues. There is sometimes strong involvement with matters to do with property and housing. There is a sensitivity towards and about one's roots with this placement which might manifest in a variety of different ways. This placement usually describes a parent that is 'hidden' from public view but also that the individual, if other chart factors agree, feels safe with that person and will return to them for safety. Sometimes, Moon on the IC is more descriptive of the individual's experience of the father than of the mother. In any event, people with this placement often have one parent who becomes very retiring and even reclusive in later life. On other occasions, the parent comes to live with the child.

MERCURY AND THE ANGLES

The immediate impression that a Mercury conjunct Ascendant individual might make is of being bright, youthful and curious – and very chatty. These people have a very pronounced need to talk, and often to write, especially about their own experiences. All contacts from Mercury to the Ascendant–Descendant axis favour autobiographical writing. As always, the sign placement, other aspects to the configuration and the houses where Gemini and Virgo are to be found, will all have great bearing on Mercury rising and form part of the overall complex.

One woman I know with Mercury rising in Capricorn (and thus Gemini on the 6th house and Virgo on the 9th house) works for an opinion poll agency. It could be said that she goes out into the world picking up opinions. Her work involves collecting other people's thoughts as to their beliefs, their politics and so on. She collects and connects people's ideas and then acts as a mouthpiece for these. Before that she worked as a secretary to a 'society' osteopath which also exactly fits the symbolism. On a personal level, as Mercury is in Capricorn, she wants what she says to be taken *seriously*. She wants to be respected for her knowledge, for being an authority on a given subject. It could be said that her life's journey is about becoming knowledgeable about herself; *the* authority on herself. Perhaps her work (6th house) and her studies and beliefs (9th house) will facilitate this process. The fact that she is a great talker is part of her persona and she also talks with her hands a lot. The first part of her that you encounter is this Mercurial quality, but it also reflects a Mercury–Saturn-type need to define exactly what she does think about things, and in particular her belief system (9th house) and areas to do with work and mind and body issues. So one might also say that a major part of her journey in life is concerned with defining her own views and ideas and communicating these to others.

People with Mercury rising usually have very strong early issues around siblings and schooling. Exactly what the issues are will be shown by the overall picture. Mercury rising people often immediately talk about their siblings and what those issues are.

People with Mercury conjunct Descendant or making other hard aspects to the axis usually have just as urgent a need to communicate as Mercury rising but the Mercurial quality does not, so obviously, constitute the individual's persona.

With Mercury conjunct either end of this axis, there is a strong need to communicate with someone else in a one-to-one setting, a need to discuss oneself, and oneself in relation to other people. Lots of people gravitate to therapy situations with these contacts for there is a need to be listened to. It is through verbal interchange with another person that the individual is able to arrive at their own position on given subjects.

Bob Dylan has Mercury in Gemini conjunct the Descendant and square Neptune. He meets the not-self (us) through writing music and singing it. He was also married to a schoolteacher. Those with Mercury rising like to be seen as intelligent and articulate, whereas the Mercury setting person is more likely to look for these qualities in a partner, in order that they might be cultivated in the self. In relationship, Mercury conjunct Descendant is often particularly looking for a brother or sister, someone they can easily communicate with perhaps.

Hard aspects from Mercury to the Ascendant–Descendant occasionally describe early communicative difficulties, especially if the configuration involves Saturn or Pluto. The urge to communicate is usually rendered far more urgent thereafter. I have also known cases where Mercury is 45/135 degrees from the axis where, following birth trauma, there has been damage to the limbs or respiratory system. In the few such cases I have known, Mars has also be implicated.

With all contacts there are often lots of comings and goings and general activity around the individual's birth. A lot of talking is also implied.

People with Mercury rising and sometimes making other contacts to the Ascendant–Descendant axis generally, often have two or more names which they may be known by simultaneously or at different times. This reflects the general ambidextrous quality of these contacts.

Mercury aspecting the MC–IC axis suggests that the individual wants public recognition for their communicative skills or their learning. This might be the ultimate goal, what they would like to be remembered for. Mercury conjunct the MC especially sometimes indicates that this is what a parent wanted or pushed for. Hard aspects from Mercury to the MC sometimes suggest that the individual wants to do these things *in spite* of what the parents might have wished. But it is rarely this clear-cut in practice. In any event the vocation will often involve writing or talking. Perhaps acting as an agent, a go-between, or an educator. A transporter or connector of ideas, people or things.

Mercury conjunct IC is suggestive of an educated background, or at least one where there were lots of discussions and perhaps plenty of books. There is likely to be a strong interest in one's roots and personal history, and it's a good combination for genealogy.

Sometimes a sibling acts as parent when Mercury is conjunct the MC or IC. More often one parent is experienced as being particularly Mercurial in some way. Sometimes the parent is more like a brother or sister than a parent.

VENUS AND THE ANGLES

Venus rising is usually descriptive of someone who approaches the environment and those within it, seeking to be as diplomatic as possible. There is a strong need to maintain or create harmony and peace. Sometimes even if the maintenance of that peace means the individual has to go along with proposals that are actually at variance with their innermost wishes.

People with Venus rising appear, and seek to be, co-operative and willing to compromise. They approach the world from the standpoint of wanting to fit in and be popular and well liked. They may meet others from the vantage point of asking 'What have we got in common?' There are often strong issues about being 'good' in childhood with Venus close to the Ascendant axis and into the first house. Often too, a desire to keep things as easy as possible, to plump for simplicity and to avoid unnecessary complications. There is sometimes a gift with comparison, whether the ability to compare is physical or intellectual. It could be said that Venus rising goes out into the world being concerned with taste. Physical taste or taste inasmuch as a sensitivity to what is or is not appropriate behaviour for a given situation.

There is usually also a strong concern with appearance and on all levels. This placement is good at packaging, whether this packaging be of oneself, or of a product or an idea. Physically, there is usually a strong need to make oneself as physically attractive and pleasing as possible; the type just cannot wear any old clothes but has to feel 'right' about their appearance. They are sensitive to the idea that they can attract or repel others by how they appear to be physically. Traditionally, Venus rising is supposed to confer good looks and certainly this is often the case. There is often a distinctive colour sense. Individuals with Venus rising and into the 1st house usually received positive strokes in childhood for their appearance, as opposed to Venus in the 12th house, where the child picks up the idea that others find them unattractive for some reason. Venus making hard aspect to this axis sometimes suggests that the individual dresses inappropriately for the outer image they are trying to convey. For both sexes with Venus on this axis the appearance may be youthful and feminine. Venus rising inclines to soft rather than rugged features, although as always the sign is of central importance.

Some people with Venus conjunct either end of this axis appear very concerned with money, perhaps naturally exude material advantage or wish to do so. Certainly the journey in life is often very concerned with value, with self-valuation and the gaining of an understanding about what is and is not highly valued in the life.

People with Venus on either end of this axis often have a gift for making others feel liked or loved by them and this does much to confer personal popularity. Venus conjunct any of the angles lends a distinct non-competitive feel to the chart but the condition of Mars can, of course, do much to offset this. Those with Venus rising for example, may appear to be more non-competitive than they really are.

Venus on the Descendant sometimes reveals itself as a concern with others' appearance. For example, a hairdresser that I used to go to had Venus on the Descendant. He could work on the issue of his own appearance through working on how others looked. Success in such a field would also confer great personal popularity. Some with this placement project their Venus onto others by seeing them as 'nice', beautiful, good or even wealthy but in so doing can find these principles within themselves. Many with this placement feel more valuable when in a partnership and I have seen this work on a literal level, as in the case where an individual becomes involved with someone who, relative to their own income, is very wealthy.

Venus on either end of this axis inevitably gives rise to a strong concern with relationship. The need for partnership may be quite overwhelming. Some with Neptune conjunct Descendant particularly, also want a relationship that looks good to others. Depending on the overall condition of Venus and the 7th house, there may be difficulty in accepting the more difficult, complicated and sordid aspects of one's relationships, always wanting to keep everything 'nice'.

Venus conjunct the MC might be indicative of a Venusian career; a vocation in art, beauty, diplomacy or somewhere where there is a requirement for taste, comparison or harmony. Certainly, whatever the actual work the individual will be able to bring diplomatic skills to it. Usually people with this placement know how to charm and get on easily with those in authority. Venus conjunct MC might also be expected to confer public popularity, or at least an urge towards trying to create it. Some with this configuration may become well known because of their romantic life or the relationships they form. Still others might wish, beyond all else, to be known as a loving parent.

Venus on either end of the MC–IC axis may be descriptive of the experience of their own parent(s) as being very loving or popular. For others it may be more descriptive of a parent's vocational activities or their wishes for the career of the child. Frequently a parent is experienced as being a very sexual kind of person and I have frequently seen Venus conjunct the IC as being descriptive of a parent who pursued secret extra-marital affairs.

Venus on the IC often suggests that the individual comes from a background which had money; there is a feeling of a 'good' home with this placement and the idea of 'good home' can be interpreted on a number of levels. Ideally it should perhaps mean a warm and loving environment and the absence of hard aspects to Venus conjunct IC may well indicate this. Certainly there are usually at least some aspects of the individual's ancestry or background that they value very highly.

People with this placement want to create a beautiful home themselves, a place with harmonious colours and pleasing music perhaps and certainly one as free as possible from emotional discord.

MARS AND THE ANGLES

Those with Mars conjunct Ascendant tend to view the world as a highly competitive place and approach it from this vantage point. Often, too, there is a vague feeling that conflict might break out at any minute. Sometimes the Mars rising person was born into or raised in an early atmosphere of conflict. Occasionally the birth itself was a violent one or involved surgery, as, for example, in cases of Caesarean section.

In any event, the persona the Mars rising person may wear is of someone always ready for action and sometimes ready for conflict too. Some people with Mars rising just seem to go out into the world spoiling for a fight. Nevertheless, the appearance of strength, courage and bravado may be all show; merely a mask the individual has learnt to cultivate in order to protect themselves.

Mars conjunct Ascendant people are keen to get on with things. This is the client who, being impatient to start, arrives early and refuses a cup of tea. I know of a 14-year-old boy whose chart is strongly Leo and Aries. He has Leo on the Ascendant but Mars in Virgo very close to it. With all that fire he is not too keen on doing homework or any kind of studying, but when he does it, it has to be perfect. He will write out a page and if there is a mistake, instead of crossing out the error or using a liquid eraser, he tears up sheet after sheet of paper and starts all over again, until either he gives up in exasperation or actually completes the task. Obviously, the Leo desire to be best and the Arien urge to be first contribute to this behaviour but it is also indicative, I fancy, of a Mars in Virgo conjunct Ascendant belief that he is in competition with the rest of the world to produce a piece of work that is perfect (Virgo) in every detail.

In appearance the Mars rising person often exudes strength. Sometimes the individual is rather muscular-looking as if armour-plated against any possible attack.

This is a very honest, go-getting kind of combination, good for any kind of initiation, although unrestrained by other chart factors and, depending on the sign involved, the individual may just be too impulsive or pushy for their own good. More positively, there is usually strong leadership potential with the placement, and it is ideal for any life-situations where the individual can legitimately compete and stretch themselves to the limit. Sport is the immediate physical vehicle that springs to mind.

Mars conjunct the Descendant, or making hard aspect to the axis, may be more combative than Mars rising. Those with Mars on the Descendant may see others as aggressive or look to others to help them find their own retaliatory impulses. This is a splendid combination for lawyers or others who have to fight on behalf of another's point of view. Often those with this placement have to put a great deal of energy and sometimes real 'push' into achieving a position of co-operation. A key phrase for this combination may be 'fighting for co-operation'; fighting too for justice and fairness as they see it.

Like Venus–Mars contacts, the Mars setting person may be impulsive about relationship, jumping into liaisons with a real spirit of adventure but not a great deal of forethought. This is a good combination for competitive relationships, partnerships that involve a bit of rough and tumble and don't rely on everything appearing to be sweet and nice. Thus relationships with people with Mars along this axis may either feel very alive and stimulating or as if World War III had just broken out.

Mars conjunct the MC is suggestive of a real sense of direction in life and great ambition. Conjunctions and hard contacts to this axis often indicate a vocation that either involves fighting to get to the top or fighting to remain there. This is the kind of combination that one might expect in the armed forces, the police force, in sales, sports or in politics. It is also very commonly found in careers in various trades, in work that involves a skill using tools or calling for decisive action. As always, the sign and its ruler are very important but examples might include: building (Taurus), carpentry, decorating, catering (Cancer), some sort of detailed craft (Virgo), surgery (Scorpio), and so on. The possibilities are endless.

Mars conjunct the IC suggests that the individual operates from a foundation of anger. Usually there is a history of conflict in the home and individuals with the placement may do anything to hide their own anger from public view and sometimes from themselves. With Mars on or contacting either end of this axis, there is often tremendous anger felt towards one or both parents, an anger that can fuel the individual into accomplishing tasks that require tremendous tests of strength or energy. This placement will often be indicative of the person who works from home or who is always 'on the go' when actually at home. The home is a place of activity for Mars conjunct IC. Whilst such activity may be of a more Mercurial nature if Mars is in the 3rd house, this placement is also ideal for more physical tasks, for these provide a way for the individual to contact and work off their anger. Often people with this placement feel cut off from their physical energy unless they actively take steps to stoke themselves up. If Mars is making hard aspects to heavier planets, this placement can be indicative of accidents or fires. Such manifestations usually only occur if the individual is not actively 'using' their energy. Mars conjunct IC can also indicate an urge to dig out one's roots. For those with this placement, courage may be about unflinchingly exploring the emotional and sexual roots of the family and their own psyche.

JUPITER AND THE ANGLES

Individuals with Jupiter conjunct the Ascendant go out into the world eager to embrace as much of it as possible. These people have an expectant attitude to life and wish to go out into the world and explore it. The houses whose cusps are in Sagittarius and, perhaps to a lesser extent, Pisces will play a part in determining the areas of life in which the individual will focus these explorative urges.

Jupiter rising people often come across as being buoyant, optimistic and as taking a philosophical stance upon life's trials and tribulations. This is the person who presents a happy face to the world, even if the rest of the chart is descriptive of a more cautious, serious and doubtful individual. They approach others seemingly without thinking twice about it. Those with Jupiter on the Ascendant often appear somewhat arrogant; in some signs much more so than in others. Often the individual sees everyone else as very positive, confident and sure of themselves and cultivates a similar persona. If the rest of the chart describes an extrovert personality, this placement will increase this tendency. Shyer individuals may be able to be quite 'up front' and confident amongst strangers but rather less so with people they know a little.

The type would also often like to appear as educated or sophisticated in the ways of the world, well travelled, physically or mentally. The journey in life is perhaps to do with exploration of the self and this self-exploration and discovery will often take place whilst the individual is in either an educative setting or abroad. As a young child, the Jupiter rising individual may have travelled a great deal or been exposed to different cultures or belief systems.

People with Jupiter on the Ascendant–Descendant axis are usually great advice-givers. Perhaps there is a need to be seen both as knowledgeable and generous.

Jupiter in hard aspect to the axis suggests that the individual's beliefs are at odds with the outer image that they have cultivated.

Jupiter conjunct Descendant often suggests that an individual teams up with a person from a different background or culture from their own, or sometimes with a teacher or religious person. Education often forms an important aspect of one-to-one relationships, with the individual either seeking to educate the other or be educated by them; the educator or the educated. There is a need for a certain amount of space with Jupiter on both ends of this axis. At the 7th house end, the individual is often particularly keen on exploring the whole realm of relationship and may not like being tied to just one person. In any event, it is through relationship that the Jupiter–Descendant person finds their own faith and confidence. They may look to someone else to provide these qualities or be able to offer them to others. Sometimes the person projects 'God' onto other people and sometimes they wish to be treated as being Godlike and wonderful themselves.

Jupiter on the MC suggests that the individual has confidence about the eventual successful outcome of their goals, although the goals can be so large that success may prove elusive. Those aims may well revolve around a Jupiterian vocation: teaching, publishing, travel, religion, politics, philosophy or law. The person would probably like to be seen by the public at large as full of generosity and good will. This placement suggests that the individual would like to 'play God' in their career in some way and they well may take on the role of advice-giver or benefactor. These people are often influential in moulding other people's beliefs and this can apply to all aspects to this axis.

The Jupiter–MC individual will usually be very 'future-orientated' and may be happy enough to put up with a less than wonderful past or present in the confident expectation of things improving in the years to come. The vocation may also deal with other people's futures in some way. One of the parental figures may have had strong religious or political views. That person may also have been rather dramatic or larger than life to the child.

Those with Jupiter on the IC inevitably will have come from a background whose chief preoccupation was either education, religion (or some other belief system) or travel. The individual will often have come from a 'good' family and often a large home. People with Jupiter on both sides of this axis themselves often want and obtain a mansion-like residence. There is a need for 'space' on the domestic sphere on all levels and a hope that one can be hospitable to all. Jupiter–IC people are often quite confident individuals; the confidence and faith is less obvious than with Jupiter rising but it is usually much more solid and underpins everything the person does.

SATURN AND THE ANGLES

The Saturn rising person will usually approach the world with a certain amount of caution, as if on some level they feel that it is not a very safe place – certainly not safe enough to venture out without wearing at least a little armour-plating. Typically, the individual feels that they must be ready to defend themselves against possible disaster. I once looked after a boy aged about 11, with Saturn rising. Whenever we went out, he used first to go around the house, checking that the windows and doors were tightly bolted and that the plugs were all pulled out of the electric sockets. Thus his persona was a serious one. The immediate impression he made was of someone older than his years and very responsible. At the same time, being so well defended, it was not so easy to see the vulnerable little boy underneath. The oldest in the family, he took on what he saw as the role of father when his parents divorced, and this is quite typical of a 1st house Saturn.

Margaret Thatcher, the so-called 'Iron Lady', has Saturn rising in Scorpio. She seems to have a very controlled persona, to have her guard up at all times. She doesn't seem very spontaneous. When she was Prime Minister she was often portrayed by satarists as a rather heavy school-teacher type, ready to discipline and control irksome cabinet ministers.

Because people with Saturn conjuncting Ascendant do not see the world as a particularly safe place, they often take steps to control the environment and those within it. They want to leave nothing to chance, and they want to be seen as being a person who 'never puts a foot wrong'. In fact this insistence on never putting a foot wrong is a common Saturnian one, whatever the configuration.

The controlled responsible exterior may not necessarily be indicative of a particularly responsible or serious person but merely indicates that is the impression that the individual initially makes.

Saturn rising is often associated with a difficult or delayed birth, as if the baby is reluctant to come out and enter into the world. Perhaps the infant is controlling the situation from the word 'go', or on some level feels it needs to. In any event, this caution about and fear of greeting the world naked and exposed, seems to persist throughout much of the life.

I know of a woman with Saturn on the Descendant whose birth was delayed because the midwife, faced with another woman coming into labour and other complicated goings on, asked the mother of the Saturn setting child to hold off giving birth for as long as she could. This story sets the scene for a feeling common to people with Saturn on the Descendant: they feel and fear that other people are in control. In relationships and, indeed, all one-to-one encounters, there are usually major control issues, with one partner seeming to keep tight control of the activities of the other.

Whereas the Saturn rising person often goes out into the world ready to be a patriarchal figure, a disciplinarian perhaps, someone older than their years and a responsible, dutiful type, those with Saturn on the Descendant often look to other people to live out these qualities, although they themselves will usually be very responsible about relationship matters and, in their own way, also very much in control. There can be a fear of relationship with Saturn contacting either end of this axis: fear of being in a relationship and fear of not being in one. At best, Saturn contacting these angles suggests that the individual is able to apply themselves to building up a relationship with another person by responsibly dealing with the different obstacles as they occur.

People with Saturn conjunct the MC often feel they have to keep up some kind of position in society, perhaps maintain a position of responsibility or duty or follow in a parent's footsteps. Classically, they feel they have no choice but to do this. There is sometimes a very fated feeling about the choice of vocation which the individual may or may not feel comfortable with. It's a common enough combination for members of the Royal Family, whose public face tends to be a very controlled one, full of responsibility, protocol, hand-waving, and never putting a foot wrong.

Very often those with Saturn contacting the MC–CI axis feel that they have to submit to their parents' wishes as to their choice of career and there is sometimes a feeling of an enormous weight on their shoulders because of this. Very often the background is a fairly conservative, middle-class one or the family aspires in that direction. The choice of vocation often seems *limited* to Saturn conjunct MC especially, and to some extent it often is limited because the individual requires that their position in society be one of respectability and security.

I have seen this placement in the charts of those who have at least one very successful parent in their field, although the success is usually very hard-won, but it's also a common placement in the charts of those whose parents didn't reach their aspirations – parents who feel a failure to themselves and their family in terms of their professional accomplishments. Thus the individual with Saturn conjunct MC carries more than their own fear around with them. There is often a fear of succeeding (for it might hurt the 'failed' parent) as well as a fear of not doing so.

Having a proper career and direction in life is often such a weighty issue that individuals with the placement often feel at a loss to decide what to do with their lives. Saturn conjunct MC are often late developers. Classically the type is frightened to take risks with their future, which is fair enough on one level, but on another it is often by taking risks, by exploring first one kind of work and then another and simply going where life and one's unconscious takes one, that an individual is able to find their particular niche in society and some sort of personal fulfilment. I have also known people who have spent their lives blaming their parents for work they happen to be doing. They feel that in their working life they are 'doing time'. Usually the parents are not to 'blame'; the problem lies with the individual who is too frightened to risk doing what they really want to do.

Saturn conjunct MC is an ideal combination for vocations that involve skills that take a long time to learn, and careers concerned with age, tradition, time or structure. The conjunction and other aspects to the axis can be associated with hard work and slow, sure success.

Saturn conjunct IC can occasionally indicate that the individual is hampered in the pursuit of their vocation by heavy family responsibilities or unresolved family issues. For many with this combination, home and family is equated with duty and responsibility, which the individual may or may not feel comfortable with.

There may have been fear around the early home life, perhaps fear of a parent, sometimes lack of a parent or fear concerning the individual's origins. People with Saturn on the IC often desperately seem to need a secure home base; a home and a foundation that is solid and cannot be taken away. Conversely some people with Saturn on the IC are frightened of putting down roots; they see permanence and security as stifling or restrictive and inevitably would have had an early experience that helped to shape this view. Whatever the issues there is usually some kind of fear attached to the issue of one's roots.

This is an ideal placement for people who build solid foundations in a physical sense; I have seen it in the charts of builders for example. Whilst there may be fear attached to the idea, the purpose of this combination is perhaps concerned with the slow excavation of one's emotional and familial origins.

URANUS AND THE ANGLES

People with Uranus aspecting the Ascendant/Descendant axis often *look* different, there is often something physical about them that sets them apart from others or makes them particularly noticeable. Frequently they are simply quite tall. Uranus always seems to increase height and this is sometimes the case even with major Uranian contacts which don't involve the Ascendant.

Whereas a person with Uranus in the 12th house may be highly individualistic but keep the more unconventional aspects of their personality, world-view or life-style to themselves, those with Uranus rising usually make no secret about their differences from others.

As always the sign involved is of crucial importance, as is the ruler of the Ascendant and other planets making aspect. As a rule though, the Uranus rising person seems to go out into the world saying: 'In what way am I different?'

Often, from birth or early childhood the individual felt marked out as being in some way unique. With Uranus rising, this is often felt to be just a statement of fact and the individual may even come to wear their 'differentness' as some kind of badge. Whatever marks them out from the rest of the family may also have been reinforced and therefore exaggerated very early on in life. Thus the life's journey is often concerned with discovering in what way they are genuinely unique from the rest of the world as opposed to merely appearing to be different from others.

Those with Uranus squaring the Ascendant, however, are usually not reinforced for their 'differentness' by the family. They often themselves feel different or think that others may find them odd. This usually feels rather uncomfortable and the individual often finds it difficult to integrate their unconventionality into the rest of their personality or life-style.

Those with Uranus rising usually have no wish to conform. The type will be highly individualistic and uncompromising in their insistence upon having space and freedom. And especially space and freedom to pursue whatever (to others at any rate) radical or unconventional life-style is appropriate to them.

People with Uranus rising and sometimes on the Descendant are sometimes born very suddenly or unexpectedly so that their first experience of themselves in the world is of their producing some kind of shock.

Others with Uranus conjunct Ascendant themselves receive an early shock to their system and thus somehow come to expect that something sudden and devastating might occur at any minute. Or at least this is my theory to explain the often very taut nervous tension that these individuals sometimes exhibit.

In my experience Uranus contacts to the Ascendant–Descendant axis are amongst the most common contacts to be found in the charts of astrologers, although if astrology ever becomes a commonplace, accepted subject amongst the general populace, I doubt whether this would remain the case.

People with Uranus on the Descendant tend to look to others to bring out the more unconventional or original aspects of their personality. It usually takes someone else to awaken the Uranus–Descendant person to the possibility of leading a more exciting or exhilarating life. It is through interaction with someone else that it dawns upon the person that they needn't conform to the whims of society but can express themselves as they would honestly wish to.

Instead of making a statement, 'I am unique', as might be expected with Uranus conjunct Ascendant, those with this placement might make a life statement which says: 'We are different. Our relationship is exciting, radical, unconventional' – or a whole host of other Uranian words. The relationships of Uranus conjunct Descendant will often involve 'shocks'. Quite unexpected happenings, unexpected choices of partner, instant marriage proposals, speedy and sudden exits from relationships and so on. And all this is usually in the service of some personal awakening, some personal radical change.

It is also through relationship that the Uranus conjunct Descendant person can rebel. The choice of partner may itself be an act of rebellion, as may the way the relationship is pursued. With the placement, the individual will insist on the freedom to pursue whatever kind of relationship they choose and with whomever they choose. With Uranus at either end of the Ascendant–Descendant axis, freedom within a relationship will also usually be insisted upon, and thus this combination might be associated with 'open' marriages and partnerships and, in particular, with relationships which are essentially based on friendship. Individuals look to their partners and their relationships for excitement, stimulation and personal awakening. If such exhilarating interchange becomes no longer possible, the individual will usually feel the need to look elsewhere for it.

Uranus conjunct the MC often reveals itself as a marked urge to rebel against the social values or conditioning of a parent figure and, in particular, to follow a line of work which might be contrary to the consciously stated wishes of that person. It may well be in line with the unconscious desires of the parent, however, who may look to the child to do all the exciting or unconventional things that they would have liked to have done but didn't dare. Uranus conjunct IC may be similar in this respect but its effects are not likely to be so obvious to the outside world.

Uranus conjunct MC may be indicative of a vocation that involves technology and thus the breaking of new ground and the breaking away from a past established way of doing things. Careers in computing are sometimes those chosen at the present time, whereas electronics may have been more common several decades ago.

Whatever the actual vocation, this combination favours self-employment. For this individual often needs to do things in their own way and without interference. Sometimes the person, having needed to rebel against an early authority-figure, continues to live out this process with bosses at work. People with this placement are too honest to want to toe the line. Their choice of vocation or the way they pursue their career must personally feel very fulfilling to them: there is usually no element of following a career for the sake of respectability or security. The vocation must be felt to be exhilarating and exciting, and as soon as the individual fails to consider it so they may well feel compelled to leave instantly and do something completely different. And not only do people with Uranus conjunct MC want freedom within their career, but that career may actually concern itself with freedom for others. Thus sometimes there is involvement in a vocation which is concerned with liberating people, whether this liberation comes through supporting free speech, feeding the world, or the usage of technology which potentially might liberate people from having to spend time engaged in boring and unstimulating occupations.

Uranus conjunct IC or even into the 4th house is sometimes indicative of great upheavals in the early home life. This placement is consistent with, for example, moving house in childhood to a location that is radically different from that of one's forebears. Perhaps being uprooted to a complete different country, culture or family, for example. Often the early upheaval is not that extreme but in childhood may have seemed so. Sometimes a parent might have made a sudden exit or been forced to do so. In any case, people with this placement often have to build their own roots; they often feel or are literally cut off from the roots of their family or their culture.

I know of one extreme case for example, where a boy with Uranus exactly conjunct the IC, because he was born illegitimately, was placed in a children's home. He never knew who his father was, never saw his mother, and when aged about 11 was sent to Australia by the home as part of a Government scheme to help colonise that country. On all sorts of levels he was cut off from his roots and has been looking for them ever since.

Sometimes, such early experiences result in the individual feeling unable to put down roots, for they cannot believe they are ever going to feel safe. For some, depending on the aspects, the lack of roots is exciting. Many others with this placement though, often become very concerned with creating a permanent home and as much security as possible.

For all its difficulties, being cut off from one's roots, like most things, can have its advantages. Individuals with this placement have freedom at their foundation. They can do what they want without having to consider the pull of the past or the tradition of the family.

Whatever the exact scenario, those with Uranus on the IC are often thrown back on their own resources at an early age. Thus the individual is usually deeply independent, not only in behaviour and choice of life-style but in their ideas and opinions. Unlike Uranus conjunct MC though, there is usually no felt need to be *seen* to be different. On the contrary, any unusual family background, eccentric family members, or unconventional views are usually kept well hidden from public view at least until the mid-life Uranus opposition. Like Uranus in the 12th house, the individual with this placement will often want to be seen as conventional in public.

NEPTUNE AND THE ANGLES

If the Ascendant is, at least to some extent, descriptive of an individual's persona (literally actor's mask) then a conjunction from Neptune may yield a number of interesting possibilities. It may be that the individual appears to the world as very Neptunian, perhaps as elusive, enchanting or other-worldly, sometimes rather vague and confused. More often though, the Neptune rising individual does not make an immediate physical impact on their environment. Individuals with this placement do not have a fixed kind of persona although the rising sign is usually quite obvious.

People whose births were induced will often have a focal Neptune in the chart and sometimes Neptune rising is descriptive of this.

It is at the Ascendant point that we are 'earthed' in the world, but those with Neptune rising seem to have a disinclination for such an earthing. For example, charts of children who have died within the first few minutes or hours of birth, often have contacts from both Jupiter and Neptune to the Ascendant axis.

Perhaps the more common manifestation of Neptune rising is of an individual whose persona and outlook is multifaceted. Like a crystal, these people can reflect whatever they come into contact with. People with Neptune rising seem to go out into the world, and approach those in the environment with extreme sensitivity. Almost as if they have invisible antennae with which they can pick up each and every nuance in the environment. It is not so much sensitivity to feelings (as might be the case with the Moon rising) so much as a receptivity and impressionability to any kind of stimuli. Whereas others will have grown some kind of skin or protection, those with Neptune rising seem, like Sun–Neptune or Moon–Neptune, to have little boundary between themselves and the rest of the world. Neptune rising people seem to go out into the world acting as, and perhaps hiding behind, a lens, a mirror which can reflect whoever they are with or whatever they see in the environment. This is an ideal placement for the photographer, the individual who physically spends time behind the camera or other types of artists who reflect what they see going on around them.

The journey in life for people with Neptune rising seems to be concerned with acting as a *medium* for the thoughts and feelings of others. Through acting as a lens for others they can both lose and find themselves. Neptune on either end of the Ascendant–Descendant axis suggests that the individual is easily influenced and thus sometimes seems to lack stamina.

Some with this placement look out on the world from the perspective of either the saviour or the victim and the individual may appear to others in either of these two guises. Neptune on either end of this axis can manifest in either the exploiter or the exploited.

Neptune conjunct Descendant, like Neptune rising, suggests that saving others or being rescued by them is a central feature in relationship and all one-to-one encounters. Those with Neptune on the Descendant may be looking for a God or a Saviour in their close personal relationships or they may play that role to others. Individuals with this placement often have difficulty in seeing others clearly, either idealising or distorting their true nature. Whilst there may be confusion about what is wanted in relationship, there is usually also often great idealism and romanticism. Boundaries in relating to others are often weak and the individual can enter into others' lives and them into theirs with the ease of a ghost walking through walls. The problem with Neptune on either end of this axis can be a tendency to live the life vicariously. On the other hand, this is a splendid combination for anyone who legitimately and consciously needs to dissolve boundaries and be able to empathise with others' suffering. There is a talent for mirroring others which also might find outlet in a variety of creative fields.

Neptune conjunct MC often suggests diffuse goals and an early uncertainty of direction with respect to an individual's choice of vocation. This aimlessness can sometimes be matched by a parent's ambivalent feelings as to how they want their child to be seen in the world. Many with Neptune conjunct the Midheaven want to be seen by the world at large as glamorous and wondrous: a saviour, a prince or a princess; perhaps someone creative or representing some kind of public ideal. Many with this placement, especially when young, can find it very difficult to get hold of the reality of what is fitting for them to pursue, given their life-situation and individual talents. In extreme cases, if they meet someone who is writing a book, *they* want to write a book; if they get to know a politician, they yearn to pursue a career in politics – and so on. They want the glamour that they imagine others have in their lives. Those with Neptune conjunct the MC tend to dream of the future; at best this can spur them on to achieving the recognition they yearn for by actually fulfilling whatever their dream is. And the dream is usually not strictly personal; the individual often wants to 'save' the world in some way. This placement is ideal for any Neptunian type careers: the arts, music, work in welfare fields, charities, at sea, with water, to name but a few possibilities.

Neptune on either end of the MC–IC axis sometimes suggests a tendency to idealise one parent at the expense of the other. There is usually a distorted image of at least one of the parents and perhaps an experience of their being some kind of victim. Neptune on the IC and into the 4th house is sometimes descriptive of a missing father and sometimes loss of family and home altogether. For some with Neptune on the MC, it is the thirst for recognition from a parent that propels the individual into weaving all sorts of romantic dreams of what they are going to do with their lives; for they feel that if the world recognises them, then so will the parent.

Those with Neptune on the IC tend to be wistful about their more recent past but unclear as to their early beginnings. Sometimes there are secrets or confusion with respect to the family that they came from. Such secrets will usually be to do with the house which has Pisces on the cusp. There may be a tendency to idealise the early home life or to delude oneself about one's upbringing or even ancestry. Sometimes there is a feeling of 'shaky foundations' with this placement but this can be psychological, emotional or physical. For example, living on a houseboat could be descriptive of shaky physical foundations, whilst a mentally ill parent might describe psychological instability. And I know people with this placement who were raised in a pub. The early home environment was 'open' to anyone and some would have been addicted to frequenting it, all of which might have a variety of repercussions.

Those with Neptune on the IC often yearn for an 'ideal home' and may put great effort into making this dream into some kind of reality; sometimes the real need is to escape from one's roots. The dream may be for a home which will be a sanctuary, a retreat, an escape route from something or a place where it's possible to transcend some of the imperfections of living in the outer, workaday world.

PLUTO AND THE ANGLES

I think anyone with Pluto conjunct any of the angles has a strong urge to power but also tends to insist upon privacy. Pluto rising people usually approach the world being very concerned with *survival*. Rather like Saturn rising, those with Pluto conjunct the Ascendant do not seem to expect the world to be a particularly safe place; they expect the world 'out there' to be something of a minefield, a place where the mines are not only hidden but potentially fatal. Intensely self-aware, the individual also seems especially aware of and sensitive to the murkier sides of life and the uglier aspects of human nature.

Pluto rising people seem to go out into the world wanting to hide. This is particularly noticeable with the Ascendant in Leo. We are used to thinking of Leo as being rather attention-seeking, but Pluto rising in Leo people seem to feel as if they *are* the centre of attention, as if everyone is watching them. The person often wears dark glasses and blushes when spoken to. In early life they may have had a great deal of attention but found that level of attention, that level of being 'watched', crippling to the development of their own personal identity. Thus there is a feeling that they want to hide.

Sometimes, Pluto contacting the Ascendant axis describes a very early life which involved the child in a family secret, something that the youngster would be unable to understand, process and even perhaps remember in later life. The 'secret' might involve almost any family skeleton but issues around sex, death, madness and rage are all implied. I have known cases where the 'secret' was merely that the person was adopted. In any event, for whatever reason, those with Pluto rising often cultivate what might be described as a 'concealing persona', an outer face that gives little away and often tightly controls each and every situation so that others too, do not reveal too much.

Sometimes the birth itself involved trauma, perhaps the near death of mother or child. And sometimes there is a brush with the possibility of death to self or others in childhood years which explains the subsequent fearfulness. In any event, there often lingers a feeling that one might be violated in some way if appropriate steps are not taken.

I have long felt that Pluto may be significator of the grandmother and largely came to this conclusion after noticing how frequently she was a dominant figure in the early lives of those with Pluto rising or in the first house. People with this placement often have lived with a grandmother in the family and often established a stronger bond with her than other family members – and this in a culture where the extended family is increasingly a thing of the past. I have also seen cases where Granny herself was not present but where another strong female, such as a nanny in the professional sense, was. What this might mean is not clear to me. However, those with Pluto rising where Grandmother was dominant usually have nothing negative to say about her but it is usually the case that she was a very powerful matriarchal figure who sometimes controlled the entire household with her sickness, money or the sheer force of her personality. Not infrequently she acted as an 'agent provocateur' between the parents but again, the results of this on the individual with Pluto rising are not clear to me, although there can be a great fear of intimacy with this placement, almost as if forming a real relationship was prevented when a child was young. Possibly the child unconsciously picked up and absorbed from the rest of the family some of the negative emotions intended for Granny, and perhaps on some level the family may have wished the older woman dead. The young child has then stood between these negative energies and the grandparent.

In any event, those with Pluto contacting either side of the Ascendant axis by conjunction or hard aspect often find it difficult to achieve intimacy, difficult to let others in. This is more likely to be the case if the axis is also receiving hard aspects from other planets, especially Saturn.

Classically, those with Pluto rising approach the world wanting to control and manipulate it and bend others to the hidden but nevertheless iron will that lurks beneath their exterior. If the Ascendant is descriptive of one's 'vehicle' then Pluto rising, especially when found in fixed signs, is rather like a tank – massively protected and defended. Inpenetrable and unyielding.

Pluto rising people themselves often live out some sort of taboo in their lives, and by taboo I mean something that society *en masse* might consider to be deviant in some way. It is as if one must get past the person's secret before one is allowed to relate to the rest of the person.

People with Pluto conjunct Descendant often tend to give their power away. They also often see other people (as opposed to themselves) as powerful, controlling, ruthless, manipulative or impenetrable. It is through one-to-one encounters that the individual is offered the opportunity of discovering the darker side of themselves. Power struggles are inevitable with all aspects to this axis and these are usually particularly obvious with Pluto setting in the chart. It is through one-to-one relationship and sometimes struggle that the individual is able to transform their image of themselves and their way of relating to other people. Those with Pluto on the Descendant are often forced to grapple with many of the relationship issues that confront Venus–Pluto people. This is a useful placement for work which involves holding others through crisis and steering them through transformative situations.

Pluto conjunct the MC is usually an extremely ambitious placement and often describes the individual as choosing a vocation which involves the use of power, one which requires the exercising of a great deal of will-power and determination to get to the top. It can sometimes be found in the charts of top sportspeople who in order to succeed have to be very determined to survive and win.

I have also seen this placement in the charts of several Asian women in professional jobs. In their culture, pursuing a career in this way is very much a taboo thing to do. I also know an undertaker with Pluto conjunct

MC. As always, a planet may be embodied in a variety of different ways, depending on the overall chart and life-history of the individual.

Pluto contacting the MC–IC axis is often indicative of a very powerful or controlling parent.

Pluto conjunct IC suggests some sort of violation at one's roots. I have known examples where the individual has discovered that they are the product of rape. Sometimes there is literal or metaphorical death or banishment of a parent. On other occasions the person may have been transposed to a completely different culture or a completely different family to the one of their forebears.

Sometimes individuals with this placement attempt to purge themselves of their history. In attempting to eradicate their past, it is as if they sit on a time bomb, waiting for it to resurface suddenly and wreak havoc on their newly built foundations.

Still others with Pluto conjunct IC want to dig and dig to see where they came from: this must surely be a very positive manifestation of this combination.

Pluto contacting the MC–IC axis suggests that the individual is forced to touch upon the darker sides of human life through parenting or vocational activities.

DATA SOURCES
AND INDEX OF CHARTS
USED IN THE TEXT

ABBREVIATIONS

AA: *Astrological Association* (data section)

ABC: *American Book of Charts*, Lois Rodden

Campion: Nicholas Campion, *World Horoscopes*

CBC: *Circle Book of Charts*

FCN: *Fowlers Compendium of Horoscopes*

LR: Lois Rodden, *Profiles of Women*

AEST: Australian Eastern Standard Time

BST: British Summer Time

CST: Central Standard Time

DBST: Double British Summer Time

EST: Eastern Summer Time

GMT: Greenwich Mean Time

HST: Honolulu Standard Time

MET: Middle European Time

IST: Indian Standard Time

LMT: Local Mean Time

PST: Pacific Standard Time

Douglas ADAMS
11 March 1952, just after 11am,
Cambridge, England.
52N11 0E08
Source: Adams to Lee Knight.
Quoted in AA *Transit*,
August 1982.

John ADDEY
15 June 1920, 8.15am BST,
Barnsley, England.
53N34 1W29
Source: Addey to Lois Rodden,
April 1979.

Hans Christian ANDERSEN
2 April 1805, 1am LMT,
Odense, Denmark.
55N22 10E23
Source: Luc De Marre
quotes parish records.

Maya ANGELOU
4 April 1928, 2.10pm,
Saint Louis, Miss., USA.
38N37 90W12
Source: Birth certificate quoted
in *Contemporary American Horoscopes*.

Jane AUSTEN
16 December 1775, 11.45pm
LMT, Steventon, England.
51N05 1W20
Source: Her father's letter,
'before midnight'.

Lucille BALL
6 August 1911, 5pm EST,
Jamestown, NJ, USA.
42N06 79W14
Source: LR. Kathy Brady
quotes birth record.

Geoffrey BOYCOTT
21 August 1940, 11am,
Fitzwilliam, England.
53N29 1W22
Source: *Boycott: The Autobiography*.

Marlon BRANDO
3 April 1924, 11pm CST,
Omaha, Nebr., USA.
41N28 96W12
Source: Birth certificate quoted
in *Gauquelin Book of American Charts*.

Vera BRITTAIN
29 December 1893, time
unknown.
Source: AA.

Pearl BUCK
26 June 1892, 12:30am.
Source: Buck to Lucie Bonnett.
(NB. A biography written with her
gives 'early in the morning'.)

Agatha CHRISTIE
15 September 1890, 4am GMT,
Torquay, England.
50N30 3W30
Source: Christie to Charles
Harvey, and the American
Federation of Astrologers
(Autumn 1967).

CORONATION STREET
First transmission
9 December 1960, 7pm GMT,
Manchester, England.
53N29 2W15
Source: Official biographies.

Aleister CROWLEY
12 October 1875, 11.30pm,
Leamington, England.
52N17 1W31
Source: CBC. (Autobiography,
Confessions, states between 11pm
and midnight.)

Bob DYLAN
24 May 1941, 9.05pm CST,
Duluth, Minn., USA.
46N48 92W10
Source: Birth certificate.
Quoted in ABC.

EDWARD VII
23 June 1894, 9.55pm,
Richmond, Surrey, England.
51N27 0W17
Source: *Times* newspaper.

Albert EINSTEIN
14 March 1879, 11.30am LMT,
Ulm, Germany.
48N27 9E58
Source: Ebertin quotes birth
record.

Jane FONDA
21 December 1937, 9.14am,
Manhattan, New York.
40N46 73W59
Source: Lois Rodden quotes
birth certificate.

FRANCE
The Vth Republic,
5 October 1958, midnight LMT,
Paris.
48N52 2E20
Source: Campion.

Anne FRANK
12 June 1929, 7.30am MET,
Frankfurt, Germany.
50N07 8E41
Source: LR. Time written by her
father in an early edition of
The Diary of Anne Frank.

Sigmund FREUD
6 May 1856, 6.30pm LMT,
Freiburg, Germany.
47N59 7E53
Source: *The Life and Work of
Sigmund Freud*, Ernest Jones.

Mohandas (Mahatma) GANDHI
2 October 1869, about 7.15am,
presumably LMT, Porbandar,
India.
21N38 69E36
Exact time of birth is controversial
but most times yield either late
Libra or early Scorpio rising.

June and Jennifer GIBBONS
11 April 1963: June at 8.10am
local time, Jennifer ten minutes
later (5.10 and 5.20am GMT),
Aden, Yemen.
12N47 45E02
Source: *The Silent Twins*, Marjorie
Wallace.

Mikhail GORBACHEV
2 March 1931.
Source: *Guardian* newspaper.

Germaine GREER
29 January 1939, 6am AEST,
Melbourne, Australia.
37S49 144E58
Source: Greer to Tiffany Holmes.

Dag HAMMARSKJÖLD
29 July 1905, 11.30am LMT,
Jonkoping, Sweden.
57N47 14E11
Source: Church of Light quotes
Drew for 'approximate time'.

Katharine HEPBURN
12 May 1907, 5.47pm EST,
Hartford, Conn., USA.
41N46 72W41
Source: Ralph Kraum quotes birth
certificate, March 1940.

HERALD OF FREE ENTERPRISE
Start of voyage, 6 March 1987,
6.38pm GMT approximately.
51N19 3E12
NB. The *Times* newspaper
(7 March 1987, p.1) gives
6.21 pm.

Thor HEYERDAHL
6 October 1914, 4.40pm MET,
Larvik, Norway.
59N05 10E02
Source: Ebertin in *Cosmobiology
International*.

Adolf HITLER
20 April 1889, 6.30pm LMT,
Branau, Austria.
48N15 13E03
Source: CBC. Originally from
baptismal records.

C.G. JUNG
26 July 1875, 7.30pm Kesswil,
Switzerland.
Exact time must be speculative as
supposed to have been born when
'last rays of setting sun lit the
room'.
Source: Various. Above data from
David Hamblin, *Harmonic Charts*.

J.F. KENNEDY
29 May 1917, 3pm EST,
Brooklyn, Mass., USA.
42N21 71W07
Source: JFK's mother to Garth
Allen.

Elisabeth KUBLER-ROSS
8 July 1926, 10.45pm (9.45pm
GMT), Zurich, Switzerland.
45N23 8E32
Source: Robert Chandler from
Kubler-Ross, November 1980.

R.D. LAING
7 October 1927, 5.15pm GMT,
Glasgow, Scotland.
55N52 4W14
Source: AA (from a copy of the
birth certificate).

Franz LISZT
22 October 1811, 1.16am LMT
(time unverified), Raiding,
Hungary.
Source: CBC. Other sources quote
1am.

Ken LIVINGSTONE
16 June 1945, midnight DBST
(thus 10pm GMT), Streatham,
London.
51N10 0W10
Source: Derek Appleby from
Livingstone.

Shirley MACLAINE
24 April 1934, 3.57pm EST,
Richmond, Va., USA.
37N30 77W28
Source: Church of Light quotes
birth certificate

Princess MARGARET
21 August 1930, 9.22pm BST,
Glamis Castle, Scotland.
56N37 3W01
Source: Joanne Clancy quotes
birth certificate.

Karl MARX
5 May 1818, 2am LMT, Trier,
Germany.
49N45 6E06
Source: Official records.

Bette MIDLER
1 December 1945, 2.19pm HST,
Honolulu, Hawaii.
21N19 157W52
Source: Birth certificate quoted in
Gauquelin Book of American Charts.

Spike MILLIGAN
16 April 1918, 3am LMT,
Ahmednagar, India.
19N08 74E48
Source: *The Astrological Journal*,
August 1967, quotes Milligan in a
Sunday newspaper article

Patrick MOORE
4 March 1923, 10am GMT,
Pinner, Middx., England.
Source: *Can You Speak Venusian?*,
Moore 1972

Eric MORECAMBE
14 May 1926, 12 noon BST,
Morecambe, Lancs., England.
54N05 2W52
Source: AA (from Joan Revill).

W.A. MOZART
27 January 1756, 8pm LMT,
Salzburg, Austria.
47N48 13E01
Source: His father's letter,
as quoted in a biography by
J.G. Prodhomme.

Richard NIXON
9 January 1913, 9.35pm PST,
Whittier, Calif., USA.
33N58 118W01
Source: T. Pat Davis quotes birth
certificate.

Enoch POWELL
16 June 1912, 9.50pm GMT,
Stetchford, Birmingham, England.
52N29 1W54
Source: Powell to the Astrological
Association.

Vanessa REDGRAVE
30 January 1937, 6pm GMT,
London.
51N31 0W06
Source: Her mother's
autobiography, *Life Among the
Redgraves*, p. 122.

Salman RUSHDIE
19 June 1947, 2.30am IST,
Bombay, India.
18N58 72E50
Source: Catriona Mundle quotes
Rushdie to Ian McEwan.

Bertrand RUSSELL
18 May 1872, 5.45pm, Trellec,
Monmouth, Wales.
Source: Ronald Clark, *The Life of
Bertrand Russell*, 1975, p. 23.

Arthur SCARGILL
11 January 1938, 2pm GMT,
Barnsley, Yorks., England.
53N54 1W29
Source: David Fisher quotes Dick
Llewellyn from the National
Union of Mineworkers.

Albert SCHWEITZER
14 January 1875, 11.50pm LMT,
Kayserberg, Alsace.
48N09 7E16
Source: Bruno Huber quotes birth
certificate.

Ringo STARR
7 July 1940, 12.05am BST,
Liverpool, England.
53N25 3W00
Source: Starr to Lynne Palmer.

Tom STOPPARD
3 July 1937
Source: *Guardian* newspaper.

Elizabeth TAYLOR
27 February 1932, 2am GMT,
London.
51N31 0W06
Source: Taylor to Bob Prince
(same in a biography by Taylor's
mother).

Margaret THATCHER
13 October 1925, 9am GMT,
Grantham, Lincs., England.
52N55 0W59
Source: Her private secretary to
Charles Harvey.

Townsend THORESEN
22 December 1924, midnight
GMT, Dover, England.
51N07 1E19
Source: Register of companies,
Holborn Public Library.

UNITED KINGDOM
1 January 1801, midnight GMT,
London.
51N30 00W07
Source: *Mundane Astrology*, Baigent,
Campion and Harvey.

Leonardo da VINCI
15 April 1452, 3am (Julian)
Florentine time, Vinci,
Tuscany, Italy.
43N47 10E55
Source: CBC (apparently from
grandfather's diary).

Raquel WELCH
5 September 1940, 2.04pm LMT,
Chicago, Ill., USA.
41N52 87W39
Source: Edwin Steinbrecher quotes
birth certificate.

Duchess of YORK
15 October 1959, 9.03am GMT,
London.
51N31 0W06
Source: Duchess of York to Penny
Thornton.

Useful Organisations

London School of Astrology

Offers weekly classes, Saturday seminars and other courses for beginners, intermediate and experienced astrologers.
Details from: London School of Astrology,
BCM Planets, London WC1N 3XX.
Tel: + 44 (0)7002 33 44 55
Website: www.londonschoolofastrology.co.uk
email: admin@londonschoolofastrology.co.uk

Astrological Association

Organisation with world-wide membership. Benefits of joining include annual conference, journal etc.
Details from: Astrological Association,
Unit 168, Lee Valley Technopark,
Tottenham Hale, London N17 9LN.
Tel: +44 (0) 20 8880 4848
Website: www.astrologer.com

There are many teaching organisations in the UK and throughout the world, numerous journals and a whole host of conferences and other activities devoted to astrology. Details of many of these can be be obtained from the Urania Trust, a charitable organisation devoted to astrology.
Details from: Dawn Roffe,
12 Warrington Spur, Old Windsor,
Berks. SL4 2NF, UK.
Website: www.uraniatrust.org

BIBLIOGRAPHY

Addey, John M., *Harmonics in Astrology*, Fowler, Essex, 1976
— *Selected Writings*, American Federation of Astrologers, Arizona, 1976

Arroyo, Stephen, *Astrology, Karma and Transformation*, CRCS Publications, California, 1978
— *Relationships and Life Cycles*, CRCS Publications, Washington, 1979

Baigent, Campion and Harvey, *Mundane Astrology*, Aquarian Press, Northamptonshire, 1984

Bettelheim, Bruno, *The Uses of Enchantment*, Peregrine Books, 1986

Carter, Charles E.O., *The Astrology of Accidents*, Theosophical Publishing House, London, 1961
— *The Astrological Aspects*, Fowler, Essex, 1977
— *Essays on the Foundations of Astrology*, Theosophical Publishing House, London, 1978

Dean, Geoffrey and Mather, Arthur, *Recent Advances in Natal Astrology*, Astrological Association, 1977

Ebertin, Reinhold, *Combination of Stellar Influences*, American Federation of Astrologers, Arizona, 1972

Faculty of Astrological Studies, *Learning Astrology*, 1982

Freeman, Martin, *How to Interpret a Birth Chart*, Aquarian Press, Northamptonshire, 1981

Greene, Liz, *The Outer Planets and Their Cycles*, CRCS Publications, Nevada,   1983
— *Relating*, Coventure, London, 1978
— *Saturn*, Samuel Weiser, Inc., New York, 1976

Hamblin, David, *Harmonic Charts*, Aquarian Press, Northamptonshire, 1983

Hammarskjöld, Dag, *Markings*, Faber & Faber, London, 1964

Hand, Robert, *Horoscope Symbols*, Para Research, Massachusetts, 1981

Hillman, James, *Suicide and the Soul*, Spring Publications, Texas, 1985

Jackson, Eve, *Jupiter*, Aquarian Press, Northamptonshire, 1986

Kubler-Ross, Elisabeth, *On Death and Dying*, Tavistock Publications, London, 1970

Maclaine, Shirley, *Don't Fall Off The Mountain*, Bantam Books, London, 1983

Oken, Alan, *The Horoscope, the Road and its Travelers*, Bantam Books, New York, 1974 (now republished as *Complete Astrology*)

Paul, Haydn, *Phoenix Rising*, Element Books, Dorset, 1988

Rodden, Lois, M., *Profiles of Women*, American Federation of Astrologers, Arizona, 1979
— *American Book of Charts*, Astro Computing Services, San Diego, 1980

Rudhyar, Dane, *The Lunation Cycle*, Shambhala, Colorado, 1971

Sakoian, Francis and Acker, Louis, *The Astrologer's Handbook*, Penguin Books, Middlesex, 1981

Sasportas, Howard, *The Twelve Houses*, Aquarian Press, Northamptonshire, 1985

Tierney, Bill, *Dynamics of Aspect Analysis*, CRCS Publications, Nevada, 1983

Wallace, Marjorie, *The Silent Twins*, Penguin Books, Middlesex, 1987

BOOKS OF RELATED INTEREST

TAOIST ASTROLOGY
A Handbook of the Authentic Chinese Tradition
by Susan Levitt with Jean Tang

KABBALISTIC ASTROLOGY
The Sacred Tradition of the Hebrew Sages
by Rabbi Joel C. Dobin, D.D.

THE ARABIC PARTS IN ASTROLOGY
A Lost Key to Prediction
by Robert Zoller

ESOTERIC ASTROLOGY
by Alan Leo

TAROT AND ASTROLOGY
The Pursuit of Destiny
by Muriel Bruce Hasbrouck

TEEN ASTROLOGY
The Ultimate Guide to Making Your Life Your Own
by M. J. Abadie

CHILD ASTROLOGY
A Guide to Nurturing Your Child's Natural Gifts
by M. J. Abadie

DYNAMIC ASTROLOGY
Using Planetary Cycles to Make Personal and Career Choices
by John Townley

Inner Traditions • Bear & Company
P.O. Box 388
Rochester, VT 05767
1-800-246-8648
www.InnerTraditions.com

Or contact your local bookseller